Nice Pinch!

Nice Pinch!

What Goes On In the Cop Shops, Inside and Out, True Stories of A Family, Four Generations of Law Enforcement Officers

Edward B. Hayes III

ISBN-13: 9781546951698
ISBN-10: 1546951695
Library of Congress Control Number: 2017908755
CreateSpace Independent Publishing Platform
North Charleston, South Carolina

Acknowledgements

As they say, some language in this book is "colorful." Hopefully you won't be bored with some of the specifics, but ya may want to know who's talkin', so I will start out with some of my background and early days as a law enforcement officer, or LEO. I am a fourth-generation LEO and very proud of it. I'm also proud of my name, if for no other reason than respect for my predecessors. My dad, Edward B. Hayes Jr., was a cop; his dad, Edward B. Hayes Sr., was a cop; and my dad's granddad was a cop of sorts, according to census records and family stories.

I don't have a real long list of people to thank other than my friend Richard Ward Fatherley, now deceased, who encouraged me to write a book; my good friend Ron Lizar, another local author who assisted me in getting this started; Keith Johnson, publisher of the *Johnson's County Gazette*, a local newspaper in Olathe, Kansas, that I write a column for; the Lisbonas, an author of children's books, Margie with help from husband Larry and some of the folks I have written about. Also some who have helped me in research and recollections; and last but not least, my beautiful wife, Pat, (she really is) who helped out and put up with me while I was writing this, as well as many other things…without *any* complaints. OK… maybe a few. And I have to recognize my dad and my granddad, for without them I wouldn't be here. They were both honorable men and true to their profession as LEOs; you will read more about them in the book's chapters. We also can't forget Samuel L. Case, my great-grandfather, father of Lena, my father's mother.

As I am "the third" after my dad and granddad, my aunts cheerfully called me "Eddie Hayes, the turd." A lot of people agree with this moniker, especially some of those under my command at one time or the other. Last and certainly not least, to those I worked with over the years. Some of them are and some were the finest human beings on the face of the earth; others not so much, but that's life, isn't it? Nobody's perfect, and not everyone will like you, especially if you are a cop. If you're smart and not thin skinned, you really won't give a shit anyway.

Contents

Chapter 1

140 Different Calls and Incidents

This book got its start from my *Johnson's County Gazette* column I mentioned in acknowledgements. In the beginning I wrote four articles for the Gazette, following those articles …Keith asked if I could do a column on Johnson County history and my career from day one as a deputy sheriff. I thought, OK, I can write a few…and pretty soon I was well on the way to writing a book, which several friends were urging me to do. The result is this book of over 140 different incidents (plus or minus) that LEOs and LEO wannabes will either enjoy or not; some of these same incidents may occur in your career as an LEO no matter where you are employed. People are people, with the same emotions and actions, making the same mistakes, or enduring the same types of incidents no matter where they are in the United States and elsewhere. Some are funny and some not so.

If you or anyone you know has aspirations of becoming a police officer or deputy sheriff or any other first responder, tell them they should read this book. It will be educational for them if they want to know what kinds of calls or incidents they can expect to experience in their career. You will read about the expected and unexpected I experienced and witnessed, all in this book. This book is not fiction. All the stories are true; they are incidents that I was involved in during my career of thirty-plus years as an LEO, incidents that my father and grandfather experienced, and incidents that some of my coworkers experienced. On many occasions LEOs, retired and active, have told me, "I had that same thing happen to me" or "We had the same things at our department." You may notice that I direct some of my comments to those who are active LEOs and those who want to be

LEOs. I'm sure readers will find these true incidents interesting and exciting, just as those who read my column did. Another comment I've gotten
is, "The writing style of your articles makes me feel like I was there."

You non-LEO folks who like to read about criminal behavior as well
as first responder incidents will find this manuscript interesting. There are
heartbreaking events, sometimes comical events, and tragedy. If you have
any interests at all in criminal behavior and its effect on the "cop shop," you
will enjoy this book. It is all true to life for a cop.

Bashing and Trashing the Cops

I really tire of buzzwords used by the media talking heads; it seems that
they cannot complete a sentence without using one of these things that
gets picked up by the public, such as "at the end of the day," "you know,"
"so," or "that's a great question." The two I really despise are "racists" and
especially "the new normal," but I will use that one once, now.

So let's talk about the bashing of law enforcement officers.

Recently it has become the so-called "new normal" to bash or judge
police officers. That seems to be one of man's favorite sports these days,
and it's generated by politicians, the media, and cop haters. Worse yet,
the killing of LEOs has become a badge of honor in some ethnic groups.
Hopefully that will soon change with the new Trump administration since
we now have a chief executive that is pro–law enforcement, pro-military,
and pro–first responder. He says it, reinforces it, and I think he means it.

Even before the Obama administration aided, abetted, supported, and
cheered on the anticop movement, some of the public were quick to judge
the police officer for supposedly doing wrong before all of the facts were
presented. The police officer is many times scorned and judged guilty until
proved innocent by the media, the cop haters, and some politicians. Cases
in point? The Mike Wallace interview with Chief Tony Lane, and remember Ferguson, Missouri, and how that turned out? It was all lies, a dog and
pony show, and several cops lost their careers with that department over
that media-generated debacle. Even after the facts and truth were known
in Ferguson, the anticoppers built a monument! In a city park! To honor

the documented armed robber and bad guy, as verified on video and then more than one million dollars was paid out in a settlement.

Then there's the Freddie Gray case, in which six police officers in Baltimore, Maryland, were suspended and went through the court system, all because the mayor knee jerked and publicly announced their guilt in her opinion *from the very beginning*. Since then a judge has found several of the officers not guilty! But now the Justice Department is looking into the case, though hopefully that will be dropped by the new administration.

Now let's not forget the "Whitehouse beer summit," I wouldn't have gone. That whole incident made then president Obama look immature, unprofessional and just plain silly but he never gave LEO's a break and in my opinion he created much of the recent unrest involving the police. Why? He obviously dislikes cops but that's Ok because I............

In the Ferguson and Baltimore cases, who looked stupid in the end? Answer, the mayors, the media, some politicians, and other cop haters. But the damage to those LEOs' careers was done. When these incidents happen, my advice to you is to kick back and chill out before you start yelling about situations you know nothing about and end up looking stupid just like the rest of them. Don't believe the media until all the facts are out. Most of the time it's inaccurately reported.

Look...here's the deal and why I bring this up, other than the fact that I am pro–law enforcement. Consider the costs:

The training period of a Johnson County, Kansas, sheriff's deputy costs $50,000—that's 50K from the date of the first interview through the trainee's time in the academy and to the date he or she hits the bricks with a field training officer (FTO), according to one who knows, Kent Brown, chief financial officer for the Johnson County Sheriff's Office (now retired). The length of that training period can vary, but it is six-plus months. And by the way, more costs, in the thousands, will accrue as this deputy develops in his or her career. Nationwide, other departments' costs are similar, more or less. It ain't cheap, folks, to train our first responders, and they and their training exceed many other professions. So be fair and think twice before you start yelling for termination just because of what is reported in the media.

I have a lawyer friend who hates cops. Cops don't have much love for an attorney like that. It's no secret that some defense attorneys love to bash the LEO on the witness stand or criticize via the media, so here's something else to think about. That lawyer, that critic, that politician, or that reporter has plenty of time to study the situation they're so critical of—if they do, and *if* they are willing to be fair. That's not the norm in many cases, which is the why behind some negative, inaccurate reporting. In the real-life situation, the officer's decision is many times made in seconds or less. In real life and time, things happen fast, and that's especially true at the cop shop. There's *no time* to study what's happening as the media, lawyers and others do, they have all the time they need.

In nationwide shooting incidents lately, LEOs have been criticized for shooting bad guys unnecessarily, they say, with too many shots fired, as the critics and the media (some of them) report. I had to laugh at Polk County, Florida, sheriff Grady Judd's answer to an attempted gotcha question from an unsuspecting and unprepared reporter:

Question: "Why did your officers fire sixty-eight rounds, Sheriff?"
The Sheriff's response: "Because we ran out of bullets."

What the reporter and most civilians are unaware of is, that officer is trained to shoot "center mass" until the bad guy goes down. Officer survival is important to most of us. It's not "shoot in the arm," or "shoot in the shoulder," and it's not a head shot unless that officer's really good; the aim is for center mass—that's the trunk of the body of the threatening bad guy—and the LEO is trained to shoot until the threat no longer exists. If it can be done without fatal wounds, we all agree that's OK in most cases, but here's the deal: When you have an officer with fourteen rounds in the magazine and one in the pipe that fifteen rounds can be fired off in rapid succession. Now multiply that by four, five, or more officers shooting at a bad guy. No one waits until someone else fires first; they all fire at will until bad guy goes down, and that's when the officer is now safe. When I fire on the range I fire in rapid succession and while my accuracy isn't what it used to be I still shoot rapidly, that's what most do in a real life shooting situation. Once on a firing range in Arkansas other shooters came to my location to see what kind of machine gun I had. What I did have was my two friends, my Smith and Wesson nine MM automatic pistol which has a fourteen round magazine, fifteen rounds when you count the one in the "pipe."

While there's a couple of different versions of this shooting and quotes by the media, it is a true event where a deputy and a police dog were killed by a bad guy, who, by the way, was an illegal alien invader who should have not been in America in the first place. Some other professions are similar to law enforcement, but they don't get the scrutiny that a police officer receives when things go wrong or *seem* to go wrong, thanks to an overzealous media. When I passed my private pilot's test, my check-ride pilot told me this: "Now's the time when you go out and learn how to become a pilot." Same thing even after FTO training for cops sent out on their own. They are prepared, but what they learn from experience is key, and they learn quickly. You're an officer when you finish with your FTO, but it takes time and experience to be what is called a "seasoned LEO." Where you go from there is your decision to make; how good you are is up to you.

So…the next time an officer seems to be in the oleo, it's your money and mine when they start yelling, "Fire the SOB!" That gets fun for some, doesn't it? The sheep will follow and scream the same, while commonsensical persons sit back, watch, and pass the correct judgment at the right time. As you can see, it takes training and time to develop an officer, just as with many other professional occupations. Is a lawyer or a doctor ready to perform as soon as they come out of the university? Nope, they have an FTO of sorts for years, and when they either make a mistake or are just accused, they are not immediately scrutinized or fired. LEOs should get the same backing, and the cop haters should just be ignored by leaders, media, or others with backbone, *if* they have one—a backbone, that is.

So there you have it, the initial costs plus the training and experience curve, and those that have the desire to stay with it are well trained in most departments—sheriff, city, highway patrol, or otherwise; they are all LEOs but not all the same.

I would be surprised if very many readers of this book would be anti-cop, maybe pro–law enforcement. I encourage you to support your police officers of any department. They support you. If one screws up in most cases and on most departments it will all be taken care of in time and in short order. Don't doubt that. Be smart and be fair to your LEOs and yourself.

Chapter 2

Differences of Sheriff's Deputies and City Police

Voting for Your Sheriff

In this book, I refer to all classifications of LEOs: police officers, deputy sheriffs, highway patrolman, feds, and others. Some of the public's beliefs are that they are all the same. While similar in ways, they are not the same, and that is why I mention this now: so you will see and know the difference as you read on. This is directed to all who read this book, including LEO wannabes—and I am not making fun of anyone when I say that; I was a wannabe too at one time years ago.

Having said that, I suggest that you research the duties of the sheriff in your state, and you will see why I make the following statements and suggestions. As you research the sheriff, you will see that by definition and opinion, the results are all over the place. Some facts, opinions, and sources will say that the sheriff is the most powerful in the land. There have been and are those that want the sheriff appointed instead of elected, giving power of politicians over the sheriff, and this is not just locally.

The position of sheriff goes back more than a thousand years, and sheriffs were and are the most powerful law enforcement officials of the land. The county sheriff is the highest-ranking LEO in his or her county, and there must be something to that or the politicians would not be concerned. If the sheriff were to be appointed, he or she would have masters other than we the people. In Johnson County, Kansas, there was, and maybe still is, the desire to appoint the sheriff. Why? So the county commissioners would have authority and control to run that sheriff's office, to be boss of the sheriff.

When you research what the duties of the sheriff are, compare that with the city police officer. City officers enforce city ordinance and can make arrests for misdemeanors and felonies that they witness on view or have credible evidence of a crime.

Your best candidates for sheriff are those who have been sheriff's deputies because they have the experience and understanding of that office, which is extensive and complicated and has duties carried out by law. You don't learn the duties by reading a book; you learn by doing the job. I had a highway patrol friend who retired and ran for sheriff in Colorado. He won, assumed that office, and his words to me were, "I thought I knew a lot having been a highway patrolman for decades, but when I went into that sheriff's office, I found out how much I didn't know. I had a good experienced undersheriff, so I just let him run that office. When my term ended, I did not run for sheriff again."

Here's another example: A man was appointed sheriff in a caucus because he and his supporters didn't realize that the duties of the sheriff were as complicated and extensive as they are. He had that sheriff's office so screwed up by the time he had to run for election on his own that it became apparent to the public, and he was defeated by a quality, experienced candidate. In addition, he was several million dollars over budget by that time due to unnecessary spending, so the new sheriff had that problem to get straight beginning on day one of his administration.

Now hopefully you know why, so…research, research, and research each sheriff's candidate if you want quality leadership in your county.

Chapter 3

Sr.

*E*d Hayes Sr. was my grandfather. I talk about him first so you can see similarities in his experience and those you will read about in my career experiences in the following chapters—history repeating itself, as they say.

Edward B. Hayes Sr.(Sr. on the right) joined the Kansas City, Kansas, Police Department (KCKPD) in 1926. In this day and age, he would not be considered as he only had an eighth-grade education. He was very intelligent despite his educational shortcomings, and he was self-educated. In reading documents and articles he penned during his lifetime, I am astounded by his communication, intelligence, and skillful use of words. He started his career as a uniform policeman and rose through the ranks to captain, the rank he was when he retired for health reasons on July 1, 1960. In my early years who would know that after thirty-three years as an Leo and first responder, I would retire at the same rank with twenty-nine years on the job as a deputy sheriff and other jobs as a first responder. As far as I know, all Granddad's injuries in life were job related, and they were all serious injuries. He was shot by bad guys several times and returned fire with his six-inch Colt revolver, killing three in self-defense, though he killed more than that, I was told. Following retirement, he lived a little more than a year before dying in bed from a heart attack.

He had worked as a motorcycle patrolman (one of the first if not the first on KCKPD), a foot patrolman in uniform, a detective in plain clothes, a member of the vice squad, and head of the Youth Bureau, which he founded, and over the years, he was promoted to lieutenant and then captain. How do I know all of this? I have his scrapbook with all of this information and much more, and I have the stories from my aunts and father, who all respected and adored him, as well as my friend Captain Byron Horn (ret.) who worked for Hayes Senior as a patrolman.

Days before I retired, I called a friend, Mike Dailey, to see if there might be some department records on Hayes Senior, and Mike says, "Yes, they would be in archives. Would you like a copy?" To which I had the obvious response, and two days later I had Hayes Senior's personnel file on my desk. That file had family history that none of us ever knew prior to this. I had worked with Mike Dailey when he was working investigations in the KCK SCORE unit when I was working undercover. It's nice to have friends and contacts like Mike, as when you work together you develop a respect, a trust, and a bond that gives benefits, such as my receiving Hayes Senior's personnel file in a timely manner.

I was excited to get the file because I knew about some of the work-related injuries and family history—I knew that he had been in a few gun battles and had busted up liquor stills and worked on other interesting cases—but there was also newer news, I thought. I called my aunt Helen who was now in her eighties and told her about his personnel file and about what I was reading. "Aunt Helen, I see in Senior's personnel file that he had shot and killed three bad guys in the line of duty, two in self-defense after he was shot." She replied, "Oh honey, he killed eight men in his career. The file isn't accurate." I didn't doubt her, because she was still sharp as a tack, and I had heard some of the stories; I just didn't know he had killed that many.

The news article from the Kansas City, Kansan" reported his request for disability retirement and stated the following:

> In numbers of arrests and solution of major crimes, Hayes' record ranks with the best in the history of the police department. His success was confined to no crime classification; he captured petty thieves and murderers with equal facility.
>
> Police files record the courage and fidelity to duty of Hayes through the third longest tenure among current personnel; only two others have served longer.

Teddy a Model

Hayes, a self-educated man, is an intense admirer of President Theodore Roosevelt and during the latter part of his career, he accepted Roosevelt's advice:

> "Speak softly and carry a big stick."
> [I wondered, damn, was he a Democrat?]

> The article went on to say, "he became the department's diplomat on crank calls and in dealings with emotionally disturbed persons. [Today that is called a "negotiator."] It was not uncommon for him to over-power a stubborn caller with the weight of multiple syllable words."

End of the article:

His intentions following retirement, according to articles he wrote, were to research psychological phases of law enforcement and write his memoirs, which I guess is what I am now doing. He died before he could do any of this, or if he did it, we never saw it.

To repeat: Senior was shot three times by bad guys and returned fire, killing them. He was also injured in a fall during a packinghouse strike in the lower bottoms of Kansas City, Kansas, according to news articles.

I remember the sometimes humorous tales about when shots were being fired at his house in drive-by shootings by relatives of one of the men he had shot in self-defense gun battles. The raids on the house started out with rock throwing, and progressed to homemade bombs, followed by several drive-by shootings. There was also sniper fire at the home, so the house was under surveillance for a while with floodlights that "would be turned on at will," lighting up the entire yard. It had become intense, and they wanted these guys before they hurt anyone in the family. I remember my aunts laughing till they cried about the evening an uncle went out on the back porch to take a leak and got shot at, and he retreated back into the house peeing and wetting himself all the way. On another night, the bad guys arrived while the good guys were waiting to capture them, and Hayes Junior, my dad, who was six years old at the time, turned on the floodlight and scared them off. Ya had to be there, but when my two aunts would tell these tales, we were all laughing until we were rolling on the floor with tears in our eyes. I can just see this guy on the back porch holding onto his bean and peeing all the way into the house; he didn't stop to "zip up," they recalled, and he left a trail behind him.

They finally captured these bad guys, but not before my grandmother was hospitalized, and she never recovered.

In Senior's scrapbook, there are news articles, crime scene pictures, and various other pictures and articles, but what I have found interesting are the pictures of alcohol stills that were raided and busted up during Prohibition. It must be true when they say history repeats itself, because I was doing the same thing with illicit drug-manufacturing labs in the mid-1970s while working undercover in the narcotics divisions.

Several other incidents were mentioned in articles about Senior's retirement. One recalls a car chase in which he and his partner were chasing the infamous criminal train robber William "Bill" LaTrasse. A news article again in the Kansas City Kansan says the following:

> Patrolman Edward B. Hayes and Detective John West didn't realize until several hours after they had captured William "Bill" LaTrasse in 1937 how close they had come to being blown to bits. As they pursued the bandits car LaTrasse tossed a half pint bottle at their police cruiser. It missed by inches and landed, without breaking, in an unpaved parking area. Police officers who later found the bottle learned to their horror it was nearly filled with nitroglycerin.

End of article.

Why that bottle didn't explode when it hit the ground is beyond belief, but it did not, according to the news. There were many bad guys or gangsters like Pretty Boy Floyd and such as LaTrasse hanging around Kansas City in the twenties and thirties before, during, and after Prohibition days.

That article mentioned two other incidents in which Senior was shot. One incident happened in 1938 when Hayes was wounded in his right shoulder while attempting to arrest a prisoner who had escaped from "the Kansas State penitentiary." The guy was found in Kansas City, Missouri, and a reward went to Hayes to go toward his hospital bill—no workman's comp or department medical insurance in those days. You got hurt, and you were on your own, except in this case the officers that found the guy refused the reward to pay for their fellow officer's medical bills. What a great bunch of guys they were and I have heard tales about them for years. In another incident, while walking his beat, Senior was shot in the shoulder by a "mysterious" gunman who had killed five people. Senior returned fire, wounding the man, who was later found under a porch, where he had bled to death.

John West was Senior's best friend and partner at the time. West tragically drowned in the Kaw River in a hunting/boating accident soon after the LaTrasse nitroglycerin incident. There's an article on that incident in his scrapbook. According to my aunts, that loss of a great friend and partner in such an accidental way hit the old man really hard. He and West were a real team. In law enforcement, when you have a friend that you can work with and trust, you are ahead of the game.

Granddad's legendary five-inch blued Colt revolver was the handgun he carried in uniform throughout his career. He was a hell of a shot with that gun, which in today's world of handguns would be an ancient weapon. When he went into the detective division, and when he was a supervisor, he carried a blued Smith & Wesson Model 60 Chief, another ancient wheel gun in today's world, some may think.

I inherited several of my granddad's weapons after my dad died. Among those is a .22-caliber Marlin derringer pistol that has at least six marks intentionally filed onto its frame. In the old days (and maybe still), the marks were an indication of how many people a weapon had killed. In this case, was it a bad guys or a bad guy killing other bad guys, or was my grandfather an assassin of bad guys? I would like to know the history of that itty-bitty gun, if only it could talk. I attempted to research who the original owner of that pistol was, but Marlin manufacturing tells me that they did not keep records on pistols in the older days. The original owner would certainly be of interest—maybe of historic interest. Note the file marks on the left side of the trigger housing.

Another "victim" of Senior was a suspect in a car theft and burglary who ran and was shot, according to the news headline that reads,

"POLICE KILL MAN WHEN HE ATTEMPTS TO ELUDE ARREST".

The article goes on to say "Hayes called him to halt but the man continued to run and jumped a 6 ft. fence" "Hayes then drew his revolver (bet he had it drawn the whole time but it says) Hayes drew his revolver and fired two shots, both of which took effect, the man dying instantly".

Yet another shooting by Senior on foot patrol was of a bad guy who was ordered to halt after he approached with a bulge under his coat, crossed the street and took a shot at Senior.

The newspaper headline was

"OFICER KILLS A NEGRO"

Different times, different verbiage folks, the article go on, saying it was:
"the third attempt in two months on the life of Edward Hayes ended in the death of a negro, Frank Williams." Williams was killed with Granddad's service revolver, the blued five-inch Colt revolver that I inherited. It's pictured here:

Williams shot Hayes with a high-powered rifle, and Hayes returned fire while lying on his stomach, firing four shots as Williams ran away. Williams was later found lying in a driveway "dangerously wounded." The rifle was found to have been used in several robberies and at least one homicide. This was the case that was involved in the attacks on the family home and the surveillance because of drive-by shootings and the police surveillance was what eventually ended the assaults on the family home.

Most of this enforcement activity was from the late twenties, into the thirties and the forties. The number of officers and members of the public that came to Granddad's funeral was impressive. It was huge even in 1960. He was also a legend with the KCK public, and I was told by many people who knew him that he was well respected. Pharmacists, businesspeople, lawyers—he had respect from all of them, and that makes me proud. They all knew him from his "community policing," and walking a beat, he was a people person. He was a worker, and he loved getting the bad guys. His "walking the beat" in old Kansas City made him a lot of friends among the civilians. My grandfather died as I was thinking of becoming a cop, and seeing the respect people had for him was a big deal to me, I never was able to talk to him about it. I came in contact with many who complimented me just for being who I am, his grandson. "You're from good stock," one said.

Chapter 4

The Roaring Twenties, into the Thirties

During this period in time, many news articles were written on stills that made rum, whiskey, and other alcohol. The articles often had pictures. My scrapbook mirrors Senior's: he busted up liquor stills, and with me it was drug labs in the seventies. According to news articles, Senior was part of a two-man squad that averaged one hundred raids a month on stills. That was in KCK alone, any questions on why they called it the "Roaring Twenties?" I am going to guess that some of them had the best booze at home, ya think? Times were different then, weren't they? Even in law enforcement. Now I could say there's a resemblance in my crew's activities and we had the best dope, but we didn't...because contrary to popular belief, I have never used recreational dope—never have and never will, and as far as I know, neither did my coworkers. On the other hand, I had friends and other LEOs that just knew I used dope to make cases. I did not. Don't believe me? Anyone? That's your problem, not mine. We did have a bit of fun dropping marijuana plant seeds in the flower beds at the courthouse as we entered with evidence. Those bags just weren't tight enough. However, we never saw anything growing.

The newspaper article states,

The raiding squad, named by Chief William McMullin, consists of Edward Hayes and Edward Wilson. These two men make an average of 100 raids a month, and the average amount of liquor confiscated is 200 gallons a month. Few large stills are found. Their method of obtaining accurate evidence has been a great assistance to the prosecutor in obtaining convictions. When liquor is found, the officers take it to the city chemist. [All of it? People that worked with my granddad say/said that he went by the book, and I'll go with that.] Both officers and the chemist testify in court.

That's a lot of raids in one month, don't cha think? My squad made a hell of a lot of raids, or search warrants as we call them today, but nothing like two hundred a month. Most likely, they didn't need as much "probable cause" in those days. The articles are a hoot. They listed everything about the bad guy but their baby sister, (oh wait, they did that too!) the names of violators, addresses, charges, and more. One paragraph lists three months' activities, for July, August, and September of 1929. In those three months, 364 liquor raids were conducted, along with 23 gambling raids, 641 gallons of liquor were seized, and a number of arrests were made. The article is a bit deceiving as it states, "Two MEN Go RAIDING," and the truth is that it was their gig, but there were other officers and sheriff's deputies involved as well. It seems that there was a lot of activity by these guys who were having as much fun as I was when I was working undercover. You will see the irony of history in the Hayes family in the resemblance of careers as you read on.

There was another case in which the "burglar" was killed by Patrolmen Edward Hayes and John West as he was running from a house [geez, these guys were good shots].

The newspaper headline on this one was this:

RECOVER ROSEDALE LOOT

Property taken From Room Occupied by Negro Burglar Killed by Police Wednesday

The article went on,
> Residents of nine Rosedale homes yesterday identified property taken from them and found in the room said by police to have been the store room of property stolen by Joseph Porter, negro prowler who was shot Wednesday night by Edward Hayes and John West, patrolman, when they found Porter running from the house with a grip which later proved to contain clothing stolen from a home.

The article then lists the homes that property had been taken from. I guess my itty-bitty aunt was right; he shot and killed more than three men. In today's world some of these—at least one of them—wouldn't be considered a good shoot, but they were then. How much do times change. It seems that in those days if a bad guy runs, ya shoot him, period. In today's world, if you shoot a bad guy even in self-defense, you run the risk of being second guessed by the cop-hating public, the liberals, gun haters, and others who think the police shouldn't even have guns.

There's a follow-up in another article on "train robber" LaTrasse, who was paroled after three years saying he was going to go straight. He was arrested with another guy with burglar tools, and they went back to the slammer. Seems as though LaTrasse went into the safe-cracking business instead of robbing trains after he got out of prison and was on parole. This article was dated 1932. For some of the articles, I can only guess the date, but they are around other dated articles in the scrapbook. I have to wonder IF all the newspaper articles in his scrapbook were all the Kansas City Kansan newspaper or were some other papers, there are no identifiers.

*Edward B. Hayes - He would
when he was promoted to
Detective on the K.C.K
police force.*

If LEO's stay in the business long enough, they accumulate a lot of friends in different stages and professions of life. I have mine, my dad had his, and my grandfather had his. One such was the famous S.J. Ray, a cartoonist and illustrator for the *Kansas City Star* newspapers for decades. Samuel J. Ray drew one of his treasures for Granddad that is a real keeper. It's twelve by eighteen inches, framed, and signed "S.J. Ray"—call it an autograph. The inscription states, "To Edward B. Hayes, Director of the Youth Bureau…"

The title on the illustration states is "ONE PART OF THE WORLD THAT SEEMS ALRIGHT" penned in lead pencil.

It's not dated, but the Youth Bureau was founded around 1955 by Edward B Hayes Sr. of the Kansas City, Kansas, Police Department. We now call those divisions the "Juvenile Division" and so on.

The very first page inside his scrapbook reads like this:

MY-CREED
I believe in hands that work,
Brains that think,
And hearts that love

Chapter 5

Family Ties

I don't know much about my great-grandfather Samuel L. Case, Edward B. Hayes Jr.'s grandfather (his mother's father). I haven't done much family genealogy research, but there were two things I wanted to know, so I went to the library. The first thing I wanted to know was how much Cherokee Indian I am. I wasn't expecting any benefits or the like; I was just curious. My dad and my aunts always said that their mother, Lena, was 90 percent Cherokee. So far, I have had no luck. I've even gone as far as to get the DNA test for a hundred bucks, only to be told, "We don't have any way of finding out about Native Americans."

My aunts, Helen James and Norma Owens, were sharp as tacks into their eighties. One or both always told me that Captain Jack Hays of the Texas Rangers and President Rutherford B. Hayes were both in our family tree. Really? I didn't pay that much attention in those days, and I really don't care so much about Rutherford B., but I would like to know about Captain Jack. Someday maybe but I have my doubts.

So the next thing I wanted to know was if my great-grandfather or anyone else was an LEO, which would make me a fourth-generation LEO, something more to be proud of. My aunts always told me he was an LEO, but other than that, I had no proof. In the library, I found in the census listings that he is listed as a "watchman." In the 1800s there was no national police, and depending on which source you read, metropolitan police organizations began forming in the 1830s. Locals had different classifications such as marshals, town marshals, constables, watchmen, deputy sheriffs, police chiefs, and so on.

My dad was an army air force veteran. He joined the air force in 1941 to become a pilot, but his dreams were dashed when they found that he was colorblind, so he finished out the war as a mechanic—never left the States. He called nearly all of his friends "Moose," and they called him likewise, although he wasn't a real big guy; he was five foot eleven and not a heavy man. Ed Hayes Jr., that's my dad, began his LEO career in 1962. His career began in the jail, as many did in those days. He worked in the jail for a few months and then transferred to the road patrol. As I recall, he was trained by Sgt. Henry "Hank" Dobson, who became his very good friend and coworker. Hank was loved and respected at the time by everyone. Sadly, he died a young man at the age of forty-four from cancer. Pictures taken of his funeral are an indication of the respect he had at the time of his death; the funeral was huge. Other than meeting Hank a few times, I didn't know the man well. I just knew his reputation as a really good guy and a good LEO.

In the beginning I rode shotgun with my dad as much as I could when my time permitted, I learned a lot from him. Until I became a reserve, he and others had tagged me as "Special Agent O'Brien." They thought that was pretty funny. Even though at the time neither one of us thought that I would someday become an LEO, he was training me by his comments and stories of incidents and calls. These ride-along experiences were fun for me and piqued my interest in becoming an LEO. It wasn't very long before I became a reserve officer. I was a reserve officer for about a year before I went full time, but that is story.

Junior was promoted to sergeant within a couple of years and worked road patrol and as an FTO. He and others were legendary, respected, and well liked by most, but some were jealous for reasons I can only speculate on. I know this from working with deputies he had trained; since I was his son, they shared more with me than some of the other reserves. I know I'm sharing points you will read later in the book, but briefly, nearly everyone he trained became very good as an LEO.

Junior didn't have any hobbies; he just loved to work in the patrol car, and he worked double shifts many days. He was either home resting, sleeping, or he was out in the field. Even as a young man, I was concerned that he was working too many hours, and I told him so. I suggested that he get some hobbies to quit lying on the couch so much. When he was at home, he was a couch potato's couch potato, as the saying goes. His response to me was, "Some guys like to go bowling, fishing, or something; I just like to go out and shake down cars and catch bad guys," and he did. In his eight years as an LEO, he made the most of it. He had years' more experience than those eight years might indicate.

His tenure at the sheriff's office was four years working for Sheriff Ralph Burger, and when Burger's term ended, Lynn Thomas became sheriff. As you will read, this was not a positive situation since Thomas did not honor the longtime tradition of allowing an outgoing sheriff's undersheriff the privilege of running for that office. Before or when Thomas took over as sheriff, half of the LEOs left the department, and my dad was one of them. Knowing how much he loved the job, I asked him, "Why are you leaving?" His response was, "I will not work for that little blanket ass. I'm going to Olathe PD." That comment in itself was humorous because my grandmother, according to Dad and his sisters, my aforementioned aunts, was 90 percent Cherokee Indian. Looking at her pictures, it was obvious that she was part Native American, but I never knew how they came up with the 90 percent figure.

When Junior left the sheriff's department, it left an opening for me to be hired full time. Before that, I couldn't be full time due to the nepotism clause. That's what they said, but I always suspected that my dad didn't want me to be an LEO at the time.

During his first stint at the sheriff's department as a road patrolman/ sergeant before he left for Olathe, most of his arrests were car thieves and burglars, and he worked at least one homicide scene. I have news articles of some of his activities but not many, and they're not very informative in nature.

When he went to the Olathe PD, Junior lost his sergeant's rank and was once again a patrolman. Olathe was a small department at that time, with only eight officers. There wasn't much that happened in his Olathe days that I'm aware of. There were some calls and incidents he experienced, and in one car stop he made with the assistance of Charles Hoy Lane (you will read about Charles "Chuck" Lane later), the driver and passenger were convicted felons, and the driver had a German Luger pistol under his seat. The driver at least was arrested, charged as "a felon in possession of a firearm," and was welcomed back into the prison system. I have that Luger pistol with Junior's and Lane's initials scratched into the frame. It's sad, but that's what they did in those days. Now property is photographed and tagged.

I don't know when or where this happened—the sheriff's department or Olathe PD—but it involves a flashlight that I have now. It's an antique-looking seven-D-cell "coon hunter's light" (these were before Kel-Lites became popular in law enforcement), and it's in sections that screw together to make it less than seven cells if ya want to. Well, the story goes that there was this disturbance, and the guy was combative. Ya know what that means…we become combative and use the force necessary to make the arrest when they do. So my dad hit this guy over the head—in self-defense, of course—and that damn flashlight flew apart. Batteries and pieces flew everywhere, they said, and it was funny. When my dad died, I inherited that flashlight, and I took it to a guy, you know "the guy," who's a welder and soldered it back together. It now proudly hangs in my office

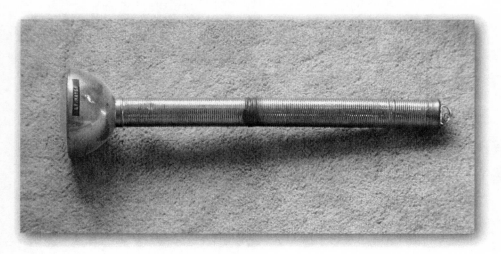

as another one of my family mementos. Another incident was when then Deputy Tom Lawrukiewicz was bent over a table by a prisoner at which time my dad welcomed the back of the guy's head with a slapper, a leather bound sizable piece of lead rendering bad guy unconscious.

My dad was involved in a stolen car incident, a high-speed chase in which the bad guys ran three stop signs at high speeds but were apprehended and booked into the county jail, assisted by Sgt. Al Bell. Strange how things happen, because Sgt. Al Bell resigned from Olathe PD and came to the county sheriff's office and was one of my district officers when I was road patrol sergeant.

I have a picture of Junior's demonstration of new motor scooters the city had purchased, for what reason I do not know, and also this one of him raising the stars and stripes at Veterans Park with Oscar Berry (O B) Deaton standing in salute. This was a daily task for Olathe officers at that time.

He was in the news for a few car wrecks, some with injuries and some not, but that was about it. One story he told was about an Olathe LEO who

was standing on the front porch of a house interviewing an occupant. As he talked he was swinging his night stick, being cool don cha know, he hit himself in the jaw, knocking himself off the porch. That guy wasn't there very long, but like everyone else, some guys think they are pretty cool.

During the time my dad was at working Olathe PD, there was a family disturbance that was one of many at the same household. After responding to several calls in a two-week period, he told the couple, "I don't want to come back here unless there's a shooting or a stabbing." The next week, the woman stabbed her husband so ya got to be careful who ya give advice to; some are dumb enough to follow your lead. This was similar to another case in Wichita I will mention in a later chapter.

Within a month of his return to the sheriff's department following Lynn Thomas's election loss to Fred Allenbrand, Junior was promoted to sergeant in charge of the road patrol. He was later promoted to lieutenant, where he remained until his death in August of 1968. He had finally taken a much-needed vacation trip to Colorado and ironically died at Hays, Kansas, of a heart attack on the return trip home.

Several cases or incidents that Junior worked on his return to the sheriff's department were armed robberies and two homicides. On one homicide, he was first to arrive on the scene where two guys had been in a fight and one killed the other with a shotgun. This was funny in that the killer kept saying, "Yeah, I shot the son of a bitch, and I would shoot the son of a bitch again." He was saying this over and over. When two of the witnesses were brought to the office for statements the woman had trench mouth so bad she later had to be hospitalized. That seemed to be funny to all of the black-hearted cops on scene at the time. That case ended in a decision of guilt by a jury.

There was one other tragic homicide case he was involved in where a local kid killed his girlfriend. Dad was first on scene, and this really bothered him because he had two daughters, one who was the same age as the victim at the time.

He was involved in a case where two locals hopped a train in Kansas City, Kansas, after a burglary, and as the train came into Olathe, it was stopped. The railroad had been called and advised to stop in Olathe. Both guys were ordered off the train at gunpoint by the brakeman in the caboose. They were both caught in short order, one while he was walking down the street, and the other surrendered at a beer joint. Both were convicted for their crimes.

He was one of the first officers on scene on several armed robbery cases. One resulted in the bad guy being shot in a shootout with Overland Park Officer Ron Thompson who shot the bastard with a shotgun, darn near killed the guy who was lucky to survive that gun battle shooting as he jumped off of his getaway vehicle, a motorcycle at a freeway entrance. Dad's picture ended up regularly in local newspapers and did on these robberies.

Chapter 6

The Gazette column

I have been a writer of sorts for almost my entire life beginning in grade school. I have had articles published in a variety of papers and most recently articles dealing with law enforcement and my column in the *Johnson's County Gazette*. Keith and Ann Johnson, the publishers of the *Gazette*, are very pro–law enforcement and encouraged me to write more for them after my initial article.

In the beginning, I wrote four articles for the Gazette, and then the column. It has run for over two years now and still at it. The following paragraph was what the *Johnson's County Gazette* publisher wrote about my column and what it would be about as well as a dedication to law enforcement:

> Introducing a new column dedicated to those in public service of law enforcement and protection from those who prey on us, titled:
> Toward Being a Deputy Sheriff By Retired Johnson County Sheriff's Deputy, Captain Edward (Ed) Hayes
> The Gazette will be publishing in upcoming issues a lawman's career from day one to retirement from the Johnson County Kansas Sheriff's Department Captain Ed Hayes (ret) is a 4th generation LEO who has stories to tell. The Gazette has confirmed many of the incidents by newspaper articles and Hayes scrapbook as well as his fathers and grandfathers LEO scrapbooks.

The first article I wrote for the Gazette was published in November of 2014 and was intended to correct the many errors that have been in a county magazine about the Metcalf State Bank robbery that happened in 1968. There were articles in another local publication, a small magazine quoting people who didn't know what the hell they were talking about—they had heard partly factual stories that they were repeating third hand. A few points that had been published were just bizarre, such as quotes by some LEOs who were not even there at the time according to some that were. That's all I wanted to do, set the record straight, because I was there from the get-go. Keith gave me that opportunity.

The Metcalf State Bank robbery was just one incident in my career where I could have (as a comedian says) been seriously killed. I was once asked by a first responder as they were transporting me to a hospital from an accident scene, "Which of your nine lives is this, Ed?" My answer was, "Hell's bells, I'm on my third set." He thought I was kidding, but I wasn't. I have had many close calls in my lifetime in and out of law enforcement. See my bio (it ain't fiction either) at the back of this book, and you may understand how. In my younger years and into my sixties I had the balance of a cat. In tight or tough situations, I have had the gift of instant and proper reaction at the right time; I credit my descendants with that. Some the result of training and doing, some was skill, and some was just plain and simple dumb luck. I have had a lot of that in my life.

The Metcalf State Bank Robbery

A short article that I wrote on the Metcalf State Bank robbery was published in the *Johnson's County Gazette* of Olathe, Kansas, on August 15,
2014. This was an interesting case by almost anyone's standards and my
first article which began like this:

> The Metcalf State Bank robbery of 1968 by Edward B Hayes, a
> 4th generation Law Enforcement Officer, LEO, a retired Captain
> of the Johnson County Kansas Sheriff's Office who was there and
> involved, not a robber, just a cop.
>
> Several articles in a local print magazine have mentioned the
> Metcalf State Bank Robbery which happened in January of 1968.
> I wanted to set the record straight because some facts in recent
> articles were in error and sparse on accurate information so I now
> tell it like it really was from personal experience. First of all the
> FBI wasn't even there until after the gunfight with the exception
> of *MAYBE* one FBI agent who afterwards said he was. A lot of
> people like to say they were at a given incident and this shootout
> was no different. The FBI arrived after the shooting stopped and
> as usual grabbed the camera shots as they always did in those days,
> maybe still today, the media just loves the FBI. At the time I was a
> young Detective with the Johnson County Sheriff's Department,
> my attendance was documented by the Kansas City Star with my
> picture on the front page as they were carrying the bad guy out of
> the apartment on a stretcher.

Oscar Smith is a veteran crime reporter with the Kansas City Star working the crime scene beat. "Smitty" was the most trusted area reporter by we LEO's who knew/know him. It's a quiet day on crime scene reporting so he is sitting near and above Overland Park's, Metcalf State Bank on a side street monitoring his police scanner covering the Kansas City area. He sees a car he will later know was occupied by Henry Floyd Brown and Andrew Evan Gipson sitting on the street near the bank. Concentrating on his work at hand, listening to his police scanner Smitty doesn't think much about this occupied car. As said, he will later know it was occupied by Henry Floyd Brown and Andrew Evan Gipson, supposed members of the radical Weatherman group which rob banks to finance their anti-American activities. Brown and Gipson are casing the bank that they will rob the next day.

"Shep," an Overland Park motorcycle patrolman has been alerted as all have that a bomb has exploded under the radio tower behind the Overland Park Police Department at 87th and Antioch. Due to the reported explosion all are on alert when another call comes out, "the Metcalf State Bank has been robbed," a car description goes out. Shortly after that broadcast Shep sees the car and follows it, gunshots ring out and Shep says he is hit in his lip. He and his motorcycle goes down. There have always been skeptics on whether Shep was hit by a bullet or something else. He radios "officer down," everyone is now on high alert and looking for that car, different than the one witnessed by Smitty the previous day.

After shooting at Shep's motorcycle the two robbers carjack a vehicle a few blocks away and we are now looking for a stolen *convertible owned by a Sheriff reserve officer carjacked from his wife and small child. At some point Gipson is dropped off at a prearranged location and leaves the area with the girls. The car jacked vehicle is located at an apartment complex in the 7700 block of West 85th street in Overland Park. Officers from nearly every Johnson County, Kansas police department as well as the Johnson

County Sheriff's Department and one Highway Patrolman con-
verge on the apartments. After a search of the apartments, an all-
clear is announced. Uniform Patrolman Bill Loveless and I get in
his marked patrol car to return to my car few blocks away from
the scene. As Loveless puts the car in gear to back away we get an
alert that one of the suspects may still be in the apartment building so we get out and surround the building. There's 150 Officers
on scene according to then Overland Park, Kansas Police Chief,
John Kenyan. We don't know IF he was even there but I didn't see
that many officers nor did others I have talked to since and I have
to wonder, were there even 150 Officers at the time in Johnson
County Kansas?

At this point gunfire from the apartment breaks out. Officers
try to enter the suspect apartment and are shot at through the door.
Six officers are on the west side of the apartment including myself
when gunfire breaks out. The window above us shatters as multiple
shots ring out, no one is hit *yet.*

The gun battle continues and some of us are positioned in the
open West side yard. Someone yells, "we need a car for cover." I
run to the marked Sheriff's car that Loveless and I had just got out
of minutes ago, it's 150 ft away. As I get to the driver's door of the
car, I see that Kansas Highway Patrol Sergeant Eldon Miller,[1] a
friend has beaten me to the car, engine is running. Miller has been
shot through the windshield of the patrol car. He is lying back in
the seat, his head back, a hole in his forehead, there's no doubt. I
move around to the passenger side of the car and report "officer
shot" over that car's radio. A Leawood Patrol Officer and I roll the
car back out of the line of fire so Miller can be moved although

1 *On May 17, 2017, HB 2203 was signed by Kansas governor Sam Brownback dedicating
a portion of Highway 75 going through Topeka, Kansas, to the memory of KHP sergeant
Eldon E. Miller. It only took fifty years to do this. Years later the reserve deputies daughter,
Debbie became a sheriff's deputy.

there's no question of his condition, we know it, he will be transported to the hospital but sadly, he's gone.

Reports will say that Sgt. Miller was knocked "all the way into the back seat" of that car, he was not, I am in the front seat with him as I radio dispatch, officer down. The firefight continues as Harley Sparks an Investigator for the Johnson County District Attorney's Office and Patrolman David Slade evacuate a lady and her 2 month old child from the apartment across the hallway through a window on the East side of the building. Bullets penetrate that apartment through the walls but luckily, no one else is hit.

KHP Sgt. Eldon Miller
Chapter #7

Brown said he was randomly firing out of the apartment and not at anyone in particular. On that day, you would not have been able to prove that to me, I have pictures of half of the sliding door either open or shot out. I emptied a box of 00 buck shells went into that apartment somewhere and as I remember through the sliding glass door, Brown disagrees but as badly as he was wounded & carried out on a stretcher he couldn't have known. That 00 went somewhere into that apartment and I had a detective and a news reporter standing behind me.

A good friend of mine, Detective David Slade[2] was handing me 00 shells as fast as I could reload and shoot them. A local news guy was leaning over my shoulder, microphone in hand reporting the action on live radio. He laughed when I said, "John you're going to get shot screwing around here." I don't remember exactly what his response was, he's laughing nervously, "it's my job!" was part of it.

The gunfight continues as I and others pound the apartment with gunfire, the occupant continues shooting back. Slade is now standing behind me at the corner of an adjacent building as I empty my shotgun into the sliding glass door of the apartment, Slade hands me ammunition as I empty the weapon several times. At that point, the sliding glass door opens and a can rolls out, someone yells "bomb" and everyone takes cover, the "nine sticks of dynamite" do not explode. The shooting continues for a short time and then stops as the apartment is entered by Sparks and Det. Jack Laptad of the Sheriff's Office. Henry Floyd Brown is found lying on the floor with several wounds. He is the only occupant of the apartment and the shooting is over with one officer fatality. No one else other than Brown is injured, he survives. Guns, dynamite and the money stolen in the robbery is recovered.

Henry Floyd Brown is the only suspect arrested at the apartment, three others including accomplice Andrew Evan Gipson are arrested within days. All are convicted of crimes and do their time. At the time, the death penalty was still the law however then

2 Sadly, Detective Slade died some years ago as he was attending a funeral for a police officer in KCK. He had moved on to the Leawood, Kansas, Police Department, where he held the rank of corporal.

District Court Judge Herbert Walton does not give that sentence much to the disappointment of most officers in Johnson County.

In the first part of 2016, I was interviewed with Brown for a documentary produced by Benjamin Meade, owner and producer of Cosmic Cowboy Studio in Kansas City, Missouri, to be aired at a later date. I had been interviewed previously without Brown presence. Ben knew I had hard feelings toward Brown, I made no bones about it. A funny thing was when my "backup" retired deputy sheriff Lee Branum and I arrived, a big guy got out of his car in front of us and went inside. We figured that he was Ben and Henry's backup in case there was a problem. We knew it, they knew it, and we all smiled. There wasn't going to be a problem.

Henry was a very angry young man in 1968 and long before that. He hated the FBI, other federal agents, and the government. He had spent fifty years of his life in fifteen-plus prisons, one of which was Alcatraz. He told me that in the gun battle he had had no intentions of hurting any local LEOs; it just happened as he was firing out the window of the apartment randomly. That could have been me or anyone, but it was Kansas Highway Patrol sergeant Eldon Miller who just happened to be in the "wrong place at the wrong time," according to Henry. I found that Henry had mellowed in his later years and was liked by almost everyone who knew him in his workplace as well as in his retirement home after he retired. I don't know what his source of income was at that time, but folks I knew said he was always complaining about not having any money. No income other than social service support was probably the case. He had very little or no social security to speak of because he had been in prison most of his adult life! When Brown was whining about not having any money Ben told him something like this, "what do you expect Henry, you robbed banks, You were in prison, much of your life you didn't work."

Brown's accounting of the robbery varies from my Gazette article, officer's reports, and news reports. He says that if I was shooting into the sliding glass door, the door was still closed when he was taken out on a stretcher. It may have been, but there was no glass, and all I can say is that a box of

00 buck went into that apartment somewhere. The news articles state that Brown was shooting out of that door, so I think Henry was wrong, and as gravely wounded as he was, he wouldn't have known. None of us believed he would survive. Henry says he didn't shoot the officer on the motorcycle and that the officer is lying—Henry's words, not mine. Brown says he was shooting at and hit the police radio on the motorcycle. He says he didn't intentionally shoot the highway patrolman, that he was just firing out the windows, and he also said that their intention was not to harm any local police officers, but the FBI was another thing. He hated the FBI for what he said they did to him, and he said that it was the FBI that put him on the path of a life of crime. According to Brown, he was first sent to prison on a bogus auto theft charge. For some reason an FBI agent had it out for him (according to Henry), and he was charged auto theft for not returning a rented car. He says he didn't steal it, but he didn't have the money to fight it. His revenge? Throw bombs and rob banks for the overthrow of the US Government.

Brown's group was robbing banks in the time of the Weathermen bombings and robberies of banks and financial institutions. Toward the end of the interview, still filming Benjamin said, "Now can we have a handshake?"

I looked at him and said, "No, I'm not shaking his hand." There was a moment of silence, and I weakened. "I'll shake your hand, Henry, but I still don't like you for what you were and did." He smiled and just gave me a nod, we shook hands, the cameras went off, and we talked more. I have to say that by the time we left the studio, I did like Henry, and I could tell he respected me, it's strange, but we liked each other. That's a large studio, and he followed me out, talking to me all the way, stopping a few times to talk. I told Henry I was writing a book and asked for his permission to include him, he gave me permission to write anything about him I wanted to, "I know you will be honest" he said..

I intended to go back at a later time and meet with Henry, buy his lunch, and talk, but I put it off too long. At the time of the interview, Brown was frail and in his eighties. Henry Floyd Brown died on March 24, 2016.

His obituary was published on March 27th. Henry is an example of what a man could have been had he put his energy to good use instead of being a crook. He did get a college degree while in the penitentiary but by the time of his release it was too late.

Chapter 8

The filming of "In Cold Blood"

The first movie of Truman Capote's book *In Cold Blood* was released in 1967. The book and movie dealt with the heinous murders of the Herb Clutter family near Holcomb, Kansas, in 1959, committed by a couple of lowlife, dirt bag criminals. What many don't know is that much of that movie was filmed in Olathe and the Johnson County, Kansas, area between Olathe and Edgerton. Why, you may ask? Because the two killers frequented the area prior to the crime, especially Richard Hickock, who lived on a small farm near Edgerton, Kansas

Scenes were of the Old Olathe Hotel on the northeast corner of the square, the Hickock farm near Edgerton, Ray's Skelly station in Edgerton, and some of the highway scenes on US 56 between Flatly Road (now 167th Street) and Clare Road and from Clare Road to the eastern edge of Gardner, Kansas.

I know this because as a young road patrol sergeant with the Johnson County, Kansas, Sheriff's Department, I was assigned to work security during the local filming of that movie. Other deputies were assigned, but I don't recall who they were.

The assignment was interesting and welcomed by me since I was a movie buff as well as knowing one of the killers, Richard Hickock. I knew him from what was then the local Olathe hangout, Zeke's Pool Hall, which was located in the middle of the block on the west side of Kansas Avenue and across the street from the courthouse. The sheriff's office holding facility is now located over where Zeke's once was. On the southwest corner was the Hitching Post beer joint where Hickock also hung out, we all did. I and others hung out there too, I bought my first draft beer at the age of fourteen,

I was kidding when I placed my order but I was served, coulda blown me over. I enjoyed hanging out with my buddies listening to beer joint music by Hank Williams, Patsy Cline, and others from the fifties. Olathe, Kansas, in the 1950s was a carbon copy of the town and kids of the movie *American Graffiti*. The cars, kids, characters, hamburger stands—it was just the same and a great place to grow up, a much safer and happy time for all of us locals.

I never chummed around with Hickock, who was older than I was; I just played pool with him from time to time, saw him in the Hitching Post or walking around town on the courthouse square sidewalks. We were acquaintances, not friends. He seemed like a misfit and a loner to me. I don't remember him ever being with anyone. We were friendly with each other, but I was friendly to almost everyone.

The murder of the Clutter family near Holcomb was big news everywhere, and when I found out Hickock was one of the suspects, it was hard to believe. A person I knew committed what was then the crime of the century? Of course, I never saw him again; he was in jail, soon in prison, and soon on death row.

I just happened to be working the nights the last four executions by hanging in Kansas were carried out, and at one time I had hard-copy teletypes (on Smith and Hickock) that were sent to all law enforcement with the announcements. That's what they did then. These victories for law enforcement and victims were sent to every police and sheriff's department in Kansas that had a teletype. The last four executions by hanging were Hickock and Smith and Latham and York. The night Hickock and Smith were hanged, I watched for and collected the teletypes. I do not have them anymore as I cannot find them.

The execution dates were as follows:

Perry Smith, April 14, 1965 (murderer of Clutter family, November 15, 1959), a half hour before Richard Hickock
    Richard Hickock, April 14, 1965
    George York, June 22, 1965, a half hour before James Latham
    James Latham, June 22, 1965

During the movie production, the actors and Director Richard Brooks were staying at the Olathe Hotel in downtown Olathe. The crew members were staying in the old motel on the west side of Provence Village (a.k.a. pregnant village because almost every female there was knocked up, and it was so named by locals) on Highway 56 across the highway from what then was the Olathe skating rink. Each morning we would meet in the skating rink parking lot where director Richard Brooks would lay out the plans for the day. We were all treated with respect, especially by the film crew who were glad to have us on board. The apparatus that held the cameras was a new invention of one of the crew, and he proudly told us all about it as it hung to the side of the 1953 Pontiac used in the movie.

The main actors, Robert Blake and Scott Wilson, were present every day, as was author Truman Capote, who at the time I was not familiar with. He was just this seemingly strange little guy who sat around on a stool with his funny hat, legs crossed, and he didn't say much at all unless asked.

The actor that played Hickock's father was around during some of the shooting, as was Jean Simmons (not in the movie) who was the wife of Brooks. A classy lady she was.

As mentioned the locations were between Olathe and Edgerton, with the main highway scenes filmed on US 56 between Clare Curve and Moonlight Road. They filmed in daylight, but in the movie, scenes were shaded to nighttime. A few scenes were filmed at the Hickock farm, which was east of the Edgerton cemetery near I-35.

I briefly met John Forsythe who played KBI agent Alvin Dewey, as his scenes were in Olathe and the Olathe Hotel only as far as I remember. My dad drove Forsythe up to the courthouse in a mock sheriff's department marked car with the Olathe Hotel sign in the background. Dad was paid thirty-five dollars for his small part in the movie. He was just a shadow in the car as it stopped to let Forsythe out at the courthouse.

Ray Braun, owner and operator of Rays Skelly, was in the movie's opening scene, but I don't recall any other local folks being in the movie, nor do I remember any other sheriff's officers who worked security on the film crew. A lot of deputies have come and gone since 1965, and looking at old rosters, I don't even remember some of them. The mind is a terrible thing.

Other incidental information about the Hickock and Smith killings came from Richard "Butch" Holland when I asked him about the Olathe Hotel history.

The Olathe Hotel was a general store operated by two men in the mid-1800s and the oldest building in Olathe at the time. It was demolished by the city of Olathe in the ignorant "urban renewal" debacle in the sixties. After the general store was hit by a tornado, one of the owners left Kansas, and the other rebuilt the structure, turning it into a hotel. It was owned by Zed Holland and staffed by the Holland family. Butch Holland was working the desk one day when in comes Richard Hickock of Edgerton, Kansas, to book a room for one night. "For how many?" Holland asks. "Two," says Hickock, and he signs the register. It turns out that Holland has to work the night shift as the regular employee is off sick or drunk. Around 2:00 a.m. the bell rings, the door opens, and in come Hickock and Smith. "You guys must've been really busy," says Holland. "Yep, we were busy," they say. As it turns out, they were returning from the Clutter family massacre.

A month later KBI agents arrived at the hotel wanting to see and search the room, which Butch let them into. Found in the box springs of the bed was a hidden pair of side-cutter-type pliers. These cutters were matched to the ropes used to tie the hands and legs of the Clutters before they were executed. This find, along with the confessions, helped seal the convictions and death sentence of Hickock and Smith.

Fast-forward a few years, and the actors and film crew of the movie *In Cold Blood* arrived and asked for the entire hotel. Rooms were booked, so it was impossible to give them the entire hotel, but they were allowed a few rooms for actors and producer Richard Brooks. The crew "wrecked" the hotel, and Zed Holland said he was angry that "they're turning my hotel into a flophouse." According to Butch, they did put everything back as it was when they were finished. Besides being in the hotel business, Zed was a bondsman, as was Butch.

Chapter 9

The Johnson County Jailbreak

T his article was published in the *Johnson's County Gazette* February 1, 2015.

The Johnson County Kansas Sheriff's Office jailbreak, September 16, 1966 by Ed Hayes 4th generation LEO, retired Captain, Johnson County Sheriff's Office 2/01/15.

Lynn Thomas Was Sheriff[3]

In the fall of 1966 during the late evening shift 7 prisoners in the Johnson County, Kansas Jail overpowered jailer Cassius "Buzz" Stanley, beat him, tied him up took and the elevator down one floor, climbed out of a 2nd floor courthouse window, jumped onto an overhang and escaped into the night. At the time, I was uniform Sergeant assisting my district officer with an injury accident in an unincorporated area of the county. My supervisor at the time, Lt. Randy Samuels AKA "shakey" had left his post to come to the accident scene which was a no no as he was duty officer; he was supposed to stay in the office. Randy and I had a definite personality conflict which was usually present as it was this day and why he came to the accident scene, he had an obvious dislike for me. He was telling me what to do and how to work the accident at which time I offered to leave and let him work it, that's how bad it got with him and me on that occasion. He ragged

---

3 Fred Allenbrand became sheriff in January of 1967. Sheriff Thomas was gone. Lt. Samuels was reduced in rank to detective in the change of sheriffs. Captain John Eulgem, who had a heart attack the day after the jailbreak recovered, returned to work but resigned when Allenbrand took office. Tony Lane stayed with the sheriff's office for a few years then resigned to work as a patrolman in Lakewood, Colorado, more on Tony later.

me each and every chance he got and was forever pissed when I didn't follow his usual ignorant and wrong instructions. Undersheriff William "Bill" Day had my back on this problem and was probably the only reason I wasn't suspended or fired.

The largest jailbreak in Johnson County history was accomplished by one of the prisoners asking for aspirin feigning a headache. As Jailer Stanley opened the door he was overpowered, beat and tied up with bed blankets and sheets.

As we were wrapping up the accident scene dispatcher J F "Tony" Lane called over the two way radio and told us to come to the office right away. I advised we were still busy with the accident at which time Tony advised us to come to the office without delay in a very stern voice. When asked why he would give no reason as it was not his place to broadcast the jailbreak to the media, it was Duty Officer Samuel's place. I knew it was something serious and Samuels must have as well as he left for the courthouse and the district officer and I finished the accident. We later learned that the dispatchers had heard a crash when the escapees jumped from a second story window onto a roof over the rear entrance to the courthouse ironically from the district attorney's office. Tony went into the jail where he found jailer Stanley tied up. Having finished the accident scene I proceeded to the Sheriff's Office to see what the hell was going on arriving at the same time as operations Commander, Captain John Eulgem. As we talked in the rear jail parking lot Eulgem filled me in on the jailbreak, at about that time Samuels exits the courthouse. Eulgem asks Samuels "where are you going Randy?" "Going out to find escapees," he replies at which time Eulgem visibly upset yelled, "Randy, you get your fucking ass back in that office. If you had been in there, where you were supposed to be this wouldn't have happened in the first place." I left the area to search for escapees with a smile on my face, I had won a battle that night and I was in celebration and I…I was going out to search for escapees without Randy getting in the way… again. I didn't have much of a problem out of Samuels after that night since he was demoted back to detective when Sheriff Allenbrand took office. He was never promoted again, remained detective until he retired. He was an

OK guy I guess but just didn't like me; Eulgem's nickname for Randy was "grandma." Funny thing was when I became Sgt. again I outranked him and ooooh, that had to hurt, remember this? Be nice to everyone you can, ya never know who ya might end up working for.

By this time besides us officers from every police department in the county and the Kansas Highway Patrol were out looking for escapees. None were found that evening, morning or during daylight the next day. We searched from Santa Fe street to the North, witnesses reported seeing some of the escapees running but we found none of them, they had a big head start. At the time, we thought that they had all gone north but later found that at least two of them had gone south to Oklahoma and were later apprehended in Texas two weeks later trying to steal a car. It was later found that two stayed all night under the bridge near the courthouse and the rest went separate directions. The main area searched the first evening was between Olathe and Lenexa where the operators of Smiley's Golf Course (now gone) turned on the lights allowing that area to be well searched and from Lenexa to the North. Patrol officers from other NE cities joined in the search. Two escapees were captured the next evening in Merriam, taken into custody by two Olathe reserve officers. The two "reserve officers" were Fred Allenbrand soon to be Sheriff who had defeated then Sheriff Lynn Thomas in the primaries (irony?) and Harley Sparks an investigator for the Johnson County District Attorney's Office.

Over the next few days the others were apprehended with the exception of the two in Texas. All were convicted or plead guilty except one who was acquitted because of being threatened and forced to leave. Another who plead not guilty claimed he too was threatened by an escapee with a screw driver but was convicted anyway, different juries? Two other inmates chose to stay in the jail avoiding prosecution.

Prisoner Transports

It seems funny now but after Allenbrand was sworn in and Lt. Samuels was demoted, I was assigned to take a prisoner transportation trip with him of all people. Now we are both detectives so he couldn't lecture me any longer, he's been busted and so have I but I understood and didn't care so much, I still loved my job. On this trip all Randy did was bitch and whine about his demotion and how he had been done wrong, I had to put up with this for two days! Was I sympathetic? Not on your life but we got along OK after that.

A trip to Albuquerque New Mexico with another Detective, Less Shriver was an OK trip. It was a long driving trip so it was over several days. When we got there we went to a movie, saw the great Gregory Peck movie, The Stalking Moon, still one of my favorites. A couple of things happened while we were there. One, we went up the tram on Mt. Sandi and while there I saw my first skiers coming off the lift and going down the mountain. It was at that point I decided that I was going to become a downhill skier which I did a few years later. The other thing was that while we were watching the movie our car, parked on the street was broken into so we had to have that repaired before we started the long drive home, nothing was taken from the car as there were no weapons or otherwise in it at the time.

On another trip, Detective at the time, Ed Schlesselman and I flew into Tampa, Florida for a prisoner. When we landed at the airport it was raining like a cow pissing on a flat rock so Ed says, "I guess we'll rent a car and go to the picture show, huh?" I say to Ed, "you can go to the picture show IF ya want Ed but I haven't seen a beach for a long time, I'm going to the beach! I've got the car because I outrank him and he decides he will go with me. It was sunshine before we left so we had a very enjoyable day on Clearwater Beach, had a couple of beers in the sunshine and enjoyed the views, had great seafood for dinner and flew home the next day. It was a lousy assignment but someone had to do it!

There was a solo trip I made to Tucson AZ to pick up a prisoner who had been an informant and had violated his parole. It was an overnighter but the agent from Sheriff Joe's squad always welcomed me during my down time any time I was there which ended up being four, maybe five trips, I don't recall for sure. When we were boarding the airplane to return the ticket guy decided he was going to flex his authority and ordered me to take the handcuffs off my prisoner which I refused. He said, "you're not getting on the airplane unless you take the cuffs off." We argued back and forth for a couple minutes to which I said, "OK, then you can take him to the airplane, he's your responsibility, you board him, we can do it that way," he thought about this for a moment and finally let me have it my way, I was right and he knew it. Air travel in that time period was a bit different then. If the captain allowed it, we carried our weapon on the aircraft or he kept it in the cockpit, we flew all over the US armed. Prisoners were cuffed until we were seated or not, this guy knew it, he was just trying to be a hard ass and it didn't work out for him.

Chapter 10

The 1968 Riots in Kansas City

Spearheaded by the assassination of Dr. Martin Luther King Jr. on April 4, 1968, the riots of April 8 in Kansas City, Missouri, had an effect on the entire metro area. With the exception of fires, rioting gangs marching, and property damage in KCMO, the streets and highways of Johnson County were like a science fiction movie, empty and eerie. If something moved, it was stopped. The only persons allowed on the streets those that had critical jobs, and no one was to be on the streets after the eight o'clock curfew except law enforcement, first responders, and the National Guard, whose weapons were not armed.

The Johnson County Sheriff's Office had recently purchased the first paddy wagon for prisoner transfer for the county and cities. During the riots, I had the assignment of picking up the folks that had no real reason to be out, those that defied the curfew, which was strictly enforced. Roadblocks were on most of the main streets coming into Johnson County cities, and they were manned by law enforcement backed up by national guardsmen.

In Kansas City, Missouri, structure and car fires were set, windows were smashed, mobs marched on the streets, and some citizens were shot. According to the news media, five were killed, but if you talked to the local police, you'd find out that the number killed was higher than that. As is the case now, the media was not reporting the truth. One local TV station reported that Kansas City was "peaceful." The *Kansas City Star* reported that there were 450 officers on twelve-hour shifts and 660 national guardsmen.

There were 150 fires were of "incendiary nature"—that's arson, folks, but it was "peaceful" in Kansas City.

A friend of mine who lived in KCMO at the time said this:

I was just nineteen at the time and a college student. I was living at forty-first and McGee, but a friend of mine's father invited me to stay with his family in Little Italy. It was far safer than any other place in KC, including police stations, but from there we could see a lotta fires, hear a lotta gunshots and sirens. Most cars had a black ribbon tied around the steering column, including mine. That meant Mafia protected, and carried a lot of weight. Panel vans with gun slots patrolled the perimeter. In the evenings, we sat on the front lawns, ate pasta, and drank wine or beer. The unrest did not exist in Little Italy.

Another who worked in KCMO said this:

I was working at the Jones Store at 12TH & main in KCMO... the Jones Store had barbwire barricades around the store windows, snipers on the roof, and at each entrance security officers.

Inside, each floor had 4 to 6 executives (myself included)... customers were allowed in to the store all day.

We had one incident where a gang of black youths walked in and took numerous leather coats off the rack to walk out with. I was in charge of that floor and had to stop them and pointed to all the personnel who were ready to stop them. They laid the coats down and exited.

During the afternoon I/we witnessed the confrontation between the marchers and the police right in front of our door, barricades were up on the middle of 12th street and the police arm in arm with riot gear, stood within a few feet of a whole lot of rioters. The street was full side to side...after a lot of shouting and arm waving the groups backed away...as an aside one of the ladies who worked for me and was inside the store, was the wife of the KC riot leader; when I drove back to Olathe that evening there were fires very visible along Southwest Traffic way.

Since my recent health diagnosis, Judy & I have been looking back at events in our life and had just recently discussed this very event.

Danny Chesney

Other than just driving around picking up those arrested, I remember two things that happened. Deputy Charlie Brazelton, who had been a KCK cop, was riding with me, and as we were returning to Olathe on I-35, we saw a patrol car that had a belligerent pedestrian stopped. Deputy Jim Malson was obviously having trouble with the guy. Charlie and I got out of the paddy wagon, and before I knew it Charlie walked up and bitch-slapped the guy and said, "Just be nice to the man." That was the end of the conversation. The attitude instantly changed, and the guy went to jail, that's the way it works sometimes.

One other incident was when a car ran the roadblock on the Eighteenth Street Expressway on the Johnson County line. A national guardsman raised his rifle as if to shoot but with no bullets. We all just laughed. I don't know what he would have done if he had had bullets, but it is best that he did not in this case. Quiet and boring for the most part in Johnson County, Kansas, it was.

Chapter 11

The Secret of Getting Ahead Is Getting Started

Mark Twain

As a kid, I marveled at what I believed my grandfather was and did, but I didn't know the half of it until much later. I always respected him and my father, as most young people do their parents and grandparents. He commanded respect, just as my father did; it came naturally for both. My step-grandmother, not so much. She was from old money in her first marriage, and as I remember she was not a warm and friendly person toward me and my siblings, kind of aloof, prim and proper she was. They both dressed like they were going to a ball or the opera, she in elegant dresses, and he in a three-piece suit. I suspect he musta been pretty pussy whipped to the largest degree; never saw him out of a suit or uniform. Grandchildren have that love and respect, especially those of us that follow in their footsteps.

You're a Fourth-Generation What?

I have his scrapbook that he kept up for many years, and in that book there is a history of KCK law enforcement. With his story and career, we could make a movie. Ironically, a lot of what he did was mirrored in my career. He was busting liquor stills early in his career, and I was busting drug labs when I was working undercover investigations for seven years. He was, I am told, a man who went "by the book." I heard this from a number of LEOs that had worked for and with him, including my friend retired KCK Captain Byron Horn, who swears my grandfather was a legend in the KCK Police Department. He most likely was, but like me, he wasn't liked by all. Some people don't like to go "by the book," some people don't like to *work* in any profession, and law enforcement is no different for some.

When I was a teenager, that old boy (Granddad) put the fear of God in me; he needed to tell me only once, "If you do anything that winds you up in jail, I will see to it that you stay there!" The Hayes name meant everything to him and my dad, and then to me as well. A name means a lot, doesn't it? However…I was like every other kid: I was ornery, and I liked to have fun. I have witnesses. Each and every time I did anything ornery, I sweated it out. I'm not talking about stealing…just being ornery, playing jokes, screwing with folks in one way or the other. I will say some of the things we did then would now be criminal, but back then it was just being ornery. Like turning over outhouses, putting Limburger cheese on the high school radiators (I didn't do this, but I was there)…ahh, let's see, what else? Climbing the water tower with OB Deaton just for fun in all kinds of weather, especially loved doin it when it was snowing, going up and down the steep hills on the gravel of Prairie Center Road as fast as a 1953 Chrysler Imperial loaded with screaming girls would go on not the best of tires—how about balding tires? How about throwing cherry bombs out the windows of a moving car, or ditching school to go swimming? That was all in my years of Olathe High School, and yep, I sweated a bit since I had been properly threatened by you know who. I had been put on notice.

My dad was old school as well. He instilled in me these quotes:

"A man's word is his bond."
"Never give up a confidence."
"Every man has his price. Mine is millions."
"Honesty is only as good as your name. Remember that!"
"Don't be a snitch!" He instructed all of his subordinates the same values.

I know where he got those old-school values—from his dad. I have always hoped I could be as good a man as he and my granddad were, and I hoped to live up to their expectations. They both died fairly young, my granddad at sixty-two. He never knew that I went into law enforcement, and my dad lived only three years after I was an LEO. He died at the age of forty-seven, ironically in Hays, Kansas, returning from a vacation trip in Colorado.

My dad didn't get into law enforcement until he was in his later thirties, but he made his mark. He was highly respected by his supervisors, peers, and subordinates whom he taught well. Some peers were jealous, but that's part of any profession where there are some that just can't hack it, some that don't, some that are downright lazy, and some jealous of success in being a good cop, a good training officer, or a good supervisor. As in each and every profession, every positive and almost every negative personality exists in the ranks of law enforcement. There's backbiting, there's jealousy for different reasons, and people will be cutthroat to beat you in the ranks or to be favored by their superiors.

Other than my grandfather, my very first contact with police was in Clinton, Oklahoma, when I was in the sixth grade working as a paper boy. Every morning I got up at the crack of dawn, in any weather, and delivered my papers, and then from there I went to school. I remember rushing through my tasks with my first pal, a brown cocker spaniel puppy dog named Ginger following along with me on my paper route and then to school. He stood by until I got out of class, and then we went home together. Ginger was my best and most faithful buddy, my first pet. One damp foggy morning, I found the front door of one of my gas station customers shattered, and the place had been burglarized, so I flagged down a police officer, reported the crime, was interviewed, and went on my way. I never knew any more about that burglary, whether it was cleared or not, but the officers always waved at me after that as I delivered my papers. I thought it was cool that they recognized and acknowledged me.

In addition, many trips were made to the KCKPD for visits with my grandfather with my Cub Scout troop, led by our den mother, my mother, Mildred. I would proudly introduce my grandfather, Captain Edward B. Hayes Sr. At that time he was in suit and tie and was captain over the patrol division of that department, but he always made time for our visits. He was the founder of the KCK Youth Bureau, now called the Juvenile Division. Other than these visits, I didn't see much of him. He would come by the house for a few minutes once in a while, or we would go by his house but never for very long. I always thought that was a bit strange, but in retrospect I don't think he and my dad were very close—maybe, maybe not. I was too young to care, and it was never explained to me…or if it was, I forgot.

There is a percentage of cops that find they cannot cut it; they just can't do the job because of the dangers that exist or dangers they think exist. All I can say is to give it your best shot before you quit and regret that you did later. Some things come natural, some are trained, and others come with experience. Some find they just don't like the demands of the job or for whatever reason just don't or cannot stick with it as a career. Some reasons are family matters, dangers, the hours, the pay, and other things, personal or otherwise. As I said to our daughter when she had been accepted to the Kansas City, Missouri, Police Department and was ready to enter the academy, "Know this, if you have to…can you or will you shoot someone?" If you have doubts now or when you get to the street, you are probably going into the wrong business. She's been there fifteen years now and is doing great, ranked as Sgt.

I made this clear to any new recruit, and I made sure that they understood. It is an important discussion to have. I will tell you that if you go into law enforcement and really work at it once you are on your own, you will have an interesting and sometimes exciting career. That is if your sheriff or chief will allow you to do your job. Only a few times was I told to hold back on a given activity or investigation by a superior, but it will happen. As you might imagine, I also was told to tone it down by a few fellow deputies, jailers, or dispatchers, mainly because it caused them to do some work. Ohh, the slings and arrows some will suffer, but in my case, I just ignored them and did my job. Now, I am not saying that they were all lazy. Some were, and some were very professional, dedicated, and a credit to the job and uniform. My goals were always to catch the bad guys, and I mean the "real bad guys," not traffic or petty violations (now called infractions). I mean burglars, robbers, and any others committing serious crimes. I wrote more warning tickets during my career than I did traffic tickets, but know this: you will find bad guys and wanted people during traffic stops and car checks as well as other activities involving the public.

Chapter 12

If You Tell the Truth, You Don't Have to Remember Anything
Mark Twain

Along the way, I required some people to work that didn't have the desire. I'm a worker, I self-initiate, so why shouldn't they? One example was radio dispatch during my days in uniform. Some dispatchers really disliked me for the work that I caused them to do. I was always checking on something or someone, and that required more radio traffic and more work for dispatchers. Some were in a position they didn't want; they wanted to be a road patrolman or a detective, not a dispatcher, but most had to do their time in most positions of the department. A few were downright lazy, not dedicated, and did not want to perform, but at times if they wanted to keep their job, they had better do it and do it well. One uniform patrolman that I remember had his mind on about anything but his job. His mind was on pussy and it cost him his position on road patrol and finally his job in dispatch. One bright sunshiny day, he was driving down the street and was distracted, looking at a lady walking down the sidewalk across from the courthouse, and BANG! He rear-ended the car in front of him. Everyone liked him, but he was a screw up. I don't remember exactly, but he had two, maybe three strikes, and he was transferred to dispatch, where he was later caught with his girlfriend in the office. He hadn't changed and was soon relieved of his job. When you embarrass the sheriff, it doesn't go well in your favor.

You will see more instances of screw-ups by LEOs, some funny and some not so funny, but cops are just as human as anyone, as you will see.

I was put into jeopardy a couple of times when I was a patrolman because of a lazy, burned-out sergeant or peers or dispatchers who wanted to go home at shift change or for some other reason wouldn't come to back me up and left me on my own. One incident at shift change was on a car check early in my career that I will never forget. I had a car stopped with three house burglars. They were out of control and all around me. I feared they might take me down, so I called for assistance and got none. That case ended in a burglary clearance in another county. Had it been today, they probably would have killed me rather than risk arrest. Bad guys like that were few and far between at the time, but you need to know that they are out there to some degree. Today's LEOs are in more peril than ever from dangers on the job of one kind or another but if you like excitement, go for it! It's more dangerous and complicated in my opinion than when I went on the job.

Johnson County, Kansas, is unique as are many metropolitan areas of the country. It is a suburb of Kansas City, Missouri, and Kansas City, Kansas, bordering or close to several counties that were more lenient with their crooks. If you got caught in Johnson County for a serious offense, you would go to jail or prison, and the crooks knew it. As odd as it may seem, most of the old-time crooks and cops in that time period had a respect for each other, even though some went to jail—crooks, that is. They didn't do anything in Johnson County or Clay County in Missouri if they were careful. Several times in an arrest of the known bad guys, I heard them say, "Damn, I wish I had known I was in Johnson County. I wouldn't have done it."

When I began writing articles for my column in the *Johnson's County Gazette*, I agreed to write on one condition. I asked editor Keith Johnson to take a look at my scrapbook with police reports, newspaper articles, pictures, letters of commendation, and atta-boy letters, anything else he wanted to see. Why? Because there would be those that may think I make some of this up, including some LEOs, working and retired. It would be easy to do, but I have always said, "If you doubt me, come and look at my records, my office, and my stuff."

The more I got into writing articles and my column for the *Gazette*, the more I remembered, and there were the retired officers who reminded me of incidents that we were involved in together. Some things I had forgotten until I was reminded. It just went on and on for a column that I thought might be around ten articles plus or minus and ended up with more than three times that many.

In my career I witnessed and worked a wide variety of calls that many do not get to experience for one reason or another, some because of self-initiation, and some just luck; others just because I seemed to be in the right place at the time—more luck, and that happens a lot. Nearly all of the calls or memorable incidents that I remember will be told in the following chapters. It may seem like I was busy every day all the time, but I was not, nor is any cop on the beat or otherwise. There are times that you will just drive around, but if you are a worker, you are not "just driving around." You are looking, and you are aware of your surroundings, and most of the time while you are driving around you are working.

I had a well-rounded career with assignments and positions beginning as a part-time reserve deputy sheriff (a reserve is an unpaid volunteer with most departments) to a full-time patrolman, with two promotions to sergeant (I got busted once), and then to lieutenant and finally captain. I worked in every division of the sheriff's department except the lab. We didn't have a lab when my career began; back then, all of our evidence went to the Kansas City, Missouri, crime lab or the FBI. My career goal was to at least reach the rank of captain like my grandfather, which I did for the last four years of my career.

During my senior year of high school, I went to school in the morning, and in afternoons I worked at Dale's Body Shop in Olathe, training to be a body and fender man under the tutelage of one of the early mentors of my life, Lawrence "Larry" Dale. They called this type of training program "industrial arts." I didn't care what they called it since I hated school. Getting out of class by noon every day that year was a godsend for me. I was the kid that watched the clock on the wall. I couldn't wait to get out of there, and upon graduation, I felt like I had been released from prison.

I had the same feelings after my divorce; some of you have been there and done that. I didn't know what I was going to do, but I just knew that I had better things to do in this life.

One evening I went to Barry's Barn, a hot local teenage social hangout that was in an old barn on the farm of my classmate Linda Barry Kurzweil's family. It was located near 119th Street and what is now I-35 in Olathe. Even though I had dreams of being a policeman, I still wasn't sure I could be one. I was just this skinny, little, insecure, naive kid with thick glasses who wasn't sure where he was going in his lifetime. While at Barry's Barn, I saw this LEO in a deputy sheriff's uniform that was my size. I watched him every time I went to the hangout. He was usually there as security. He was professional looking and very businesslike. He looked good in the uniform, and at that time I was thinking, "Darn it [I didn't cuss much then, yet] if he can do it, I can too." That gave me a goal. I would need to age some, put on a few pounds, and go for it. It took a while, but my childhood dream was in motion.

Prior to graduation I had made the decision that body work was not for me, so after graduation I went to work for a couple of local gasoline stations. Then I worked a few months at Sun Master Corporation, which manufactured large commercial-sized grass and weed mowers. I was the metal shearer operator, cutting commercial mower parts, which was quite a responsibility for a young man of eighteen, and it was dangerous—if you weren't careful, you could lose body parts. I still have all of my hands and fingers, and I never hurt anyone before I quit for another job at the GM Delco battery plant in Olathe, just down the street from Sun Master. Delco, for those of you that don't know, was a branch of General Motors that built car batteries for GM and others. That plant is now gone, leaving a large, unattractive, fenced field, but it was huge in its time.

I worked a variety of positions in Delco, and as I recall, it had around 450 employees at the time, all union members with the exception of three or four brave persons who would not be bullied into becoming union members. The Delco Union called two strikes while I was there, one right after my first month, and I couldn't figure it out. I was making more money than I had ever made in my life, and I was striking? On strike, unions have frequent meetings, and ya had to go. I listened to these radical old guys standing up there calling management every vulgar name under the sun, and the sheep were just nodding their heads in agreement, but I didn't. I couldn't wait to get out of there, and it didn't take long for me to realize I was not cut out to be working inside any building my entire life to go on strike whenever the union bosses wanted us to. There had to be a better way. At Delco I was able to bid into some pretty cushy jobs. I was able to work on my private pilot's written exam along with my friend Terry Griffin, who also wanted to be a pilot, we both passed. I was also able to read all of the Ian Fleming James Bond books, Nero Wolfe as well as other crime books, I just loved that stuff. On the midnight shift I napped a lot, so you might ask, "Why did you leave?" Answer is, it was the boredom of that inside job, which was not my life's goal. By now I was sure, I wanted to be a cop!

So I was still working at Delco in Olathe when my LEO career began. My coworkers were laughing at me as I start out as a reserve officer under Sheriff Ralph (Pappy) Burger. "Why do you want to be a cop? Ya have a good job here," some said.

Now a cop, I worked (still not cussing much) dang near full time in the evenings and on weekends riding with deputies trained by my dad. They were all good at what they did, as he was, and I received the best training there was at the time. They all took me under their wing as I was getting my duckies in a row, although I didn't know it at the time. It didn't take long. This was what I wanted to do with my life right then. When I quit Delco, coworkers were still laughing at me. They'd shake their heads and say, "Why do ya wanta be a cop? You will be back." To which I said, "No I won't." I had a plan, and my plan was this: work at the cop shop for at least two years, and if I didn't like it or couldn't cut it, I'd go on to something else. I was still unsure, but I was going to give it a shot.

Chapter 13

Advice and Words to the Wise

*B*efore we go on, here's some more advice for new hires and wannabee LEOs or even those on the job. Some of these nuggets are from personal experience; others are lessons learned by others and advice from the old school.

1. Be aware of the three Bs that can get you in trouble if you indulge: booze, broads, and bucks. Remember them, and be honest with yourself, your family, your department, and your coworkers, and you will be comfortable in your own skin. I add another B and that's B honest, Mark Twain once said "IF you tell the truth you don't have to remember anything." Many LEOs get in the oleo over one of these things or more. Distractions, especially looking at pussy, while driving can cause accidents, transfers and may cost you your job, ask Bennie. Going after pussy? Same thing, especially if you, she, or he is married.

2. When an individual calls the police for any reason, it may be the first personal contact with an LEO he or she has ever had. The problem they are reporting can be the most important issue in their life at that point in time. Treat them and their problem with that in mind, show interest. Or the person calling may be one who has had several or many contacts and hates the police. At that time in either case, what you have is an opportunity to make a good first impression, which may change how that individual sees the police for the rest of his or her life, and you may make a friend out of that anticop person.

3. Some of the "old days" advice—such as "your word is your bond"— is the same or similar in today's world. Use that old advice; following it will help your success in the cop shop. Your word is your bond, be honest, don't be a thief, thieves are caught and scorned, families and loved ones are embarrassed, and all pay the price if you screw up.

4. If you work hard and do a good, competent job, you will be noticed, and if you work hard, you will also occasionally get lucky. Don't let anyone tell you different. Luck, good or bad, will come when you least expect it. Good luck is good, good luck is needed.

5. Learn for yourself and train your subordinates in good report writing. If you produce good, competent, honest, and factual reports, excellent. It will pay off in spades. Many people read and use your reports and documents, including your bosses, your peers, district attorneys, defense attorneys, judges and the courts, insurance companies, the media…you get the picture? A lot of people see them, and what you say and write is a direct reflection on you, your person, your department, and your competency. Maybe you'll even write a book some day.

6. Be careful what you say and to whom you say it. Remember that the pets, snitches and bosses relatives may use your words against you. Be kind to everyone you can. Ya never know who you will end up working for. That person you're talking to could be your boss in the future.

7. Save what you are allowed—daily activity reports, newspaper articles, pictures, reports—and keep it all in a scrapbook. Keep a diary.

8. If you have any doubts about the courage to shoot someone who needs to be shot in short order, do something else, be one of those "hero" fireman, an EMT, or something else.

9. Ya do not have to follow unlawful orders. In fact, you have a duty to defy that unlawful order and to report it through appropriate channels to higher-up command officers. If ya have to, go to the top and

be aware of "vicarious liability" as it pertains to law enforcement. Look it up.

10. Not all cops like each other. Jealousy and envy exists in the cop shops, and additionally there will be snitches, pets, and snakes that will do anything to get ahead, and that includes taking your job. They are few, but some may be those you least expect. When you go for promotions your friend is now your competitor.

11. Don't be a snitch. There will be incidents you will have to report; you will have no choice if you're smart, but leave the small stuff to others. You don't have to be boss to be a leader.

12. Prison is not a good place for cops or ex-cops. If you go to jail—and this is a fact—here's your asshole before you go to prison: o. Here it is when you get out: 0. *If* you get out, think about it IF ya don't get it. (I got this from a joke and most people think it's funny, my bride thinks it's "tasteless")

13. Have a plan for retirement. Retire early or when vested if you want to. Stay as long as you want, but get vested so you can draw retirement pay. I know many who couldn't stick it out and left early with no retirement and then regrets.

14. If you stay on the job, you will most likely get promotions if you want them, each of which equals a different shield. Save all your shields/badges for mementos. Shadow boxes work well.

15. Consider this book and the incidents in it "incident awareness."

16. Learn military time.

17. IF ya have a police dog make sure it's trained to not chase rabbits on investigations.

I have written many opinions about people and situations. Some LEOs I worked with may have different opinions on some people mentioned, but you will have mine.

Chapter 14

Two Sheriffs

I don't mention Sheriff Fred Allenbrand in this chapter since he is mentioned throughout the book. The following two were the last of the old guys and into a new era in law enforcement in Johnson County. Initially Sheriff Ralph Burger could or would not hire me full time because of the department nepotism clause.....that's what they said.

My dad was full time, so I could not be hired except as a reserve......
that's what they said. Thing is there were already relatives working, but I was too young and naive to make an argument. I had decided, however, that one way or another, when I had some experience under my belt, I was going to be an LEO, if not at the Johnson County, Kansas, Sheriff's Office, then somewhere else. I always suspected in the beginning that my dad was

the reason they wouldn't hire me full time. He either didn't think I could cut it, or he worried about me being on the street.

When I started out as a reserve, I was christened "Little Ed" since my dad was "Big Ed," and that stuck until Dad died in 1967. Following his death, the moniker Little Ed eventually faded away, and after that I was just Ed. I have been called many other names since then, and you folks that go into the job of being an LEO will be called many of the same things. As in my case, you will be threatened, shit at and missed, shit at and hit, and for those that threatened, me I just told them to get in the long line over there on the left. That included one bad cop you will read about later on.

Sheriff Burger's term ended in 1965, and during that election a Delco coworker, John Persell, who was a former sheriff's deputy, was filling me with stories about some of the deputies he had worked with and some of the calls and incidents he had been involved with. As I recall, John had quit because of the hourly shifts, the work he didn't like, and a better salary at General Motors. John and I remained friends even after I left for the sheriff's office, and he stayed with GM until he retired. I always thought he hated to quit as an LEO, but he needed to for the good of his family. John was a big laugher in about any conversation about anything—couldn't tell his stories without laughing. One of his biggest regrets as an LEO was having to arrest anyone. He didn't laugh much in talking about "those poor bastards' faces when you handcuff them and put them in jail." He hated that part of the job, and it was probably one of the reasons he opted for a career change.

One day John was talking about the upcoming election and said he was supporting a man named Lynn Thomas who was running against the current undersheriff. Lynn Thomas had been sheriff for four years, which was then two terms. The unwritten rule was that when a sheriff's time was up, his undersheriff would be the heir apparent for sheriff, so Thomas was breaking the rules. Most sheriffs at the time would stay on as a deputy after their terms were up, and Thomas did, but now the laws had been changed to allow unlimited terms for a sheriff in Kansas.

Unbeknownst to me, my dad was like most of the rest of the working deputies: they were all angry at Thomas for breaking the unwritten rule, and they were backing Undersheriff Tom Lawrukiewicz. Well now, in my immature naivety, my pal John conned me into putting a "Lynn Thomas for Sheriff" bumper sticker on my beautiful red 1959 Ford convertible, and oh, how it showed up. Not knowing what it would hurt and wanting to help friend John, I stuck it on. Soon I found the error of my ways when my dad came home and saw the "Thomas for Sheriff" sticker on that car…in front of the house…on a busy street…with heavy traffic. I can only remember a few times when he was that mad. Needless to say, the bumper sticker was removed before he stroked out. John got a big laugh over that, he laughed much more than I needed to see, and he never let me forget it nor I him.

Soon after that, Lynn Thomas was elected sheriff over Tom Lawrukie-wicz. Tom stayed on as a detective, but there was a huge exit of really great, knowledgeable deputies from the sheriff's office. None of them, including my dad, would work for Thomas at that point. I did though; I wanted to be a cop! My dad quit and went to the Olathe Police Department, going from being a sheriff's office sergeant to a uniform patrolman. This was January 1965, and he remained there until Fred Allenbrand, was elected sheriff over Lynn Thomas, who had run for his second term of his second stint as Johnson County sheriff and lost. Many were happy over that loss, including me. Thomas's sheriff's office had self-destructed with Lynn at the helm due to bad judgment and inexperienced people assigned to positions that they were incompetent in and some with very limited LEO experience at all.

In defense of Thomas, the reason he broke the unwritten rule is that the state statute changed. Instead of being able to serve only two terms, the sheriff could now run as long as he wanted, as long as he could win elections. There were no more term limits, and therefore he had his sights set on a long time in office. But due to his management downfalls, he only served one more term before being ousted by Fred Allenbrand.

Many other deputies did the same thing: quit and went somewhere else because they wouldn't work for Thomas, who now hired me as a full-time deputy since my dad no longer was a sheriff's deputy. I left a five-day-a-week job at Delco for a job that was six days a week, sometimes seven for $100 less a month, and no overtime pay. If you had to work your day off, it was without pay, but I didn't care. I loved being out there in the hunt for bad guys; I loved the excitement. Times were different then. I loved the job, and I had found my place in life, although I was totally unsure at the time. I still figured that I would work there for a couple of years, and if I wasn't happy, I would try something else. It took twenty-nine years for me to find that something else…retirement. Following my retirement, I worked four more years as a first responder of one kind or the other, and I was actually a volunteer fireman for two weeks in Cotter, Arkansas. Why two weeks you may ask? Here's why, I couldn't take the smoke but it isn't what you might think. I went to two meetings where I could not see the walls on the far side of the room because of cigarette smoke, so I quit. Those Cotter Arkansas boys really loved their tobacco.

Chapter 15

First Days

There are those that will tell you that being an LEO is 98 percent boredom and 2 percent absolute terror. I call that (I cuss a little bit now) bullshit, because if you work, if you self-initiate activities in between radio calls, you will have an interesting and sometimes exciting career. I'm not saying that every day will be exciting, because it will not be. Some days will be interesting if you work hard and steady. After a short time on the street after the academy, you will know what to do and how, and you will continue to develop if you work at it. Where you are geographically has a lot to do with how busy you will be and what activities and types of calls you will have to deal with. Larger cities have larger call volumes, and of course, larger populations experience more crime (Chicago, for example). If you want to be really busy, apply at a large city or county department. If you want less, go to a small town or the suburbs. In my opinion, if you want a well-rounded career, be a deputy sheriff on as large of department you can find. There's a lot of difference in the activities and assignments of sheriff's deputies and the career of most city policemen besides arresting people. Most of the calls and uniform activities are the same or similar, but there's a lot more to it than you may think. Believe me, if you don't want to spend your entire career in uniform in a patrol car, you need to do your homework and see what the different agencies or departments have to offer. About the time I was getting a bit tired of an assignment, I usually was able to transfer to another. If I had had to work in a uniform in a marked patrol car my whole career, I probably wouldn't have lasted. I know some who did and liked it, but I needed a change every now and then; I needed challenges of different types.

Shortly after I went full time, I was shift relief deputy. I worked dispatch two days a week, the jail two days a week, and in a patrol car two days a week. This went on for about a year. I didn't like working the jail or dispatch, but I did what I had to until I was back on the road full time. The jail and dispatch in a sheriff's office are good for the career and good for learning. In the jail, you learn how to communicate with the bad guys. In dispatch, you learn about your county and the cities within, and you meet a lot of fellow cops in person and on the radio. A good dispatcher is liked and respected by all and deserves all the accolades he or she gets.

One thing you will hear frequently from the media and others in reference to an LEO's career, usually when an officer is interviewed or retires, is this: "This officer never had to take out or pull his gun." They seem to love to say this. All I can say is that it wasn't so for me. You will see in some of my incidents, calls, and activities on the job in following chapters (and I'm not bragging), my weapons came out a lot!

In movies and TV, there's background music and sounds: sinister music for unhappy scenes, exciting music for exciting scenes, boom-boom and loud bang sounds to startle you. There's happy music for happy scenes, and there's laugh tracks, which to me are silly—I don't need anything or anybody telling me when and how loud I should laugh. In real life, real time, real events inside or outside, there's no accompanying music or sounds for effect. There's only the sound of what's going on around you, what's live or worse, traffic and train sounds, sirens, common noise of your surroundings. It's the same in a cop's life, but additionally there's the sounds of the constant crackling police radio, the sirens, screams, yelling, fear, the injured, the grieving, and not very frequently…gunshots. No music!

Patrolman Charles Hoy "Chuck" Lane, the deputy working off-duty security at the Barry's Barn kids' sock-hop hangout, became one of the most respected and qualified deputies, detectives, and supervisors in the history of the Johnson County, Kansas, Sheriff's Office. That's the opinion of many in the greater Kansas City metropolitan area as well as nationwide with some LEOs. When I began as a full-time deputy, Chuck and I were at odds for a while, but we eventually got over it and became trusted friends who respected each other and each other's abilities, and not just as lawmen. For one thing, I had to prove myself, as you all will. Most of you will know if you are cut out for the job by the time you get out of the academy; others will not. I don't know what the turnover rate is in law enforcement now, but early in my career, it was high. Reasons were the hours and meager pay rate. Later on, it seemed to level off as salaries between the metro police departments became about the same.

Chuck attained the rank of major before he retired. He once told me later in our careers that if he could put together a squad of seven detectives, I would be at the top of his list. He mentioned several other detectives that I respected. I was proud to be on Chuck's dream team, his list of professional LEOs. Chuck died about a year or so after he retired. The funeral was huge, as some officers' funerals are.

My First Days on the Job

I say this to anyone going into law enforcement and anyone in law enforcement who has not done this: Keep every document, every picture, and all the notes and reports that you can within the law and your department rules. Keep a daily diary, and keep it up to date. Keep a scrapbook of news articles of incidents you are involved in. If you can't keep pictures or reports, keep detailed notes. If you stay in the profession, you will be glad you did. Some do, some don't. I didn't keep a diary. I wish I had, but I did keep some things that have been very helpful in writing my column and the writing of this book, things like news articles, reports, and the scrapbook. If you do this, keep it to yourself, because defense attorneys will subpoena everything you have if they know about it and some of your coworkers may be paranoid by your record keeping. I have witnessed this. People keep notes, and people talk and wonder why.

I also have copies of all of my good-guy and bad-boy letters—letters of commendation and my two notices of suspension—one of which was silly, in my opinion. It was when I was snitched off by a subordinate for a dastardly deed. I'll touch on that later. The other suspension was for a practical joke that went bad—really, really bad. Did you ever see the movie *Porky's*? We still laugh about this caper. More on that later.

As said, I went on the job as a reserve in 1964. I was a young, naive kid who had watched my grandfather while growing up. In addition, I had ridden "ride along" with my dad many times, and he told me often things that I would use in later days. Because of all of this, I decided that I wanted to be a reserve officer, which meant no pay, just doing the job. As a reserve, I was able to ride with seasoned officers who knew their stuff, and I did that for nearly a year before the aforementioned politics took place. I didn't see a lot in the way of crime happening during my reserve days. There were a few accidents and a few calls, but the main thing was the guys I was riding with. Most of them were those that self-initiated and really worked during their shifts. I learned their methods of operation and the way they thought about different situations, and I heard the stories they told about their experiences. Now I'm telling you mine in this book. All of this helped me develop into a beginner who had a leg up on other rookies, and in the process, I developed my own methods and my own ways to operate, and all the while I was just loving it. There were a few that I rode with that were just plain lazy, hated the job and didn't do much. They didn't like reserve officers riding and watching them. Imagine being in a car with some asshole while he pulls off into a field and takes a nap, or some guy who continually bitches about the job, people he works with, his supervisors. I didn't need to hear all of this. I said to myself, "That will never be me." I never did any of that, but as a supervisor I had some of the same type of people. By the time I retired, I spent nearly 50 percent of my time on deputy personnel matters. Consider this before you attain rank, especially as you get higher and higher up, this is what ya do.

In our department we rotated from a month of days to evenings and then midnight shift. I liked evening and midnight shifts because there was more activity, more calls, and more excitement. There were two district officers working half the county each and the sergeant who was our only backup, with the exception of city officers if one was close. For the most part, you were out there on your own. Both districts had cities and unincorporated areas, most of which were patrolled by the sheriff's deputies. District 101 was the north half of the county, which had the largest cities, and 102 was the south half with a few smaller cities with only a couple of small-town police departments. My first day at roll call, such as it was, the captain tossed me the keys to a patrol car, smiled, and said, "Hayes, you are 102. Be careful out there," and off I went.

My very first day as a full-time deputy sheriff was on a day shift. My car needed to be cleaned, so I went to the drive-through car wash in Overland Park, Kansas. It was one of those automatic car washes that handle several cars at a time being towed by a chain. Once you're in it, ya don't get out until it's done, and as I'm sitting there about in the middle of the wash cycle, I get a call: "Calling 102."

I answer, "102."

"102, proceed to 175th and Mission Road. Take a report on a 1040 [a fatality] at the side of the road."

I'm sitting there waiting, waiting, waiting, and finally I get out of the car wash, turn on the reds, turn on the siren, and south I go down Metcalf Avenue through 101 District in Overland Park.

The city police department, mainly some officers and staff, didn't like cars from other agencies and especially the county sheriff working in their city, but too bad—we did what we could do. I had been briefed on this situation as a reserve, but it didn't bother us; we had the law on our side. The sheriff had jurisdiction over the entire county, and the folks just had to get used to it.

I arrived at the crime scene and was greeted by a postman who had found a dead aborted baby on the side of the road by a mailbox. It had the appearance of a rag doll and had been there for more than a day. My job was to protect the crime scene until detectives arrived, interview any witnesses, and make the initial report. Then I was to leave the scene, and the detectives took over. I don't remember anything else that happened on that first day, but a hell of a first day, and sad day, it was.

Chapter 16

Like a Dog, Either You're a Hunter or You're Not!

He Hit Her with What?

I had been on patrol for a while and I'm not remembering much to tell other than a few minor incidents, car checks, accidents (some not minor), a few cattle calls, disturbances, and just mainly routine calls, if there is such a thing. But I got this one call—it was around 4:00 a.m. on dog watch (the midnight shift). "Calling 102."

I answered, "102, go ahead."

"Proceed to a family disturbance on Mission Road and 171st Street. A man beating a woman with a baseball bat."

Away I went.

When I arrived at the residence, I was met by a woman who said her husband in fact had taken a baseball bat after her, and when she called the police, he ran into the wooded area behind the house. Soon after I arrived, several cars with detectives and uniform officers arrived, so we did a search around the house and outer areas in the dark. Into the woods we went, but we didn't find him. The woman was sent to the hospital for treatment of head wounds, and all of my backup left. A warrant would be issued, but I wasn't leaving yet. It wasn't a dark, rainy night; it was a cool, damp, misty morning. I stayed, set up shop, thinking the guy wouldn't stay out very long. There was no outbuilding to get shelter and no other houses in sight. So I sat in the nice, comfy, warm car, listened to the radio and waited.

I couldn't see him, but I knew he could see me, and by now, he knew I wasn't leaving. I don't remember how long I sat there for sure, but the news articles say the bad guy was in the woods for four hours. As daylight broke, out he came with a grin on his face. I searched him and found a small .22 handgun in his pocket, handcuffed him, and off to jail we went. "You did good, Hayes," says my commander. Wow, an atta boy right off the bat (no pun intended—but yeah, why not?).

As Paul Harvey used to say, "Now, here's the rest of the story!"

I was at the station, and as I was interviewing the victim of the battery, the wife, I found out that I needed to go back to the house, either with her permission or with a search warrant. That's to retrieve the baseball bat as evidence, he had told me it was somewhere in the field he had been hiding in. She broke down and admitted that she and her husband had been committing burglaries in the area for some time, so now a search warrant was needed and was issued by a judge. We executed the search warrant on the house, finding a lot of items from area burglaries in Kansas and Missouri. Mission Road is near state line, so they didn't have far to go to get to Missouri. We found firearms in the house and a handgun in his car from the burglaries or not, those finds, plus the gun in his pocket, along with the fact that we found that he was a convicted felon, meant he was now charged as a felon in possession of a firearm. In addition, there was an outstanding warrant for the wife's arrest, so both were arrested. So what started out as a family disturbance and an assault turns out to be, a felon in possession of a firearm and he's going back to prison, the wife being arrested on an outstanding warrant, and both being charged with the burglaries.

This call is an example of how a near-routine call can snowball into a larger and more involved case to remember. The *Kansas City Star* reported, "Parolee Is Arrested, Johnson County Man Was Object of Manhunt."

By this time, I was loving my job more than ever. I was having fun and knew that more fun was to come. It was like I was hunting—not birds, not animals, but bad guys, some of which I found out were worse than animals. Delco? I never looked back.

Disturbances are never classified as routine, nor should they be. It is said that more officers are injured or killed on domestic disturbances than any other types of calls. They can be dangerous, and that is especially true in today's world. We always thought that they were kind of fun and exciting, but then no one on my department was ever killed on a disturbance call. Some, including myself, did get bruised up a bit on occasion, but no one shied away from a disturbance call. There was usually always a backup either there or on the way. Later in my career, we were required to wait for backup for officer safety reasons. We had become more "civilized" and "modern," but it is an officer safety issue and a smart procedure.

Another call on the midnight shift was one in Stanley, Kansas, a small city at the time. This guy calls a homeowner and says, "I know you have been fucking my wife. I'm coming there, and I'm going to kill you!" I get the call from dispatch. It was just before daybreak, so my sergeant at the time, John Zemites, and I went the scene. It was a large house on acreage near 151st Street just west of Metcalf Street. They were obviously either wealthy people or heavily in debt. We set up a roadblock, got behind the cars, and waited. Again, it was a cool, damp night. We waited and we waited…for over an hour, there's no traffic. I was standing beside the car with a shotgun for all of this time, and when we decided for whatever reason the anger of the caller must be over for now, we left, figuring he wasn't coming. After we left, I found that—are you ready for this, new officers and LEO wannabes?—my shotgun had not been reloaded after Sunday morning roll call, which was when we cleaned shotguns. Someone had put the shotgun back in the car unloaded, and I had not checked it when I took the car out.

Laugh at this if you want, but I don't think there are many officers out there that won't admit that the same type of thing has happened to them… either an unloaded gun or leaving it atop the refrigerator when they left for work, getting to work before they discover they are unarmed. That ain't good; that ain't safe. As a comedian says, "It could happen" and it does.

So here's the deal: check ALL of your equipment at the beginning of your shift and during your shift, whether required or not. I certainly did after that. It's what's called a cheap lesson.

Another time I was in the oleo and didn't even know it until it was over. A deputy had checked out a patrol car, damaged it, and returned it to the lot without reporting the incident. The car was a mid-1960s Mercury four door about half the size of an aircraft carrier. The next deputy to drive the car felt a vibration, returned it, and informed the duty officer, who had to launch an investigation; someone had taken that car out, damaged it, and put it back in the lot without reporting it, that's not cool..

At the end of every shift, our deputies were required to park the car with a full tank of gas and the car ready for the next deputy's watch. With the tank filled, the officer signed a gasoline records card with the time, date, and mileage. So guess whose name was on that gas sheet as the last person to drive that patrol car. Mine…Ed Hayes! That's me! So now, guess who they suspect damaged the car? ME! All this happened without my knowledge until the mystery was solved and I found out I was almost called in and suspended or fired. It turned out that one of the sergeants from another shift took the car out, tried to drive across a concrete median, bent the drive shaft, took the car back and parked it with a nearly full tank of gas, and did not report it. Did he get suspended or get a written reprimand? I never knew, but here's another reason to check your equipment before you leave the station.

Chapter 17

It Was a Dark, Damp, Rainy Night

During your career, on evenings and dog watch (midnight to eight, plus or minus) on some or on most departments, you will be checking buildings for security, open or unlocked doors and windows. As you look for evidence of business break-ins in between calls and during quiet times, you may be surprised at what you will discover. Much of the time I seemed to be where things were happening, crime, incidents and others, just seemed to be in the right or wrong place at the time.

A couple of incidents in my earlier uniform days were burglaries of restaurant bars. One was a bar next to the railroad tracks in Spring Hill, Kansas, another small city at the time on the southern edge of Johnson County. Investigating the burglary that had been discovered by one of my district officers, Robert Basore and there were at least three of us checking this building and finding nothing. We were about to leave when all of a sudden Basore sees this guy just standing in the very dark corner of a storeroom. Hells bells, we had flashlights and we didn't see him, we then found two of them and they got their free passes to jail.

Here's another bar burglary I found as I was checking buildings on a slow midnight shift. It was a dark, rainy night, and as a guy in a movie once said, "It was raining like a cow pissing on a flat rock!" Plus, it was cold. This will be in the test! What movie was that quote from? OK, so it was raining, and I was driving around checking buildings, and I see this guy soaking wet climbing into a front window that he had just shattered. I lit him up with the spotlight, he froze. I placed him under arrest, called the district car to come, and waited for a detective and the business owner, and off to jail I and the bad guy go. This was similar to the ball bat incident in that in interviewing this guy, I found out about other crimes. He was wet, cold, and I was being nice to him (I always was when someone's freedom was going bye-bye), giving him blankets and drying him out so we are friends. So now he wants to talk to me, he needed a dry place to stay, so we talked. He had traveled from Boston, and he admitted to burglaries in Boston, Massachusetts, and a few others in between here and there. One large burglary he admitted to was a Swift binocular factory. Two-plus burglaries cleared in one pinch—that's a pretty good arrest, don't cha think? Dad would have told me "nice pinch!"

Here's another piece of advice for those of you that do a good job and make a good arrest. Cover your ass, and don't be bullied by your superiors, I was and I took it. Go over their head if they do to you what they did to me and others. It turns out that the management or owner of the Swift factory sent three brand-spankin' new pairs of Swift binoculars as a reward: one to the officer that caught the guy and got the confession, and one each to the detective and his captain. Well, two pairs went to the right place, but one didn't, that's mine. At the time I was a patrolman, so what did I know? I found this out in a roundabout way and found that two captains (one the sheriff's brother-in-law) and a detective kept the binoculars, and the guy who made the pinch didn't get shit—that's me. I challenged one of the captains but got nowhere. What I should have done was take it to the sheriff. I did not, and I have always regretted not saying more, but I never let them forget that I knew what they did. If anyone tells you that cops are like brothers, let me tell you that it ain't always that way, in some cases, some departments, and with some people.

During your academy days is where friends are made before you even prove yourself. That ends for some when they get into the chain, where it sometimes gets to be dog eat dog for promotions. Then there are those that are snitches who will snitch you off in a heartbeat to get ahead; they'll make bad things out of good. There are also those that are jealous and envious for other reasons, and they will tell tales. I am not trying to put a negative face on all LEOs, but be aware that there are some who are like this. We will get into some of that later, but for now, I am getting ahead of myself.

As mentioned earlier, as said when I was a reserve officer, I rode mainly with the guys my dad had trained. They took care of me and trained me as he did them. I learned a lot from them, so I had a jump-start when I became a full-time deputy, sworn in on March 15, 1965. I thank him and them for my success. I watched them, paid attention, observed, assisted on many different types of calls, and saw them in action, watching how they performed. I watched their actions on calls, listened to their words, and digested their advice. They were my police academy at the time, such as it was. We had some really great deputies at the time that I will never forget; they "had the nose." Sadly, a lot of them resigned when Lynn Thomas became sheriff in January of 1965 and some did not come back when he left. Times and laws have changed; it was a different time then in law enforcement.

I will never forget a few wintertime accidents when the roads were solid ice. In this particular accident in January, we were working an accident in below-zero weather, standing on State Line Road. One side of the road is Missouri, and the other, the west side, is Kansas, and unfortunately for us that was the side of the road this accident was on. We stood directing traffic until we could no longer feel our feet. Expect it, it's all part of the job, and you do what ya gotta do. We also had a fine tuned measurement, the rule of thumb on these types of calls, ask any old cop to explain that one to ya.

I had been on the job for over a year and had made many good arrests by that time when I received a compliment from my then shift sergeant. This was really big, I thought, because this guy was really full of himself. At roll call, he mentioned the many good arrests I had already made. He commented that on evenings and dogwatch "while the rest of us are all in the alleys or under the K7/K10 water tower napping, Ed is out there working and making arrests."

A guy asked me, "How do you do it? How is it that you make all of these good arrests, Ed?"

My smartass response to him was, "Ya just have to know what you are doin', John."

There was a lot of laughter at my response. My comment was a bit short with him, and I just smiled. I wasn't about to give away all of the secrets of my success to some. Some got along, and some did not. There was some jealousy, and some personalities clashed, just like everywhere else. Some were just downright lazy, they didn't stay long and while some might disagree, it got worse in later generations; however, we had more people on the department by then. There are some very dedicated officers out there, but before I retired we all noticed the decline in determination and loyalty to the cause by some. To some it was just a job, and at the end of eight hours, all they wanted to do was go home. I am told this has improved somewhat these days, but who knows where this is all going to go with the assassination of police officers? Will many of them quit, deciding that being an LEO is not for them? Time will tell.

Eight hour shifts? When I went on the job, I rode with my relief deputy after my shift. I just didn't want to miss anything. And it wasn't just me; it was that way for most of us at that point in time. Day shift rode over on evenings, and evening shift rode over on midnight shifts. I remember more than a few times when we were a carload of officers working overtime with no pay, just because none of us wanted to miss anything. It was usually on a Friday or Saturday night, but on any night when it was busy, we didn't want to go home. A carload of us just rode around talking shop, politics and answering calls.

You will see a lot of different scenarios during your career if you stick with it. Some will make you nauseous, some will make you just sick, and some will make you itch. Such was the case in some of the apartment duplexes in an old army housing development named Sunflower Village built for employees of the Sunflower Army Ammunition Plant that operated through several wars, including World War II, Korea, and maybe part of Vietnam. There was a line of about six to eight duplex-style apartments, and some were similar in nature to slum housing, people being poor. It was evident when you drove through the area that not many middle-class citizens of anywhere were living there. I felt sorry for most of them. Junk cars, trash in the streets, run-down buildings, filthy little kids running about… you get the picture. Most of the people were very poor. It was a slum, and you hated to go into some of the apartments because of the bugs and filth.

There was either a murder/suicide I don't recall for sure, but what I do recall is that we had to go in to interview family and witnesses. This apartment was like most: dirty, in disarray, dirty dishes all over the kitchen, sink filled, worn furniture, and *cockroaches*. In this apartment we sat at the kitchen table with cockroaches covering the walls. They had to be in every apartment in that line of apartments. These apartments, some of them, were cockroach- and mouse-infested ranch style. The complex has since been upgraded into a very nice and attractive little village located on the western edge of Desoto, Kansas.

During this interview the lady in this apartment offered us a drink, coffee or tea. My partner and I looked at each other, smiled and shivered at the thought, and respectfully declined. Even the coffee cups were filthy.

Chapter 18

She Shot His What Off?

As Mark Twain, maybe Yogie Berra, Bear Bryant or someone once said, "It ain't braggin' if it's fact."

On most shifts if you have a full crew, some will dine together as you can, you've seen them. We had several hangouts where we ate. These did not necessarily have the best food but were in the best location should someone get a call and have to leave. They were in kind of a central location for all district officers involved.

When my dad was working for the Olathe Police Department, we would meet for breakfast before we went off duty when we both worked the midnight-to-eight shift, if we were not busy. One morning we stopped into a local restaurant in Olathe, and we sat and talked as we were served. This was the best quality time I had with my dad in those days, just he and me, meeting for a meal or just riding around together. We always talked about what was going on, previous calls of the shift in the county as well as the city. OK, so out came the food, pancakes and eggs for him and probably something different for me—hell's bells, I can't remember what I had yesterday for breakfast, so give me a break.

So here's why I remember what he had to eat: He had a stack of three or four pancakes, so he lifts them up one at a time, slapping on the butter, and when he gets the top two, he freezes, and looks at me still holding them up. "Look at this," he says. I looked down and saw a cockroach about as long as a half dollar is wide. Dad looked at the kitchen, and the cook was looking out the service window and disappeared after Dad points at him. He calls the waitress over, makes a few comments, he wasn't rude with the waitress but we got up and left. That incident had to have an effect on policemen eating in that restaurant, because we let every cop in the county know what was served up on that day. A waitress recently told me that in those days when they turned on the lights in that restaurant in the mornings at that time, cockroaches covered the walls. Yuck!

So the moral of this story for you wannabe cops, newbies, or anyone else, is to be careful where you eat if you are in a uniform. Ya never know who spits, flips a bugger, or adds some sort of additional treats to your food.

One group of cops who frequently ate together tells this story about a deputy who would get nauseous when they talked about "eating pussy." This guy would start gagging, near puking, and stop eating. It didn't matter how many times they pulled this on him, it was always the same, they say, I was never there. After he stopped eating, they would eat his breakfast in front of him. I believe this, as a couple of these guys were ornerier than me, and I have witnesses and victims of my pranks that would tell you about me. This was pretty cold, and it is an example of what black hearts some cops have, but this prank was OK with me. I always thought it was funny because of who this guy was, ya couldn't trust him, at least I couldn't, didn't, many did not. Here's another piece of advice: Watch out who you tell what. Some guys will set you up, and that's what this guy was all about. He would get you to say something about someone and then go tell them what you said. It didn't take too long for me to find out that he was a snake, and I let him know that I knew it. I showed him no respect, just did what I had to do when I was around him and other people. Once you lose the trust of your fellow cop, it's very difficult to get it back, and you may never get it back. Had everyone known what I knew about this guy, who knows where he may have ended up.

Another of our antics was throwing cherry bombs beneath one of our buddies' patrol cars on the midnight shift when we could catch them making building checks or sitting somewhere for some reason. It was always fun, especially if you nearly caused the guy to crap or wet his drawers. This worked especially well if he was napping. We could have cherry bombs back them, legally. On midnights there will be times that you will have to pull off and rest or chance having a wreck. It didn't happen to me but a few times but I had to park on the shoulder of the highway or I was going to wreck, what ya did was open up windows, turn on the police radio as loud as it would go so if your radio number came on you would be awake. Some guys nap almost every night. I didn't; I was too busy trying to find bad guys and I did sleep during the day so I was ready to go.

Another cop friend of mine was colder than I. Jimmy Briggs walked in on his brother in law pretending to be extremely angry, ya didn't want Jimmy mad at you. He walked in on this auto shop screaming and yelling, pulled his pistol, and started shooting blanks near the unarmed, unsuspecting brother-in-law. It's a wonder that even that healthy young man didn't have a heart attack or wet himself, he may have, Gene, did ya?

There was this bar out in the county that had a great deal of business, and along with a great deal of business, there were more than your average problems. Disturbances, shootings, and stabbings were more frequent here than most places of business. There were even a couple of homicides. The bar owner was a policeman's friend who had moved from Chicago, my dad nicknamed him "Frank Nettie." Nettie rode with some of us at times until Sheriff Allenbrand stopped unscheduled and unauthorized ride-alongs, but Nettie liked all of us just the same, and most of us liked Nettie, Allenbrand didn't.

Nettie was the victim of some of my jokes whenever I could think something up. Any time we found something wrong with the bar tagged the Teepee on midnight shift, we would call Nettie, who would come to check out his building inside and out. If we weren't busy, Nettie would buy our breakfasts for taking care of his interests and business. Well, after this happened a few times and we kept finding this one window unlocked, I figured out that if ya jimmied the window, the lock would fall open, and it was then an open window—a possible burglary, if you will. After about a half dozen times of this, Nettie was tired of getting up in the middle of the night, he says, "Hayes, it's taken me a while, but I know what you're doing. Here's a goddamn key. If you find something really wrong, go on in, check out the building and contents, and if nothing is wrong, lock it up and leave me the fuck alone! And by the way, when you guys get off shift, you can use the key to get in, play pool, drink beer, whatever you want." It wasn't too long before the sheriff found all of this out so now the Teepee and Nettie were off limits for all LEOs. You will see how close Nettie and I was when you read about the *Porky's* caper in chapter 22. What a loyal friend he was under pressure. I was a bit surprised.

In the end Nettie was a sad case because he and his wife developed into terrible alcoholics, partly because after a while the county attorney and the sheriff started closing his business down because of the disturbance injuries and a couple of homicides. So at this point, Nettie and his wife were fighting a lot. And I mean fighting. He would smack her, and she would smack him, and then she would call the police, so now we had frequent disturbance calls at the residence. The beginning of the end was when his wife shot him, separating him from one of his testicles/balls/nuts, ya get it? After that, some black-hearted cops would joke around, saying, "He better be careful, someday she will shoot off his other nut." And lo and behold, she tried it. She shot him again, making him a paraplegic. Nettie lived for a few years after that and died of so-called natural causes complicated by his gunshot injuries from his lovely wife.

Some of my peers and supervisors including my dad said I "had the nose." Some of us did, meaning that we could find the bad guys, we could smell things out. I made a lot of good arrests, and so did guys on my shifts, partly because I trained them to work as I did. All I can say is that in any position or any assignment I was placed, be it uniform division, detective plain clothes, undercover, or otherwise, I made cases, and I made arrests. I seemed to have the knack, the luck or whatever to be in the right place at the right time when things were happening. Part of my secret? I profiled and I profiled and I profiled. Ya hear that, you politically correct loonies. *I profiled!* Many of us that knew what we were doing, *profiling!* Nowadays? Some departments have many tools that I/we didn't have. They don't have to search for stolen cars as we did. Electronics collect information from all vehicles and report when a car owner is wanted or the car stolen.

One of the worst things politicians have done with their political correctness bullshit is to try to stop or slow down one of the best tools the LEO has-Profiling. I did it, I still do it, and it still pays off. There are different methods of profiling that include a number of things: car description, condition, and type; time of day; day of the week; driver's actions; location and actions of said vehicle and occupants; body language, and yes, race. ***News flash!*** As I am writing this book, some of the media is finally talking about profiling in a positive way; they are finally waking up.

Times were very different. Johnson County, Kansas, and Jackson and Clay Counties, Missouri, were avoided by the bad guys because they knew that if they broke the law and got caught, they would go to jail. We LEOs knew many of the real crooks, and some were good crooks, so to speak—good at what they did. They had respect for us, and we had professional respect for some of them; however, we still sent them to jail when we caught 'em. Back then they didn't hate cops, they didn't shoot cops, and for the most part, they respected cops, unlike today.

Chapter 19

Unincorporated Areas Are Similar

When I retired I thought I was out of it, really out of law enforcement, but I still keep track of my surroundings, and I still people watch. Other LEOs, working or retired know what I am talking about. Most just can't help it. Since retirement, I've seen things and have made some phone calls that have resulted in some good information and some arrests on serious investigations and crimes. One such incident was one of the biggest cases of its type in Johnson County and maybe Kansas state history I was told. I can't share any more about that because of some of the circumstances of that case, but before it was over, it involved the city, the county, and the feds.

It was such a great case that the detective I initially met with (who wanted to give the case to the city) received all kinds of accolades before he retired. The rest is history; he was even invited to the white house.

Me? I didn't even get a good-job letter from the sheriff or anyone, just arrogant comments from a DEA agent when I quizzed him on the bust.

In another incident, I reported a telephone call to the feds about a guy from the New York area who was interested in an ad I had placed on selling my airplane in *Trade a Plane*, an aviation ad magazine for airplanes, parts, services, and so on. The man's heavy accent was obviously Middle Eastern, and he told me that right off, "I am from the Middle East living in New York, but I'm not a terrorist." The questions he was asking about my airplane were suspicious to me or any pilot; it's hard to explain this to a non-pilot. He was asking about how much of a load my little airplane would haul, which was strange because that type of information is easily found by simply researching that type of airplane other than the fact that as airplanes go, mine was a hot rod. But that wasn't the only suspicious question. So I called the FBI and finally was able to talk to an agent who was very interested. I don't know what happened with that, but I did my part.

Now let me tell you about calling the FBI: If you are in a hurry on something of importance, call your local sheriff, they will contact them for you IF they see the importance! This may have improved since this was a few years ago, but you hear all of the advertisements that say, "Call the FBI," but when you do, your call will be fielded by a secretary, and this case wasn't the first time for me since my retirement. It took me two weeks to talk to an FBI agent, and that only happened after I called the local sheriff, whom I told about the suspicious call. He got me in touch with an FBI agent, not a secretary. In my experience after I retired, it's been the same thing when you call any federal investigative agency, any of them. When I was on the job, I had contacts, but once you leave the department, in time you lose nearly all of your connections and contacts—even personal friends and acquaintances, because in time they too retire. So now some retirees know very few who are working in law enforcement, and the longer you're out of it, the fewer you know.

Another phone call I made was in regards to a couple of suspicious men in an Overland Park, Kansas, Circuit City electronics store (before they went bankrupt and closed down). It appeared to be a father and son. They were obviously Middle Easterners, and they were buying all the cell phone batteries they could find. I couldn't understand what they were saying in Arabic or something like that, but it was suspicious to me. I followed them to the parking lot, got their car description and license number, and reported it to the Overland Park Police. Again, I heard nothing in a followup, but I did my part. So as you can see, some guys never really retire, but once you do retire, you are out of the loop.

Most retirees will tell you that they seem to be dinosaurs and are treated as such by the active-duty cops, with not much respect. Until I began writing my column and this book, none of the younger guys knew anything about what I did during my career. About all they will remember you by is what your last assignment was before you retired and for some that is just OK. I know a few guys who brag about the one thing they did in their career and do their best to impress the uninformed.

In this book, times and dates may be off a bit in a few instances because I have to go by memory on some things. If a mistake is made, it's not intentional; I want this book to be the absolute truth.

I worked at the Jo Co Sheriff's Office for twenty-nine years: one year as a reserve and twenty-eight full time. After retirement, I moved to Colorado, where I volunteered in search and rescue (north) for three years with the Chaffee County Sheriff's Office. I will say this about that: In my lifetime I have never worked with a more dedicated bunch of first responders than those folks in search and rescue, other than in law enforcement. The S&R guys and gals are the same as cops in a way except they are all volunteers. They risk their lives on many rescues to save someone, the same as cops, but for no pay. Being retired with time to spare, I was available to go on any "mission," so I worked and witnessed the operations firsthand on scene. My LEO experience caused me to be interested in the S&R team, I wanted to learn about the mountains, and boy, did I. Some of those old boys that have lived there all their lives know the mountains like the back of their hand. They know every crack, crevice, and drainage in their county as well as some of the rest, and they can name them all. Some of them are retired LEOs and first responders, and like me, they just wouldn't quit. So I joined up, even aside from that, it's a lot of fun to play and work in the mountains. I did a lot of history research for S&R and put together an album of news articles from the local library and the local newspaper, *The Mountain Mail*, while I was there, so I know a lot of the history of their missions in Chaffee County, Colorado. I learned a lot about the rescues they have made and lives they have saved, but that's a story for another day. Some rescues were incredible, heroic, and miraculous, just in Chaffee County alone.

Most old-timers, retired LEOs, and others remember that there were at one time many small towns in Johnson County, Kansas, that have been nearly lost to history as they got annexed into the larger cities. There's a museum dedicated to most of them you will find interesting if you check it out. Have you ever heard of Wilder? Virginia Village? Have you heard of Zarah? Holiday? Most of Holiday is now buried under Deffenbaugh's Landfill…a dump, we used to call it. There was a general store in Holiday that was also the post office. Bonita? Aubry and Stillwell, Kansas? Some are buried in neighborhoods with streets named after them, but they are all now in a larger city.

How about Monticello? Monticello was a stage stop with saloons and a few stores in the 1800s, when Kansas was just a territory. Did you know that one of the first law enforcement officers in Johnson County was James Butler Hickok (a.k.a. Wild Bill)? He was elected constable of Monticello in 1858 and stayed two years before he moved on. I found this out from a friend who worked in the Jo Co archives department. When I was talking to him one day, he showed me court records from 1858, records of Hickok being a witness in a grand jury hearing for a murder charge in which a true bill was returned. The suspects however were not convicted, they were released due to the Peace Act of 1859.

My point in all of this is that the sheriff's office answered calls and patrolled every small city in Johnson County until some of them hired their own police officer or chief. After that, they received backup on calls by sheriff's deputies until they had enough officers to man their departments. Examples are Edgerton, Lenexa, and Gardner, Kansas.

At one time, Edgerton and others had a light on a telephone pole that notified officers of a call or incident. There was no communication other than the telephone pole light turned on by telephone operators when an emergency was reported to them. The officers then drove to the pay phone, where they call the telephone operator and received information.

Sometime around 1965 Lenexa, Kansas hired one officer who worked days, and the sheriff's office patrolled and answered calls after 11:00 p.m., so for the most part Lenexa was patrolled by the sheriff's department. For some time now, the sheriff has contracted with Edgerton and Desoto, both in Johnson County since some cities know that this is more cost efficient than having their own police department. Public safety within those departments is as good as it gets, as are all of the unincorporated areas of Johnson County today—same as in the past, in my opinion.

Buildings from the 1800s and early 1900s are still standing in some locations, and while most towns had a general store and post office, saloons, and a grain elevator or storage, most are gone. Take a drive through the small town of Morse Village (now in Overland Park), which is on the east side of Executive Airpark on Pflumm Road, and you will see the buildings that were the business area. They still house a small mom and pop type business, but they are ancient. Some were built in the late 1800's or early 1900's.

If you drive north on Monticello Road from Eighty-Third Street, you will experience what nearly all rural roads were like in Jo Co before the sixties and into the early seventies: very narrow, with hills, and very dangerous. There were a lot of terrible accidents during my uniform patrolman years due to road conditions in all kinds of weather. Old Highway 10 in Shawnee and west to the county line was a killer. Also extremely hazardous were US 169, 56, and 69. My years in uniform took me to many fatal accidents and gruesome sights on these old roads.

Chapter 20

Snapshots in Your Mind

To this day, I still see some of the dead and injured people in or around vehicle accident scenes, sometimes an entire family. Some are unforgettable—they're snapshots burned in your mind. Gruesome sights they were: people who'd been killed in an instant, their eyes and mouths wide open. I have 'em, but I deal with it. Some stay, while some fade.

In the training of new deputies, I included a trip to a postmortem (autopsy) to expose them to what they were going to see, what they would witness and record on the roads and cities of Johnson County in their career. The purpose was to acclimate them to the incidents they would be required to investigate and record such as homicides, suicides, car wrecks, plane crashes, and victims of other carnage. The sights, smells, and broken bodies in a postmortem are never forgotten, the same as some incidents. Around a fatal car wreck or plane crash, it's very quiet. Only the noise of traffic and other daily activities is heard, along with the whispers of LEOs working the scene. Some of these scenes you can't forget, but ya don't dwell on it. Except for the grace of God, it could be you or me.

Now, there's no one who supports our military more than I do, but the question I have that no one talks about is this: Do some LEOs have PTSD like the military? Ya don't hear about it, and I don't understand it, because I've been there and I'm OK, but there are some that are not, so it is a debatable question.

By Kansas statute, the sheriff's office is required to assist other agencies of any size as needed, and in some cases the sheriff takes over. In the Katherine Carpenter School and surrounding area following a tornado in

1965, there was a lot of damage to the school and houses in the area. The sheriff had as many deputies on site as Overland Park PD did. We patrolled the area for several days, some on days off and on unpaid overtime, to discourage thefts and looting.

While a plainclothes detective sometime around 1969, I was dispatched to an after-hours burglary of a small restaurant in Lenexa, Kansas, located near Interstate 35. A Lenexa officer shot at escaping suspects as they ran east across I-35 into Overland Park, where one was lost around an apartment complex; one was arrested. The sheriff's office assisted, as usual, and as the on-call detective, I was called out. The burglar that was caught by Lenexa officers fingered his accomplice. Chuck Lane, who was then my lieutenant and I went to the suspect's house. That was a couple days later on the Missouri side. We received no response with a door knock, but I saw the shades move, indicating that someone was inside. Since he wouldn't answer the door and we had a warrant, we kicked in the back door and arrested him with little resistance. The odd part of the story is that this missing suspect had been shot in the foot as he made his escape. While in jail awaiting trial, he fell asleep with his wounded foot in a bucket of ice for swelling and suffered frostbite before he awoke. Pain medication? Probably, but who would know? Or remember? Or care? Back in those days.

Dyn-oooh-mite!

I say this over and over, I wish I had kept a diary during my career, but I didn't, and because of that, in most incidents I mention, I don't remember many of the deputies who were with me at any given time. Some names are mentioned in this book with permission, as I remember those people or have them documented in some way, such as newspaper articles, notes, or reports.

In conversations, I am sometimes reminded of happenings, some funny and some not. Some that I absolutely have no memory of until I'm reminded of them. Thankfully, there are not many of those, but they still are there. That's part of growing older, I guess.

Back in the sixties, before the Johnson County Sheriff's Academy was started, spearheaded by Sheriff Fred Allenbrand and then Lenexa Police Chief John Foster, the training was adequate for the time, I guess. The "academy" was sessions of one day to up to a month (once) of seminars of one kind or the other. Experience on the job was where the real education and lessons were learned. Training classes we attended were just OK as they demonstrated what one might expect in different scenarios, but in my opinion, the best teachers were the officers that had lived it, shared it, and taught it. These were the best instructors; I rode with them, hung out with them, and listened to them. For instance, there was an EMT class that lasted for several weeks around 1966, and when ya got through that boring class, you were an EMT, card and all.

Another seminar was a bomb class that lasted for a day. The bomb class was interesting. The instructor gave his best advice right at the beginning of the class. With a straight face, he shared the following: "If you encounter or see a bomb or anything that looks like a bomb, and if you intend to disarm it, here's what you need to do. The first thing ya do is remove your watch, then your rings, then any other jewelry or valuables including your wallet, car keys, and anything else of value you may have in your pockets. You hand this over to someone to keep for you, as you will want to be leaving mementos to your loved ones to remember you by. Lesson learned or not? Leave bombs alone; leave 'em to someone who knows about bombs! Someone who knows how to disarm bombs or explosives, who will hopefully not blow himself up."

The rest of the class was a waste of time for me, but here's another case in point. We had a guy at the time who responded to a fire call, he rushed into a burning building for some reason and had to be transported to the hospital for smoke inhalation. Ya leave burning buildings to the firefighters if you ain't one.

On the subject of things that go boom. Let's talk dynamite, OK? This is about a location in Johnson County that is and was one of the best little secrets in the area. It was similar to the smaller towns that are now history and which most don't know ever existed. One midnight shift, dispatch receives a call from the Olathe Hospital regarding victims of a vehicular accident (that's a car wreck). When we arrived, we found that it was a couple of Springhill, Kansas, boys that we all knew. I don't know if they are still alive, in jail or out, but they would tell you that they were ornery and in the oleo a great deal, always in trouble for something. We all knew these kinds of guys from each and every small town as well as the larger burgs. There were and are many local boys and now girls just like them. It's kind of like grade school, or high school; we had the guys that want to be straight and those that sit around and dream up shit to do, something to just screw with, someone or the public in general, or something to just steal, as in this case. This was before the Weathermen and people were trying to blow up police stations. We never confirmed what they were going to do with the goods, they didn't say, other than they wanted dynamite for fun.

So we were dispatched to the hospital, and in we went, me and my district deputies. The victims were pretty bloody, bruised, and banged up with multiple injuries. "We had a wreck," they said, so taking the information required a lot of questions, as you know if you have ever been in a car wreck. Some of the first questions ya ask are "Where did this happen? How did this happen? Where is your car now?"

Well, "Our car is in the hospital parking lot," they said, but as far as where and how this happened, they were very evasive, kind of tap dancing around those questions.

We took a break while they were being treated (leaving one deputy), and we went to the parking lot to see the car to record the damage. That's another item for the accident report, cost damages. Now this car had damage to the entire front end. There was a deep crease across the front fenders, and the grill and anything else on the front end was heavily damaged from right to left, headlight high. This extensive front-end damage indicated they had hit something very hard, huge, and very solid, but what? They wouldn't tell us. It was hard for us to believe that they even drove it to the hospital. Photographs were taken, damage recorded, and back into the hospital emergency room we went.

We were all on a first-name basis from past experience—disturbance calls, fights, arrests, investigations, and so on—but John Doe One and Two were still very evasive about what and where this happened. So they were released from the hospital, and we were sitting in the patrol car talking. After a short time, they knew that we weren't going to give it up; we were going to know what happened before they went anywhere. They knew by now they were had, and they had to tell us. Here's their story, and it was a funny one because these two misfits were having one of the worst days of their life.

For some reason they decided that they needed some dynamite. Why? As I said, I don't know, but they intended to blow up something in orneriness, so they decided to burglarize a dynamite storage shack. It's at the Holland Quarries, an industrial rock quarry at a dead-end road at the time, Ninety-Fifth Street now in Lenexa, Kansas.

So knowing about the quarry, these two guys drove out there, broke in, got their dynamite, loaded it up in the back seat of their car, and took off at a high rate of speed. In their escape—Are you ready for this? Are you sitting down? They took off at a high rate of speed as some burglars do making their escape; they made a wrong turn, and guess what? They crashed into a huge steel industrial rock crusher! It's at a dead end blocking the entire road, built into the road and harder than a brick wall. It didn't move a fraction of an inch, but parts of the car did, and that's what caused the huge, deep crease across the front end of the car. So now, broken, bruised, beat up, and bleeding, and with a box of dynamite still in the car, they left the scene to go to the hospital. All the way they were tossing dynamite out of the car onto the side of the road.

When someone is injured like these guys were, you don't arrest them, or the county or city pays the hospital bills. A warrant will be issued and arrests will come later. So we released these two guys and proceeded to the burglary scene, picking up any dynamite we could find on the way but not much, and yes, we should have handed our valuables to someone—you get the picture—but we were lucky. We figured if the dynamite didn't blow up in a car wreck and didn't blow up when it was thrown out the window, it would be safe to pick it up. We shouldn't have done this, but we did, and the day shift continued after we went off shift. At the burglary scene, we drove into the caves to see if there was anything else disturbed, and it was nothing but pitch black except for the headlights of the patrol cars. We had a good time playing on the radios; no one could hear us but us. We drove around until we were satisfied that nothing else was disturbed, and back into service we went, meaning we were ready for more calls as needed.

---

*The quarries are now under new ownership, probably several times since then. This Quarry was operational until around 1986 when quarry operations ceased, it's now an extensive labyrinth of tunnels that go on for miles, tunnels large enough for semi-trucks to drive through. The caves house and contain business offices as well as storage and other facilities.

Chapter 21

Inmates Beat the System

I had been on the job for a little more than a year when three of us were promoted to road patrol sergeants. Not so much because we had experience and leadership abilities but mainly because around twenty-five deputies had left that year because they wouldn't work for Sheriff Lynn Thomas. Some went to security jobs, some became insurance investigators, others went to other police departments, and one went to the railroad. Tension was high because of the election results and exodus of experienced people. I was a sergeant for a while; that is, until Sheriff Fred Allenbrand came into office. Many of the folks that had quit returned, some never did. Some that returned had more experience than I, so I was demoted back to patrolman. Although disappointed, I understood, and it wasn't hard to do my job since I loved it—the excitement and having an outside job, catching bad guys and all. The following year I was promoted to plain clothes detective. Although I wasn't in plain clothes for long, about two years, I did get to work some interesting cases, investigations of one kind or the other.

There were some guys that were not real bad but just liked spending the winter in jail. They were petty crooks, a few ornery guys who would commit a misdemeanor crime so they could stay warm for the winter, get three squares a day, a warm roof over their head, a nice warm bed—well, not too nice then, but it was better than on the streets. One such guy was Junior Henry. Junior had somehow lost a leg, but he got around OK with a cane. When he was jailed, he would always be a trustee since he had been in jail a number of times. A trustee was a prisoner who did chores, did cleaning, mopped floors, washed cars, and helped the cook. He wasn't paid; he just had a bit of freedom other inmates didn't have. He was unsupervised much of the time. Ya told him what to do, and he went and did it. Junior was on a first-name basis with almost everyone since he was sort of like a seasonal employee. Junior liked all of us, and we liked him even though he was using the system, he and we all knew it. He and others were allowed to run errands in the downtown area until two trustees walked away one day. After that, trustees were not allowed outside jail except under close supervision, usually to wash cars.

Another story about Junior Henry is from a friend who was a reserve deputy for years, Jim Conrad. Jim was as good a deputy as some of the regular officers were. We had several of those capable reserve officers. During my time as a uniform road patrol sergeant, if I had a district officer who couldn't work for whatever reason, be it sickness or whatever, I would call on the reserve deputies who could work a district, and they would fill in. Conrad was one of those.

Jim wrote a comment regarding one of my articles in the *Gazette* regarding Junior Henry:

Ed, you mentioned Junior Henry in the article. I remember a Lieutenant giving me an envelope with cash in it to purchase a train ticket for Junior along with some money for Junior to get something to eat on the train. This was for a scheduled trip to a VA hospital for treatment for something but I don't remember what. I drove him to the Union Station in Kansas City and was told to make sure Junior got on the train which he did. The next day KCMO PD called and said they had Junior in jail. The next day the Lieutenant sent me to go pick up Junior at KCMO PD. What Junior did was to get on the train at the loading area and get off on the other side which I could not see. I don't know if Junior ever made it to the VA on another day. The only other thing I remember about Junior is that he caught some other trustee pissing in the deputies' coffee pot, he was loyal to us. signed......Jim.

It just so happens that the two trustees mentioned that walked away were on my dad's shift soon after his career in law enforcement began. He was working in the jail as most new deputies did—jail or dispatch. Jail was good experience for new or young deputies, they learned a lot from the inmates, how to deal with bad guys, how far the bad guys could go, and what a deputy could allow. These two prisoners were thought to be among those that could be trusted to go about errands. When these two walked away, I have to tell you that it was tense around the house for a while. I didn't understand why. I was still in high school and really didn't care. It was explained to me, but at the time I didn't realize the big deal. The tension all passed after Dad found out he wouldn't be suspended or fired. It could have happened to anyone, but he just happened to be the deputy on duty. At the time, all I was interested in was sports, playing pool, girls, and having fun. I soon lost interest in sports when I found out that girls were the real deal.

As I said, I was the kid at school who watched the clock on the wall, but I have to recognize two of my favorite teachers. Both who were coaches— one football, and the other basketball. William Mace and Ralph Dennis are now both ninety-plus years young at the time of this writing. Two of my classmates, Buck, JD comes in once in a while and I have lunch with these two almost every Wednesday. A few others show up from time to time, and it's a hoot with these two, whom I call "the odd couple" since they are both widowers and have only each other and us to nag at, and they do, on steroids. In my public education years, we were taught civics, history, government, and the rest of the essentials not taught today, and we had teachers like these, plus Bud Selves (another coach), *Marshal Ensor, and Ed Compton, to name a few, who did just that. They taught, and they should all have received a medal for their efforts.

Chapter 22

"Porky's?"

My first suspension was a result of the following caper, which caused police cars to be dispatched from all over the county for an assist-the-officer call miles away. It made all of the newspapers and was reported as "Practical joke goes awry."

When I was working at the Delco Battery Division of General Motors, coworkers in my section of the plant had this practical joke they just loved to play on unsuspecting victims, usually horny newbies. In an earlier chapter, I asked if you've seen the movie *Porky's*. Well, this was about the same gag, only years before *Porky's* came out on the big screen... Ya don't suppose...? Any gullible friend or coworker could be a victim if he was a horny bugger and fell for this practical joke. They'd get set up by their "buddies" to get "something strange"—you know, a strange piece of ass. Some were married guys and some not, bad boys all! I'll bet their wives would agree if they knew what they did, but they received their just reward in the end.

Here's the deal. "Strange pussy" was a ruse. It would all start with someone whispering, "Hey, ya wanna get some strange pussy? I know these two sisters who live together. Their husbands are truck drivers, and they're never home, and these two sisters just love to screw." Well, as you can imagine, some took the bait, and while I was never out there watching, I heard the stories, and they were funny. This little three-room abandoned house (we had permission to use it for this "mission") was at the end of a dead-end road about the length of a football field off the road with a creek in between.

The "host" would take the guy or guys to the house, park the car, and as they approached the house which was lit up with a lantern (no electricity), a door would slam, and a female voice would scream, "Run, run! My husband's home. He's got a gun, he's gonna shoot!" Then came the noise, multiple gunshots: bang, bang, bang! The unsuspecting victim of this gag wouldn't know if he was getting shot at or not, and therefore some frantic escapes took place. I heard stories about cars hitting trees, transmissions getting ripped out, and guys getting hurt running away. While this was going on, I left General Motors for my sheriff's office career, or I would have gone out to watch, but believe it or not, while I was gullible, I wasn't that gullible. Being quite the jokester myself I have never been an easy mark.

As deputy sheriffs, after our shifts were over, we would sometimes enjoy our cops "choir practice." That's just a different name for a beer party, and some used to get pretty toasted (drunk). Occasionally we would go to the old Olathe Hotel across the street from the courthouse; we had a key, courtesy of Butch Holland to the bar for after hours. We would sometimes watch the black-and-white smut films of the day—you know, the ones with the vertical lines and streaks and snow all through the nasty production. So, one evening we're sitting around watching and telling war stories, other stories and lies, some funny, some not, and I tell the story about the "strange pussy" caper by GM employees of days gone by. This was one of my stories that everyone thought was funny for a change. Now ya have to know that a bunch of LEOs who uphold the law wouldn't do such a thing as this, don't you? Well, think again, and if you said no, they wouldn't do such a thing, you're dead wrong. Cops like having fun just the same as everyone else. So the question "Why don't we do that?" was quickly posed by some smartass. It was discussed a bit and decided that this would be a good way to initiate new deputies or anyone else that would fall for it, single or not. Why would any deputy, new or experienced, do such a thing to another brother deputy? A hazing of sorts, that's why.

So here we go, Initiation 101 on unsuspecting new cops and friends that take the bait, and I'm the biggest duck in the puddle in the arrangements…but I wasn't the only one that suckered them in. I only did about a total of four. Our plan was a bit more reserved than what the Delco boys did. We made sure that all guns were locked in the glove box and that the driver, not the "victim," had the car keys so there would be no cars wrecked or damaged or people hurt. We had all the bases covered, or at least we thought we did. Some resisted having to leave their gun, but they were told, "That's the way it is. It has to be that way or no pussy for you. These gals won't let anyone in the house with a gun, and we don't want them to know we're cops anyway." OK, so a horny cop always leaves the gun; we made sure of it, and we locked the glove box and the car. This thing got so big that we had LEOs from area city police departments, highway patrol as well as our sheriff's office. One observer was the Olathe police chief at the time. My dad was there, and my sister, Kathy was the door slammer and screamer. There were other command officers in the audience, which would usually total about fifteen people plus or minus at any given event. They were hiding behind trees and anything else—out of sight, of course. My dad loved hiding behind one of the close trees, which he circled as the victim ran by. Anyone and everyone that knew about this caper wanted to be there and see this thing happen. The car had to be parked on the far side of the creek, so about halfway from the creek to the house, the action would commence.

Now you have to imagine the setting, bugs and crickets chirping, frogs croaking, and ya might hear a cow or horse moo or whinny, but that was it, nothing else. It was stone silent and pitch black, dark and humid with the summer heat. There was nothing around this house but the road, an open field, and a wooded area to the east. There were towels on the windows for curtains and a lantern lit to simulate light. This house was abandoned and run down, but ya couldn't tell that in the dark. So when the "victim" was about halfway to the house in the silence of the night, a door slammed as loud as the door slammer could make it, and in that silence it was loud. "Run, run! My husband's home! He has a gun!" Again, in the stillness of the night, bang, bang, bang, bang! And I mean this guy was now running full speed to the locked car. With the adrenaline pumping, it actually was faster than full speed.

Anytime I tell these stories, and as I sit here writing this, I still am nearly rolling on the floor, tears in my eyes. It was *Your Show of Shows*, the Academy Awards of practical jokes. It was the greatest show on earth, a movie, and we were in it. I'm telling you, *Porky's* (made in 1981) was very similar to our caper.

So hopefully before this guy gets to the car, someone would jump out and say "gotcha," and everyone would come out, and we'd have a good laugh and a beer. Every newly initiated victim was now a part of the game and wanted to be there to see it as well; they couldn't wait to see it happen to someone else. Due to our precautions, we didn't have any cars damaged or anyone hurt…but we did have a couple of situations, and neither was good. We shoulda stopped while we were ahead, but we didn't.

Jim was six foot six at least—he was a huge man. Other than being an LEO, his claim to fame was that he was a cousin of a well-known Hollywood movie star. So after the gunshots, Jim vanished into the trees; he was gone, we couldn't find him. We were yelling for him to come out, driving up and down the one-lane road, trying to tell him everything was OK, it was a joke. He didn't believe us, his response for about thirty minutes was, "Fuck you!" Even big guys don't like getting shot at, so over and over, "Fuck you!" He didn't trust us; he was back in the woods to stay. As I say, it took about thirty minutes to locate him and get him back. I followed his voice through the trees and found him standing in a slouch near a cliff with an arm over a large tree branch, hanging on. He was soaking wet from sweat, out of breath, and about to collapse because he had been running through the woods since the gunshots. We got him to the car and took him home to his bride, got him in the door, and left without explanation. I don't know what he told her, but he did say it was some kind of an initiation of sorts. This guy came down with a bad cold, near pneumonia, and was off sick for three days. Now this isn't so funny is it?

The next guy was Nettie. He was my target, our trusted Teepee bar owner friend who brought along a friend, Calvin. I was OK with this, the more the merrier, I knew Calvin too. This part of the caper demonstrated what true and loyal friendship is, a portrait, how far a guy would go for his buddy when the chips were really down. We got out of the car and approached the house, getting closer than we ever had. The door slammed, Kathy yells, "Run, run! My husband's home! He's got a gun!" Bang, bang, bang! I yelled, "Help me, I'm shot!"

Now…Nettie and Calvin were history, running faster than a little guy and a fat man ever could. Calvin yelled, "Mike, we gotta help Ed."

Nettie's reply, "Fuck the little son of a bitch. He's the one that got us into this mess," and off they went.

The surveillance guys were able to stop big Calvin—he didn't move so fast—but Nettie? Not so. About a half hour later, we found Nettie walking and running, going east in the middle of the narrow county gravel road, and he's nearly walking backward looking over his shoulder. I still to this day have to laugh at Nettie's response to Calvin as he yelled at the top of his lungs, "Fuck the little son of a bitch. He's the one that got us into this mess!" And he meant it. He was in overdrive, leaving me to die alone.

As said, by now we should have cut our losses and quit this gig. But we didn't.

So there were a few other capers in between Nettie and Calvin and now the last guy, Benny. He was the deputy who wrecked a patrol car looking at the girls, was reassigned to dispatch because he couldn't pay attention to drive, and then fired, but this was before all of that. He was pumped; he was wearing his best boxers, slacks, and silk shirt. He had so much cologne on that he reeked, and when the car door opened, the steam glowed in the dark, well, almost. My buddy OB Deaton, who was bringing him to the caper, later said that all he could talk about was the pussy he was going to get that night.

They arrived and got out of the car. There was a huge audience—all the aforementioned LEOs—they get very close to the house, just on the house side of the creek. The door slammed. "Run, run! My husband's home! He's got a gun!" Bang, bang, bang! And off Benny went. OB yelled, "Help, help, I've been shot!" Benny didn't slow down, and all of a sudden he was among the missing. We couldn't find him. We were looking in the woods, the fields, and all over the area, so we started driving up and down the road looking for him, it had been a good half hour. I was driving slowly, and as I passed this house that was around a mile east of the gag house, it was all lit up, door open. As I was going by, I was thinking, "No! Please, no!" I went back, and through the door I saw Benny…he was on the telephone!

I knocked on the door and went on in. This man and his wife were sitting on the couch, and Timmy was still on the telephone. He was dirty, sweating, and out of breath, and he didn't smell good anymore. I don't remember anyone else in the house other than LEOs who followed me in, including my dad, but the living room was full. Benny, who had entered the house without knocking, told the occupants he had to make a call, he needed help, an officer had been shot. He saw me and said, "How'd you get here so fast, Ed?"

I say, "Benny, what have you done?"

Fearing the worst, I took the telephone from him, finding a dispatcher on the other end. I asked the dispatcher what was going on, he said, "Don't worry, Ed. We have cars on the way. Do we know how OB is?"

I said, "Cars on the way from where?"

He said, "From all over the county for the assist the officer who's shot."

"Dave, the call is unfounded. Call them off. No one has been shot! It was a joke!" I made sure he understood me, because when you get any "assist the officer" call, the troops come running, adrenaline flowing, red lights flashing, sirens blaring. The home owner is hearing all of this and he isn't amused at the invasion of his home.

We all left and home I went to suit up since I was working midnights. So was OB; he was on my shift. Anyone that picked up that telephone to talk to the dispatchers was going to be in trouble; it just happened to be me.

My wife one time asked, "What did your father think of you being suspended?"

I said, "What could he do?"

Then she asked, "Why didn't he get suspended?"

To which I said, "Who's going to suspend him? His chief of police was there!"

"Well, why didn't the sheriff know?"

You may realize by now that she asks a lot of questions. Anyway, I told her, "The sheriff wasn't going to find out. It was kept quiet because everyone wanted to see it happen at one time or the other."

At some point ya run out of victims, but when what ya least expect to happen and ya don't want to happen, happens, it doesn't last long after that. That's until a newbie comes along. Do this in today's world and someone would be arrested.

Chapter 23

OB's Fired! I'm Suspended!

I need to go back a bit because the "Porky" caper all happened at the end of Lynn Thomas's last term. Within a few months he's gone and Fred Allenbrand was coming in as sheriff. We were all walking on eggs because we all were, most of us were against Thomas getting another term, and he knew it.

Oscar Berry (OB) Deaton was a childhood friend, a high school classmate and now a fellow LEO. We had a lot of stories to tell even before this that go back when he and his brother, my cousins and other kids in the neighborhood stood at the creek under the bridge between our houses to see who could pee the furthest across the creek. OB was one of the guys who climbed the water tower on the west edge of town, there's too many stories to tell but we were ornery and we did have fun even up to the aforementioned caper and there's other stories about OB after he departed the sheriff's office but I will leave that to another day.

OB had laid the groundwork for his own demise as an LEO at the Johnson County Sheriff's Office since he had not been holding back any of his remarks bashing Sheriff Thomas and other staff members. The uniform division squad room was just down the hall from the sheriff's private office. OB didn't care; he just kept going on, loudly, night after night, even though I kept telling him to tone it down, saying, "They're going to fire you if you don't." He was loud enough that I feared I was going to get fired for just being around him, and the sheriff, who was very hard of hearing, was hearing some of this.

So I showed up for our shift, it was 11:00 p.m. OB was already there, the sheriff was there, and OB had already had his "interview." He informed me, "They are going to fire me." He told me that Thomas wanted me to report to his office, so I did. Sheriff Thomas was sitting behind his desk looking down, and he was visibly pissed off. It was his department, his employees that had embarrassed him in the eyes of every police department in Johnson County as well as Fred Allenbrand's supporters; he now had to deal with it. He looked up at me and softly said, "I take a very dim view of what happened tonight." He paused and then said, "What do you have to say for yourself?"

"What can I say, Sheriff?" I said. "What happened was a practical joke that just got out of hand. Other than that, I have no excuse." What else could I say without a lie?

He proceeded to tell me about the phone call he received from the folks who had been terrorized and subjected to a home invasion until they found out what the problem was. He had to apologize to them for our actions he said. He told me how embarrassed he was, and then said, "I cannot fire you because I need my sergeants, but I am going to suspend you for two weeks starting Monday."

And I, also a bit embarrassed, said, "OK, Sheriff, whatever is best."

"You are relieved."

"Yes, sir." There wasn't anything I could do other than to walk away with my tail between my legs.

So I'm suspended, two weeks off. I worked construction for one week, making more than I would have at the sheriff's office in two weeks, and I take a week's vacation. When I returned to work, it was like nothing had ever happened. They did fire OB, but that had been coming; Thomas had been looking for a reason to fire him for a long time and we handed it to him. I can't say I am proud of how this caper turned out and the ending results, but I do have fun telling the story. To this day, the memories of the caper still make me smile and laugh.

The sad part was that OB was fired and there was no defense for him. He had been working on it very hard. I tried to tell him, he wouldn't listen. He hated Thomas. I didn't, but I didn't care to work for him and was glad when he was gone. Later I talked to incoming sheriff, Fred Allenbrand, and told him I was going to resign. His response was that I shouldn't quit, because if I did, he wasn't sure that he would be able to rehire me. Needless to say, that was the end of the "bang, bang, run, run" caper. All's well that ends well, or not.

You Arrested who?

By now you know that most LEO's enjoy a bit of black humor, probably because of what we see and experience over the years, and it's refreshing sometimes to laugh, don't cha know? In some cases, we create it.

Eye doctor Marvin (Doc) Wollen was a beloved local doc, city father, and social volunteer who enjoyed being Santa Claus in every Christmas season. He did some of his appearances at the courthouse for courthouse employees' kids, as well as deputies' kids Christmas party, every Christmas season. It's December 25, 1971, "Santa" was in the sheriff's office on his annual children's surprise. I said, "Santa! You are under arrest!" (No children were present.) He and I were both laughing, as I escorted him to the jail booking area, handed him the block of numbers, and took the picture of him holding the numbers plaque. So Santa is now identified as a prisoner in Johnson County and the state of Kansas, we both had fun with that "arrest" for years to come.

I have had a lot of fun with this over the years with my kids (I guess I was a cold bastard, wasn't I?) I'd tell them that there would be no Santa Claus that year because Santa was in jail! I would show them the picture as proof, I messed with my kids every Christmas over the Santa thing. Now I would probably be arrested for child abuse. I also told them that Santa and his reindeer were hit by a train at a railroad crossing in Olathe. My kids were easy marks, very impressionable. They believed their daddy, but I never strung them along very long. I had fun with it, but it was more of that cop black humor. We all laugh about it today, especially me. Here's a picture of the youngest person I ever arrested, more black humor, it's my son Chris when he was two years old.

When an incident was found to be funny or out of the ordinary, the district officer would make the announcement, and we tended to gravitate to the scene if we were not busy at the time. One such incident happened on the shoulder of I-35 just outside of Olathe late on a midnight shift. I saw this parked car on the side of the four-lane, engine running with two occupants, asleep in a very compromising position. A local drunk known to all of us, who knew us all by first name, was asleep on his knees on the passenger side floorboard of the car, facing her, in her lap. He had one arm over one leg and the other arm over her other leg with his face buried in her private parts. OK, I tried to keep it clean. He fell asleep eating pussy. Ya get the picture, don't cha? Initially I couldn't get them to wake up, and in describing my car check with dispatch, with a male and female unclothed on the roadside, of course I was unable to keep from laughing, so everyone else was curious. By the time the guy woke up, the car was surrounded by snickering LEOs, deputies, highway patrolmen, and city policemen. He looked up through the open window and saw me. Looking at me, still in position, he said, "Wasssssss goin' on, Ed?" He passed out, so they were left in the car without any keys. The keys would be returned by the next shift, when he would be sober enough to drive away.

We did that a lot in those days, leaving a cooperative drunk in his car without keys. That changed about a decade or less later for reasons we all know. A lot of things changed thanks to incidents and ambulance-chasing lawyers. Sometimes we would leave the car and take the drunk home. That also changed. It came back to bite us in the ass when somewhere a drunk was left in the car, had an extra set of keys, drove off, and either injured or killed another driver. It only takes once, and we all learn from our own and hopefully others' mistakes, don't we? In my career, I let a lot of drunks sleep it off in their car and took many others home. This seems a bit ignorant by today's standards; I admit it due to deaths caused by drunk drivers. Population is greater by far, and another side of the equation is the influx of drunk drivers from south of the border. To them it is very "macho" to drive drunk and sadly, their customs come to America right along with them. While there are organizations out there that beat their chests about

Nice Pinch!

all they have done with the drunken driving problem, they ignore illegal aliens driving and killing Americans.

By now, some of the Delco boys were glad I became a cop, because I took some of them home instead of to jail. The word was out, I was told, that Sheriff's Deputy Ed Hayes was OK by the union members.

Chapter 24

Equipment Failure!

One of the many tasks uniform police officers do on their shift is after-hours building checks as mentioned. Banks and post offices are checked, as well as all businesses, even if they only look at the business while driving by during quiet periods. Two banks that come to my mind are the Spring Hill and Stanley Banks. Stanley Bank is now a model train shop in Overland Park, Kansas. I can't tell you how many times I rounded the corner of the Spring Hill Bank and had the hair stand up on the back of my neck. It was always very well lit up, on a wall visible through one of the south windows was a life-size portrait of some guy, probably a past president, founder, or owner—I never knew. When you see a burglar/person in a business, it gives ya the willies at first. You have to process what you have just seen if ya have time, you deal with it, but this looked so real, it pulled my chain no matter how many times I had seen it.

In checking the Stanley Bank one evening, my reserve partner, Pete Lorenze stood atop of an air conditioner to look in. When he stepped down the south end of his pants went north, equipment failure! His ass was hanging out, his boxers were exposed…oh, what an ugly sight! Oh, the humility! Needless to say, we had to get an equipment repair to continue our shift. Luckily, nothing happened in between the time of the failure and the time repairs were made.

A similar incident happened to me in Desoto, Kansas. While working an accident, I bent over with a crowd of people around to lift something, and my pants fell apart. Yep, you know what was hanging out. I worked the rest of the accident walking around with my clipboard covering my ass. Once again, equipment failure!

Driving by the Gardner, Kansas, Post Office on one of my midnight shifts, I saw through the front window that the safe was open—wide open! I called dispatch while checking the outside of the building. Finding nothing wrong, I waited until the postmaster came to secure the safe and building. We checked the inside of the building, and I went back into service. An appreciative postmaster sent an atta-boy letter for that event, so you see, self-initiating activities are rewarding in one way or the other in some cases. Some expectations are null and void; they just happen, but ya kick ass and take names, getting nothing but bruises, and a simple thing like this generates and atta-boy letter. I was told by the secretarial staff that I got a lot of these, but the higher-ups trashed about half of them. They didn't want me getting too many.

It was during this time period that I worked some horrendous vehicular accidents with fatalities. Car wrecks before mandatory seat belts or involving occupants without seat belts are as gruesome as you may imagine. In transportation accidents, the only thing that is worse than head-on crashes are plane crashes and car-train crashes, especially in the era of no seat belts. I only mention this because the following were some of the worst accident investigations I worked. Anyone who has aspirations of being a cop should know this is what they may witness and investigate during their careers. The sights, smells, and sounds will stay with you a long time, maybe a lifetime—in my case it's been lifelong—but most are able to deal with it, no PTSD. As I told our daughter before she began her career at the Kansas City, Missouri, police academy, if you don't think you can deal with mayhem such as car wrecks and crime scenes and—I know I'm repeating myself—if you don't think you can shoot someone in self-defense or to protect others, you should consider choosing another career. My advice to a few that were already in the career and finding some things hard to deal with was "Maybe you should consider another profession." Our daughter is now a sergeant with the KCMO Police Department and doing very well.

Back to the vehicular (that's car wrecks). One such wreck involved a family—a man, his wife, and young son. This accident is a prime example of hauling and loading goods on or in trucks or any vehicle. This accident involved a two-ton flatbed truck with a large load of bricks stacked against the cab of the truck. They were traveling on the four-lane highway rolling down a slight grade when a front tire blew out. The truck didn't go very far before it left the roadway and went into a ditch, where it came to a sudden stop hitting a berm. Upon impact the load of bricks shifted into the cab, crushing and pinning the occupants, and it probably killed them instantly. It was all over when I arrived, but if they didn't die instantly as we believed, they burned to death because the truck caught fire, with the cab involved. The fire had been extinguished by cement truck drivers carrying water for their load, but the damage was done. Fuel tanks in many trucks in those days were in the cab behind the seat. After many crashes such as this, safety became a factor and gas tanks were moved towards the rear of the truck bed.

Another car wreck in that same area around the same time happened when a man lost control of his two-person sports car going into an exit and skidded into a light pole. The driver's side of the car was crushed, and the impact killed him instantly. When I arrived he was still sitting behind the wheel as if he was going somewhere.

Two more wrecks in that time period were just as tragic. One was a Volkswagon Bug containing four young men out having a good summertime day on one of the very narrow, hilly, county roads. The VW and a large car collided head on, killing the four in the VW instantly. Some were ejected, some not. Both cars were total wrecks, and the driver of the larger car was seriously injured but survived. As I recall, both cars were in the middle of the road going over the hill. To this day that road is just as hilly but a bit wider, though it's still not real safe in my opinion. An ironic side note on that accident is that in telling my wife later on, I learned that she had been in school with these four youngsters who had graduated.

We all have heard of the first responder who goes to an accident and finds that a victim is a relative. This happened to a couple of officers during my career. That's sometimes in the back of your mind on the way: Will it be someone I know or a loved one?

Another accident that could have been much more tragic ended with serious injuries to some young people that lost control of their large-sized convertible on a county gravel road and left the road at a bridge, coming to rest in a shallow creek. One of our deputies saved one young lady from drowning by holding her head out of the water until the car could be raised enough so she could be extricated. A very passionate letter of thanks was received on this one to all of us on that accident scene by the victim's father. Believe it or not, atta boys don't happen very often and especially during my uniform years. While we are all aware of the fact that we are just doing our jobs, it's always nice to know that someone you helped has been appreciative of your actions, I have a few such letters in my scrapbook.

Other car crashes were gruesome and involved multiple victims, more snapshots in your mind. When it comes to some aircraft crashes, they are beyond gruesome. Just imagine human bodies cut into random-sized pieces, That's what you get when ya hit the ground in an aluminum tube or container that comes apart along with the human body. It's worse than body parts in a post mortem, except plane crashes and car wrecks are outside on the open roads, fields, and properties. The following aircraft crashed while doing a loop over the runway, the day before the pilot completed the loop with him only in it. The next day he did it again with a passenger forgetting that an added 180 lb. person required more sky for that maneuver thus killing both pilot and passenger.

One such example was the airplane that stalled, fell out of the sky, straight down onto a concrete driveway killing two men. Imagine the sights in that crash, too gruesome to tell about. A search and rescue friend in Colorado told me about a plane crash he worked in which a couple and their dog were killed. That airplane, according to him, hit a mountain rock wall. The largest human body part found in that crash according to him was the man's penis. Here's yet another plane crash following a VFR pilot taking off into weather, a low cloud cover and here's why ya don't do it:

During these days there were only private ambulance services in the unincorporated areas of the county, some of the cities had them manned by policemen, firemen or volunteers. Many times it took an ambulance way too long to get to an accident scene and all you could do was to comfort the injured any way you could. It's pretty tough standing by while the injured are screaming in pain but we did it.

Chapter 25

At First You're Dead. Then You're Not?

On a midnight shift I was advised, "Calling 105, call (105 was the sergeants call number) dispatch for information!" When there was a call or information that should not go out over the police radio, this was what we did at the time. This was to protect persons, victims, and their families privacy from media so notifications could be made by us and not them. At that time the only portable telephone the sheriff's office had was the size of a lunch pail and weighed as much as a car battery. It was so heavy that no one really wanted to carry it around even in a patrol car, at least not me. It was usually used only during disaster emergencies and for command posts when needed, such as a tornado, a dive recovery, or other special operations.

So I drove to a pay telephone, gave dispatch the telephone number, and they called me, it saves a dime. This was the sixties. A dime was a dime, and for cops...as I say, contact at the time was the police radio and pay phones. When I got the telephone call, I was advised of a notification of death, which we did on occasion. These calls are a real downer, but as they say, somebody has to do it. It gets easier after ya do it a few times but you still don't enjoy doing it, giving folks bad news. At times we had a sheriff's office chaplain who would handle these notifications with the assistance of an officer. When a chaplain was not available, usually the sergeant made the call, which was the case on this this night. So I was given an address to make the notification to the parents of a robbery victim. Their son had been murdered in New York City, NYPD said, our office got the information from NYPD via teletype. My partner, a reserve deputy, and I went to the residence, which was located out in the north end of the county. We had to bang heavily on the door to wake up the victim's mother and father. They knew when a couple of deputies came to their door at that time of night that the news could not be good; you could see it on their faces. We stepped inside, and I informed them of why we were there as kindly as I could, surprisingly they took the news fairly well. We were surprised because some of these are so sad, and the notified person understandably just goes to pieces. In this case there were no relatives or friends to call to come and stay with them to comfort and support them so we remained until we felt they would be OK. Eventually we went back into service.

An hour or so later, I got the same call, "Contact dispatcher for information." Back to a pay phone we went, I got the call, and are you ready for this? I was now advised that New York Police Department had made a mistake. We had another notification to make. We were now told that after further investigation, NYPD has found out that the dead guy is not who they initially thought he was; he's an armed robber. This dead guy had robbed the person they thought had been murdered, the guy we had just made the death notification on. Good news, the dead guy had the robbery victim's identification and wallet and someone had murdered him, it had been assumed that the robbery victim was the dead guy.

So here we went, back to the parents to give a "living notification," a first for me. The lights were on, and the parents were still awake. We were once again welcomed into their home. Their faces indicated confusion, but this was good news for a change. I felt a bit embarrassed, but I gave them the news, and all were relieved. We couldn't apologize enough, but they understood, and they understood that it was not our department's mistake. What a relief it was, but that situation could have had a very different outcome with an elderly couple losing a loved one. I would never have been able to forget it. Goes without saying, I haven't forgotten this, but the positive outcome just makes this an interesting incident that ended up happily for all. During your career you will remember the good times and you will remember the bad times at the cop shop but no one knows unless they've been there.

On another evening shift, the city has an operation 100, as it's called today. An operation 100 involves a person who refuses to come out of a structure, car, etc. to follow law enforcement's instructions for one reason or the other, many are standoffs and most are dangerous. As I listened to the radio traffic, I realized who the subject of this standoff was. I knew what and who this was about, it was my friend and former Deputy, OB Deaton and the officers were very hesitant to take him on. After a short stint with the city of Desoto he was now out of law enforcement. I advised dispatch that I was proceeding toward the conflict and why. Upon arrival I met with the Olathe officers, who as said were very reluctant to go in. OB when he wanted to was a real bad ass, and he had the reputation and history to prove it along with his brother Donnie, also a childhood friend. So I volunteered to go in and try to talk him out. First of all, I am not a badass, but I do have the talent (if that's what you want to call it) to reason with people, which is what has saved my ass on many occasions. So I approached the front door and walked in, I was greeted, not in a real friendly manner. We talked, and talked and I convinced him he was already in trouble and this wasn't going to end in a positive way for anyone, especially him. Having been an LEO, and given the fact we were longtime friends, he agreed to surrender and proceed to jail. We emerged from the house, and it was all over. The Olathe officers were relieved that no one got hurt, and so was I.

In about the same time period another operation 100 in Overland Park was in an apartment. My partner (a reserve officer) and I stopped by to see what was going on. It was a quiet night, and we were just curious but it's called "Jumping a call.". We saw LEOs outside, in the hallway, and on the stairs, all with weapons pointing at the very confused-looking guy in the apartment. The door was wide open. He was walking around the apartment with a shotgun—not pointing it at anyone, just holding it. I asked the leading officer what was going on, and he said, "Well, Sergeant Hayes, there appears to be a threat. We received a call about this situation on Mr. Hayes, is he a relative?."

I said, "Mr. Hayes? Maybe I can do something to help?"

Now I am going to tell you that this was not one of the most intellectual moments of my career, but I decided to walk in and talk to Mr. Hayes, much to the surprise of the city officers. I didn't make very many friends that night for jumping their call, but the situation seemed to be at a standstill. So I walked in and announced myself. "Mr. Hayes? Hell's bells, that's my name. We may be related, ya think?" He looked very confused, I reached out for his shotgun, and he handed it to me. Once again, no one was hurt, everyone was relieved, and I left. They thought I was looney tunes, and maybe I was? Now days they would assemble the swat team and sit on the house for a day or so trying to talk the guy out, that's much safer than what I did.

On another guy three of us just went in, he ran to the bathroom and almost got the door shut, it took all three of us to restrain and arrest him and we got some bumps and bruises but no purple hearts that day.

Then there was Charlie years later who was holed up with the police all around his house after an argument with his wife. I was watch commander so I am hearing the radio traffic and I know who and where this is so I called Charlie. He gets pissed off at me because I am not telling him what he wants to hear so he hangs up on me, I call again and he hangs up. This happened four times so I give it up, now Charlie calls me and I hang up on him. He apparently decided to give it up getting no help from me and he immediately walked out of the house and again, no one hurt.

Dispatchers are the lifeline of the street deputy or police officer, be he a detective or in uniform. At the time the Johnson County Sheriff's Office dispatched calls for around thirty-plus police cars from the sheriff's office, the cities, and the highway patrol, for nearly every city in Johnson County, every patrol car, and all cars, whatever their assignment was, plus detective units, all at one time. There were others, such as the coroner, some reserve officers, the DA on call, and so on. Most, not all, but most good dispatchers had road patrol experience. Some that didn't would ride along to educate themselves to make themselves better dispatchers. Dedicated dispatchers pay attention and have the backs of the patrol officers. If something seems odd, the patrol officer doesn't always have to ask for backup; the dispatcher has backup on the way. Dispatchers are required to keep command staff in the loop as events occur and keep them up with the details of what is going on at the time. My sheriff's department had some of the best dispatchers in the world at the time, and I'm sure that has not changed.

A funny thing happened after President Ronald Reagan fired the air traffic controllers who went out on strike in 1982. Three of the fired Olathe based controllers were hired by our sheriff's office. All three were excellent as dispatchers and all three were excellent in their jobs. One retired as a lieutenant, and the other two have retired as detectives.

Some dispatchers had "pipes" (a term meaning *voice* used in radio broadcasting), and I always wondered why some of them didn't go into radio or TV. I guess everyone can't make it there, so they probably made the wise decision to go to the sheriff's office. They had already lost their job once, hadn't they?

Here's the headline: All three of these guys told me that being a dispatcher with the sheriff's office was harder than being an air traffic controller. It was more difficult to keep track of a bunch of police cars at one time than it was to pass airplanes off to another center without putting them together at thirty thousand feet. So much for the difficult job of air traffic controllers that they whine about.

There are many different personalities in law enforcement, as in any other business or occupation, and Johnson County was and is no exception. I will note some in future chapters. Some are memorable and make a lasting, positive impression on deputies and public alike. Such was the case with Deputy John Boase. My first exposure to Boase was in the early years of the Breathalyzer instrument, the testing instrument to determine the amount of alcohol in a person's system; it's mainly used on vehicle drivers, as most of us know. This was somewhere around 1967 at a Shawnee, Kansas, Police Department class. Johnny, as we all called him, was a volunteer for the police department and fire department and was conned into being the "crash dummy" for the class by his friend, the Shawnee police chief. Johnny was NOT a drinker, so this was cruel and unusual punishment, and Chief Charlie should have been arrested for doing this (smile). Johnny had downed a few drinks before we arrived for class so he was well on his way to oblivion.

Drinking straight bourbon he was for the demonstration (a lot), and it didn't take long for him to be just a funny, falling-down-laughing drunk. Now most classes were not this funny, but this was a real hoot because of Johnny's demeanor. The pain would come later, both from the hangover and from what he was going to endure from his wife, Dorothy. As I said, a falling-down, happy drunk, laughing all the way, Johnny needed help on all fronts. After the training class he obviously needed a way home, so another deputy and I took Johnny home. That was not a good move on our part, because when we arrived, we were introduced to the "wrath of Dorothy." It was as if the two of us had done this to him, and she wasn't listening. Dorothy was not happy with him or us, as we had to carry him inside, and that's no shit—we HAD to carry him in and deposit him on the couch, and needless to say, we left him in marital hell (as he described it later) as soon as we could get out of there. Before we left, we managed to blame Chief Stumpf for Johnnie's condition, but Dorothy wasn't hearing it; we brought him home, so it was our fault. With our tails between our legs, we retreated to the car and left poor John to fend for himself.

Until my friend John's death, we laughed about that lapse in his and our judgment many times. After that class for some reason John had not had enough. He joined the sheriff's department and worked in dispatch for years, did some civil work, and then was the "aide de camp" and office backup for the watch commanders on the busy evening shifts until his retirement. We worked together a lot during our careers. I'll say it again, dispatchers are the lifeline to district officers and Johnnie was top notch and so was his son in law Larry Bruce; I remember all of them, good or bad. The good ones had your back and were highly respected and appreciated by all. The ones who were not so good for whatever reason did not last long in the profession. In my earlier days, we had some dispatchers that were where they wanted to be, a dispatcher, and most of them were really good at their job. Some of us worked dispatch for a short time or occasionally, and some were even good at it. A smooth, calm radio voice makes for a good broadcaster, and it's the same in dispatch. Deputies with uniform road patrol experience were among the best, and some transferred in and out.

John's dedicated service to his fellow deputies and the department was respected by all, including city officers. He was excellent in every position

he worked but was known by all for his work in the dispatch center covering his fellow officers' asses as good dispatchers do. The following picture is Johnny, wife Dorothy and Sheriff Fred Allenbrand.

Horses, Dogs and Henry, Jeff Who?

A frequent problem in the unincorporated parts of the county is livestock on the roadways. Driving on 199th Street in Stillwell, Kansas, on a midnight shift, going the speed limit, which was sixty miles per hour on nearly all narrow county roads at the time, I topped a hill only to see the south end of a horse going north. That sucker was walking away from me smack dab in the middle of the road. As I have said, these things happen quickly, and the only way I could miss this horse, if I could miss it, was a decision made in a split second, to go the left of the horse. The horse was startled by my presence. He looked at me, and his eyes were wide with fear, looked as big as a full-size paper plate…well, maybe a little smaller than that, but he bolted and went in the same direction as the patrol car. The rear protruding door handle hit the poor thing in the butt, taking out a sizable piece of flesh; however, it did not seem to hamper said horse's mobility. It took off running at a gallop down the middle of the road, leaving behind what horses leave behind for some distance. Ever see a parade? It scared the livin horse………never mind. The owner was located by the day shift deputies the next day by checking with area veterinarians so as to collect damages to the patrol car. Loose animals on the highways that cause damage to vehicles are the animal owner's responsibility, if the owner can be located. There are cases where the owner will not step up because of this responsibility and just accept the loss of their horse, cow, or other animal as the cheaper way to go. That is when the damages go back to the driver's insurance company.

One accident that I recall, though I did not work it, was when a car hit a horse, and the horse came through the windshield, killing the occupant.

This happens more than you may think, and the main culprits in car-animal crashes are usually deer and other wildlife, but large farm animals are frequent in rural areas. In some states ya have elk and moose, much larger that a deer. I was south of Buena Vista, Colorado, at night when all of a sudden there was this moose standing partially on the road, and that sucker was huge. His head and neck were out over the roadway, while the rest of his body was on the shoulder of the highway. Even though he was only partially on the road, I swerved to miss him—or maybe it was a she? But whatever, it would have probably totaled out my car and walked away. Experts will tell you that if hitting a large animal is inevitable, you should not try to avoid the collision; just hit it straight on. That has to be your call at the time because all things are not equal. In my case with the moose I didn't follow my own advice did I? But I missed him so I apparently did the right thing for that incident.

South of Gardner, Kansas, I stopped an obvious drunk who was driving all over the road. He was really toasted and very uncooperative—his personal pass to jail. Uncooperative folks nearly always get to go to jail, as was this guy. He wasn't going to pass go; he was going to jail because of his attitude. In my career, I wasn't interested in numbers, just good arrests, and if I wrote a traffic ticket or arrested a drunk, it was usually because of their attitude. Some guys like to work traffic and write tickets. I did not like working traffic any more than I had to. Back to this drunk driver. I was taking him to the car after his sobriety checks, which he failed miserably, as my backup pointed and said, "Go on up to the passenger's door," so the guy could be put in the car. I'm on the driver's side at the rear, and he's on the passenger's side. This guy started walking, not in a straight line, and he just disappeared! I'm thinking, "Where the hell did he go?" I ran around to the passenger side, not knowing what happened. Did he run? Did he try to escape? As I got to that side of the car, I found that there was a very deep concrete culvert, and I saw the guy flat on his back about eight feet below the roadbed. He had walked off the shoulder and fell into a culvert. Was he ever pissed at us! I have to admit he had reason to be. He was flat on his back in a spread-eagle position. Ya had to see it, I guess, but it was funny, and funnier since he wasn't hurt. If he had been sober, it might have killed him. We couldn't help laughing our butts off at this picture, and that made him madder than ever. He accused of us of letting him fall on purpose, but that wasn't true. His anger passed before we got to the jail. By that time we were buddies. I can only guess that when he woke up the next day, he was very sore and the worse for wear.

All persons under arrest have very different attitudes, such as another drunk. He started out arrogant, combative, and uncooperative, which got him arrested in the first place, other than being drunk. Then he accepted the fact that he was going to jail. Some are uncooperative, while some just accept the fact that they screwed up and got caught; they are the folks that are more pissed at themselves than the LEO who is just doing his or her job. Some will shoot at you to avoid arrest, such as Henry Floyd Brown in the 1968 Metcalf State Bank robbery although he was just in the process of suicide by cop, didn't work out, he lived another 40 plus years.

With other prisoners under arrest, personalities to consider are those on drugs, especially mind-altering drugs of one type or the other (PCP, for example). Some drugs give superhuman strength, as cases have shown. Here's an example of a prisoner that was probably on PCP. Pappy Freyler must have been off that night since it took five of us to put the guy down and restrain him. Pappy probably could have held the guy down by himself. This guy had been booked, and whatever he had taken was really now taking hold. As I said, it took five deputies pinning this guy down on the floor to get him in a straitjacket so he was no longer a threat to us or himself. Anyone who is familiar with the Rodney King debacle in Los Angeles can understand the problems caused by druggies taking PCP.

Chapter 27

The Average Dog Is a Nicer Person Than the Average Person

South of Gardner on a day shift, another deputy, the district officer
and I were attempting to serve a felony arrest warrant on a local bad
guy whom we all knew since he was a regular crook, always in trouble for
something. As I recall, this was a forgery warrant of some kind. This guy
was like the dynamite burglars; he just couldn't stay out of trouble. We
were all standing in the driveway by a locked gate, and I was explaining to
the bad guy's father why we were there and what the warrant was all about,
but the bad guy wasn't home, the father said.

Ya always want to be alert when dogs are around until ya know the dog
isn't a threat. In this case the dogs were friendly and hanging around us,
but one of them was waaaaaaay tooooo friendly. I didn't notice—yep, not
alert this time—and one of the larger dogs hiked his leg on my partner as
I was talking with bad guy's father. All of a sudden, I heard this commo-
tion as my partner said, "Son of a bitch! Goddam it!" I took notice of this
because I didn't know what the hell was going on, and it goes back to "staying aware of your surroundings," even though your partner is supposed to
have your back. When something happens, no matter what, your sense of
awareness kicks in. So this pooch shows us what he thinks of law enforcement, probably the same thing as his bad-guy master does. My partner,
Don, who was paying attention to the conversation, kicked at the pooch
that had just peed all over the side of his long left leg from his knee to
the ground. Don was tall; the whole side of his leg was soaked, making
it a much darker blue than the normal color of his uniform pants. Quite
humorous, I thought, since it wasn't my uniform pants or my leg. Don

didn't think it was as funny as I did, and the bad guy's dad, who was not a law breaker, was speechless, embarrassed, and apologetic. Bad guy wasn't home, so all of this was for naught.

I found a couple of stolen cars in this time period just by making car checks/stops. One driver acted strange—body language was the key—so I stopped him and found the car stolen along with a stolen "gasoline card," as the news reported; now we call them credit cards. One other was a stolen car with three young men from Florida; the news headline was "Trio Admits 5-State Spree." They admitted to burglaries in Georgia, Tennessee, Indiana, Illinois, and Wisconsin. They were all over the place.

And another was a car I stopped out in the county containing stolen articles. Included were tires, wheels, and other car parts from a farmer friend's barn they had just left. Didn't get far on that caper. We had to really work at it to find stolen cars in those days. Ya had to visibly note the numbers, call dispatch, who ran the numbers, and if it had been reported, you stopped it if you hadn't already.

This chapter ends with my "Brush with Rush." On a late evening or early midnight shift, I found a couple of youngsters parked in a car out in the county. I could be wrong, but I am 99.999 percent sure one of them was young Rush Limbaugh (a.k.a. Jeff Christy). I don't remember exactly what they were doing, but as I remember it could have resulted in the arrest of both. They were smoking weed or something like that; I just don't remember. One thing you learn as a young patrolman is that "ya don't have to arrest everyone; you can let some go just as the judge" (that's a quote from my father). So for whatever reason, I elected to take these two guys to the office and call their parents instead of arresting them. I did this a lot when I believed it might improve attitudes. This heavyset, baby-fat, talkative, jovial kid enjoyed telling me about himself. He was a DJ in radio under the name of Jeff Christy in Kansas City he said. I made the call, and it didn't take long. It was either his dad or grandfather who came to pick him up, at which time he became REAL quiet. The parent was a big man dressed in a very expensive three-piece suit, and he wasn't laughing or smiling. He thanked me in a very nice way. No doubt he was a businessman of sorts. Rush's dad, grandfather, brother, and others were/are lawyers.

I have attempted to contact Limbaugh on several occasions but have never received a response to verify this Jeff Christy who worked at a local radio station was him for certain. If it wasn't Rush, it was someone very similar. He might think that I want something from him, but I don't. I'm just curious since I started listening to him when he became a national broadcaster, shortly after he left Sacramento.

This was following a local talk show guy here in the Kansas City area who committed suicide, shot himself in a hospital parking lot. That was sad; he was very good locally and may have himself eventually been a national personality. Depression takes its toll on many, and people become a threat to themselves and others in many cases, and it gets ugly. This guy just did himself in, and I have always have regretted not hearing him longer. Besides being interesting he was funny and entertaining. One funny conversation he had with a lady on air was trying his best to convince the concerned mother that her son would not go deaf or blind and would not grow hair on the back of his hand if he continued to masturbate. As my partner Billy always said, "My daddy told me that if I didn't quit jackin' off, I'd go blind, so I quit when I had to start wearing glasses."

Chapter 28

Pappy

I mentioned earlier a deputy respected by all, Charles Leroy Freyler, who was a jailer for many years, called "Pappy" by all who knew him. By now, he was approaching his years of retirement, but even at his age, he was tough and stout as ever when he needed to be. Pappy was nearly as big around as he was tall and solid as a rock. He had been a block ice deliveryman and a wrestler in his early years and then worked as the sheriff's office midnight Jailer until his retirement. Officers through-out the county knew the "turnkeys", same as dispatchers, especially in the early days. That was the guy to whom you delivered your prisoners, one jailer a shift on evenings and midnights. Pappy was a legend, just as steady, low keyed, and even tempered as one could be, but ya didn't screw with Pappy if ya wanted to stay healthy. Those that did soon found the error of their ways.

It was really funny on one shift when Pappy called *me* to assist *him* in the jail. He had a prisoner who was just going berserk, running from one end of the drunk tank (about a twenty-five-foot-square jail cell) to the other, hitting the thick steel walls, which, believe it or not, bowed with every collision. The drunk tank was one of the most famous rooms in Johnson County with the drunks and bad guys. This guy was going to kill himself if left alone, so Pappy and I went into the tank, Pappy restrained the guy (in a bear hug or "Pappy hug" while we worked him into a strait-jacket and got him shackled to a bench.

Pappy worked for a few more years after that and retired. Sadly, like many old cops, Pappy died soon after he retired, which happened a lot in those days. Some of these old boys would stay around way too long, and after retirement they didn't survive for very long in many cases. Pappy was the salt of the earth. He showed his respect for others and me as well. We all certainly loved and respected him.

All of us, well, nearly all of us, liked to "one up" our fellow officers, and here was one such case that involved me and a highway patrolman friend. I was on US 69 at about 141st Street (it's now called Old Metcalf Highway), and I saw two guys walking on the shoulder of the road carrying nothing and trying to hitch a ride. I stopped to check them out, and after visiting with them for a few minutes, I radioed to dispatch to check for wants and warrants. I was informed by a very aggravated dispatcher that a highway patrolman had just checked the two and had let them go; there were no warrants. This anger happened frequently, as some dispatchers bitched at me a lot because when I was working, it made them work. I was always checking on someone or something, and they had to do the checking on their end at the time with a card file, teletype, or telephone call. We didn't have the luxury of modernized communication; thus some inquiries had to be done by teletype, which was also time consuming. We also received the most current news, good or bad, and wanted-person and stolen-car information by teletype.

I knew these two guys were good for something, and I questioned them long enough that they could see I wasn't going to let it go, so they admitted to me that they had escaped jail in Thief River Falls, Wisconsin. Now I went on route to the county jail with two prisoners. A still very aggravated dispatcher asked me what the charge was, and when I advised him, "Escapees," it got really quiet. The highway patrolman who had let them go prior to my contact with them was at the jail when I arrived. He was visibly embarrassed—a sheepish grin he had. He had blown it, and he knew it. I loved it! Over the years he never mentioned it again. I didn't either, but he always knew why I was smiling.

On another midnight shift, I was in the Desoto, Kansas, area and found a couple, their car stuck in a ditch. They were on the way home from their wedding, they said. As I was helping to push the car, the husband was at the wheel when the new wife asked me for my telephone number so she could call me sometime. Funny things happen, I have my doubts that this marriage lasted very long. We got them out of the ditch, and they went on their way to their honeymoon.

I was road sergeant on this night when my district deputy "Jim" called me on the radio and said, "Ed, I'm on 119th Street and Nelson Road, and ya need to get here fast." He was shouting on the car-to-car frequency, so not knowing what he had, I was running hot. He had not notified dispatch (they can hear car-to-car transmissions), so I needed to get there pronto. I got there, and Jim was sitting beside an vehicle on the county road. He said there was a dead woman in the back seat of that car. I checked, and there was a woman who had been beaten so severely her head was swelled to the size of a basketball. She was breathing, so I notified dispatch, and they called an ambulance. The woman came around enough that she could communicate but not real well. She mumbled, "He tried to kill me," and I was thinking, "He may have." We had no idea how long she'd been here, but the ambulance arrived, she was transported to the hospital, and the situation was turned over to a detective unit.

I recently found out from one of our lab techs of the time, Lee Branum, who remembered this case, that the woman was a local bartender and knew the guy who beat her. He was the last person when the bar closed and said he needed a ride home, so since she knew him, she offered him a ride. He started beating her and attacking her with an object that he also penetrated orifices with, and then he left her, thinking she was dead. Well, she wasn't. Jim found her, she lived, and her attacker was found guilty, so there was some justice in that case. No one knew why he did this. He was a regular that everyone knew at the time. Lee Branum continued in the crime lab until his retirement. When he retired he was lab director.

Profiles in Crooks & Bounties

I have mentioned that I "profiled"—you know, that nasty no-no of some of today's politicians that are guided by their bullshit political correctness. I profiled and never quit! I did a lot of sitting. I liked to call it observational surveillance (another word for profiling), and that is exactly what it was/ is in my case, and they came to me. I was sitting at the old intersection of Kansas Highway 150 and US 69, mainly watching northbound cars, many of them coming from Oklahoma. A lot of Texas and Okie crooks traveled that road, and most of us knew it. This was a four-way-stop intersection. It was one of my key spots when I wasn't busy with calls, but I had others, and you will too as you develop your career. During my second year (1966) at the sheriff's department, there was a budget crunch that put a freeze on hiring as well as funding for operations, so then Sheriff Lynn Thomas restricted us to one hundred miles per shift on our patrol cars. This really put the pressure on those of us on the road patrol, and we really had to measure our activities. No problem for this rookie cop. I just sat at my favorite places and watched and stopped at a lot of the businesses in my district and visited with merchants and their employees. The term "community policing" in most areas was in its infancy, but the strategy was used in our department, especially by me.

As said, US 69 was the place to catch bad guys coming up from Oklahoma, Texas, and other places to the south and west. There was a gas station at that intersection, and the attendants felt pretty safe whenever I was in the area. I shared with them the method of my madness, since they were thinking that I was just watching the intersection for traffic tickets. That was one of my little secrets; I was watching and profiling. When a car stopped, I took a visual inventory of the car and its occupants. If they appeared nervous, I stopped them at any time of day or night. I made a lot of good arrests by this method, catching burglars, thieves, escapees, AWOLS, and illegal aliens, whom we were able to arrest at that time. When we made the arrest of an illegal alien, an AWOL, or a deserter from the military, a bounty was paid, just like coyote ears were paid years ago.

Metro area law enforcement departments worked closely with naval security when there was some type of violation. One evening my dad arrested the same AWOL sailor from the old Olathe Naval Air Station two times during the same shift, in less than an eight-hour time frame. This poor kid was determined to go home or somewhere, so he escaped, was caught, got out again, and was caught again by Dad. Another one of those stranger-than-fiction things in law enforcement it was. The bounty amount per escape was fifteen dollars (plus or minus) at the time, so my dad collected thirty bucks that night, which was worth a lot more in 1966 than it is now. The bounty paid out came from the AWOL sailor's paycheck, so he paid for his own capture. That's more salt in the wound for him it was. "*Good pinch*, Dad," as he would say to other officers who made a good arrest, and he made a lot of them. "*Good pinch*," he would say, and coming from him it was always appreciated by his subordinates. It was an atta boy in cop talk. At the time of his death. he was lieutenant over patrol. He had made many "*good pinches*," Now you know the why of the title of this book.

In my time in uniform, I made several AWOL arrests, but that perk dropped away for the most part when the Olathe Naval Air Station was decommissioned. My brother-in-law told me a funny story about when he tried to go AWOL at the Olathe naval base. He said he was climbing a fence to make his escape when a .45 caliber shot caused him to immediately change his mind.

I'll throw this in since I am on the subject of bounties and rewards. In the sixties and before to somewhere around 1972, if an officer found an illegal alien from anywhere, that officer received seven bucks per head. Again, coyote ears? In the Desoto, Kansas, area and all along the Kaw there were many farms since the grounds near the Kaw River were very fertile for melons etc. Farmers hired a lot of folks from the south as day laborers, and some even provided housing. I supplemented my income many times with the arrest of Mexican laborers. That's just what we did. On a midnight shift, I stopped a van loaded with eight illegals, and the dollar signs were in my head. I called dispatch, telling them what I had, and a short time later I was advised to release them all. The feds had decided that they would no longer confine illegals from our area. It was probably nationwide, as we now know.

One summer evening I was sitting at my favorite spot with the car windows open, leaned back watching and waiting for something to happen. The gas station at K 150 and US 69 was closed. I felt the car shake—it really shook—and I turned my head to look out the driver's window, and there was a huge black Great Dane leaning on the car looking in the window at me, his head filling the entire window. That dog lived at the gas station. Needless to say, it startled me, but when I saw it was him it was OK. We were buddies, so we visited for a while. He was just lonely, needed attention, and I always gave attention to my puppy dog friends who didn't want to piss on me. Remember Don and the warrant attempt? Are you paying attention?

Chapter 29

Bouncing Around and Dusty

W hen I took the deputy sheriff's oath, I also took a $100-a-month pay
cut from the job I had, I went to working six days a week on shifts,
and if I had to work on my day off, I didn't get paid extra. For this, I was
raking in $330 a month, instead of the $400-plus I had been making for
working five days a week, plus overtime.

There was no air conditioning, no seat belts, and no AM radios in our
patrol cars my first year. I'll never forget bouncing around in a patrol car
going on a hot call down a dusty dirt/gravel road with the windows up on
those hot summer days. Ya took the heat as long as you could and then
rolled 'em down, and the dust stuck to your sweat. The rest of the shift, you
felt grimy and dirty. As you see, patrol cars had to be cleaned quite regularly if they were to look presentable since a great number of the county
roads were dirt and gravel. Any officer you see driving around in a marked
or unmarked patrol car, be it a city policeman, deputy sheriff, or otherwise, can be subjected to absolutely terrible working conditions, and a hot,
dusty car was one of them. Blizzards, dust storms, smoke from grass fires,
freezing temperatures, heat—this is just some of what all first responders
have to endure on the job. I'm not whining—nor would they (well, maybe
a little), but it's part of the job. Winter was better since we had car heaters
even in those olden days.

The seat belts...it was around 1968 when seat belts were required in
cars. Many deputies didn't use them for some time because they felt that
it restricted their movement, but I used them. When I began my aviation
career, a seat belt was required, and I felt that it was just as good in the car

as in the airplane. I felt like a part of the car when I was strapped in, especially on emergency calls. Any officer be it a city policeman, Deputy Sheriff or otherwise you see driving around in a marked or unmarked patrol car can be subjected to absolute terrible working conditions to work in, a hot dusty car was one of them. Blizzards, dust storms, smoke from grass fires, freezing temperatures and heat is what all first responders have to endure on the job. I'm not whining-(well maybe a little) but it's all part of the job.

In the early days, there were procedures we could implement that may seem a stretch now, but they were not illegal or unlawful at the time. For example, around 1966 was the time period that the "Miranda warning" came into effect. Most of us thought it was bullshit and stupid, and so did some of the bad guys. Resisting, initially some of us didn't use Miranda, but it was very soon when we all had to take it seriously. We had a little card to read from so we didn't slip up and forget something, and we had that backup for court; you better be able to recite it in court or read it from the card, or you would lose your case.

Another thing in the early days of my career was "hold for investigation" arrests. District attorneys at the time would authorize "hold for investigation" arrests where the suspected bad guy would sit in jail on suspicion or a hunch until he was completely checked out. We could hold them for about a week. If I had a guy that was good for something, and I knew it, he knew it, but he wouldn't tell me, all we had to do was to call the DA, anytime, day or night, and get the authority to hold the person. I only remember a couple of these incarcerations where they were released without being charged. Some didn't mind since they were getting three squares a day and a temporary roof. The number of days of those holds is unheard of today, and some would probably not believe it. It was reduced somewhere around the late sixties. To get a DA's OK, it helped if he knew you and your competence.

Car chases are dangerous, and depending on location and time of day, in some cases they're extremely dangerous or deadly. Years ago, chases were regulated by the chase officer or his sergeant. When you are chasing someone, you may not know why he's eluding; adrenaline is charging, and common sense may not prevail so much. In my entire career, I only had two car chases. There were some guys that had them frequently, and a few had them all the time, but if ya don't turn on the lights until you are on their bumper, they usually don't run.

In a car chase I had going out of downtown Olathe, the stop and capture of the perp was a result of a roadblock out in the county south of US 56 on Clare Road on the bridge over I-35. Gardner police chief Robert "Bob" Eaton blocked the bridge with his patrol car, and the bad guy—who was arrested for several violations, including carrying a concealed weapon—had nowhere to go, so he gave it up. The city presented me with his pistol as a memento.

My other chase was in the Aubry/Stillwell area and proceeded into Miami County. On this night, I attempted to stop a car, and the chase was on. I lost the car South of Aubry, so I backtracked and parked, blacked out, on a side road just inside Johnson County where I could see for a mile, give or take, in all directions. A short time later, I saw this car coming down a side road driving very slowly, no lights. When he went by me, I lit him up. He was had, and he knew it. Capture number two.

In yet another car chase incident, Gardner police chief Bob Eaton was chasing a car out of Gardner. This chase ended when the car left the road and hit a huge oak tree on the east side of Lakeshore Drive north of 151st Street, sadly killing both young male occupants. This turned into a sticky situation upon my arrival on the scene to assist on the accident; it was in the city of Olathe and it was being worked by a police officer who was a friend. Sometimes the district attorney's office will send a DA to the scene of a crime or serious incident to observe. In this case it was the district attorney, Jim Wheeler who arrived on scene and directed me to work the accident. The Olathe officer was visibly and emotionally pissed off. I tried to calm him down, but he wouldn't. I resisted Jim's instruction, since it was an Olathe incident and I didn't want to take over the Olathe PD case, but Jim was insistent, so I worked the accident with the assistance of my district officers.. The Olathe officer became enraged and verbally challenged Wheeler. Ya don't challenge the DA at a crime or fatality scene, at least in those days. The officer was allowed to resign later that day. I was saddened to have been a part of that.

District Attorney Jim Wheeler was an officer's friend if he knew you were honest and competent. The Olathe officer was honest and competent; however, Wheeler wanted it his way for legal reasons. He wanted the sheriff's department working the accident because it was a city officer–involved car chase. The Olathe officer just didn't understand this, but that's the way it is.

The sheriff or his deputies can take over any investigation in any city in the county for extenuating reasons, and that's whether the city likes it or not. It didn't happen very often during my career, but it happens, and normally it's with an agreement of both agencies. Usually the city is happy to pass it on. In this case, I am sure that the Olathe police chief agreed with Wheeler and welcomed the sheriff's office's investigation; there really was no other choice.

Accidents sometimes happen on county lines or city boundaries, and when there were no extenuating circumstances, we would do our best to pass them to the proper agency, it's their jurisdiction. Many times in accidents on state highways we were happy to see the highway patrol show up. The highway patrol in those days were not out patrolling all night many nights, they went home. IF it was a serious accident we had dispatch call them out and stood by until they got there securing the accident scene.

Chapter 30

A Pretty Pattern, Surprise, Surprise! I'm called a Thief?

I'll be bouncing back and forth here from being in uniform and being in plain clothes, but in real life that's what I did at times as assignments changed. Early in 1968, I was transferred to plainclothes detective, working that assignment for about two years. Around 1970 I was promoted to sergeant, and back to patrol I went until 1972, at which time I was in undercover assignments for seven years.

When I transferred to the detective division, I was assigned cases, and some that I self-initiated and worked were interesting. Up to that point in time, the only investigations I had done were in uniform, when I'd work the case until it was taken over by a detective, and then I was off it. In plain clothes, I worked burglaries, home invasions, suicides, accidental deaths, theft by deception, the Metcalf State Bank robbery gun battle, one rustling case...you name it. Some of those investigations will come up in following chapters. There were twenty cities and townships, plus or minus, in our county, and most didn't have a detective since some were small. We worked cases in the unincorporated cities and areas as well as to assist those departments that had no detective or were short on manpower.

The Kansas City Area Metro Squad was formed in 1963 by KCMO chief Clarence Kelley, who placed Major Elza Hatfield as commander. The " Metro Squad" was for all departments in the Kansas City metropolitan area where a major crime had occurred. Crimes such as a homicide or similar serious major crimes that needed the manpower for a short time were considered. The metro squad was very active; however, I never worked a metro case other than some that occurred in Johnson County, and my assistance was not as an investigator, more like a gofer, you know, go for this and go for that.

At that point in time, home invasions nationally were on the rise, and had been in recent years. One of my first cases in plain clothes was a home invasion robbery that was in the county, behind Chet's Tavern on old K 10 Highway just west of Shawnee, Kansas city limits at the time. The tavern owner, Chet and his wife lived in the small house behind the tavern. Many patrons knew that at the end of the day, Chet and his wife closed the bar and took the money of the day to the house. So, there was this guy named after a movie cowboy who was a security guard of some kind. He and his cousin knew about the tavern's procedure for the proceeds at day's end, and they thought Chet would be an easy mark. What they didn't know was that Chet was a retired cop (I don't recall from where) who slept with his itty-bitty Colt .32 automatic pistol.

One night Chet and his wife were awakened by this guy who was standing halfway inside the bedroom doorway in low light aiming his four-inch .38 special Smith & Wesson revolver and yelling at the couple. Chet sprang into action, grabbed his itty-bitty gun from the headboard, and shot the most perfect bullet-hole pattern down the wall through the Sheetrock and into the bad guy's torso, hitting him, as I recall, about five times. All seven holes were in a tight pattern in the Sheetrock just to the left of the door trim. What this bad guy found out was that Chet was really a good shot! Later it was rumored that Chet shot the guy after he was down, but that was never proved, and no one really cared much. Ooh, I hate it when I say things like that!

Leaving the crime scene, my partner and I went to KU Medical Center, where the bad guy was in the ER with a room full of medical students. Ya shoulda seen the look on some of the faces as the doc was explaining to them bullet wound by bullet wound, explaining why this guy who was conscious, breathing violently, in shock was going to "expire," he was gonna die! At the time I thought this was kind of cold, but believe me, you don't lose much sleep over a home invader threatening old people. The newspaper reported that he was shot three times. I remember more than that; I think there were at least five or six bullet holes. We had the information we needed on the crook, and back to the crime scene we went for follow-up. Now here's the kicker. The guy didn't "expire"!

His cousin who was just outside the house thought he was dead and left him. He was later arrested, and they both talked. We found that the bad guy who was shot was privy to some private information through his job as a security officer, and he used that information to his advantage, or so he thought. But in the end, not so. Several burglaries were cleared as a result of solving that crime. One was from a coin collection that included a good-sized footlocker nearly full of silver coins of all denominations, paper money, silver dollars and some gold coins from a coin collector. Some of the recovered collection came from residence burglaries and some from a local hock shop that was also a coin shop. In my mind, I can still see that box of money and coins and feel a great deal of satisfaction that we were able to clear that case and return the property to the owners. In the beginning of that case, it didn't come from great investigation techniques; however, the follow-up was satisfying, and it was one those fun cases to work. I was still having fun being a cop!

During my career, I was twice accused of being a thief. There was this burglary of a small gun shop in Olathe, so it was an Olathe PD case until I got a call and received information from an informant who said the stolen guns were hidden in the barn on a farm near Gardner, Kansas. It now became a joint sheriff's office and police department case, so since I had the information, I went to a judge and got a search warrant. An Olathe detective and I served the search warrant, in which we recovered a fifty-five-gallon cardboard barrel full of guns and ammunition. I don't remember how many guns were in it, but it was full to the top with handguns, some in boxes and some not, and a few long guns. So, the bad guy was arrested and the guns taken into evidence.

On the way to the sheriff's office, the Olathe detective said, "If we take a couple of these, who would know?"

I said, "I would know, and it ain't going to happen."

Would he have taken anything had I agreed, or was he trying to set me up? I don't know the answer to that, but he had to agree; that conversation was over. I probably should have said something to his superiors and mine, but I did not. This was not handled well on my part, but no crime was committed; it was just conversation, so I let it go. I can remember several cops getting in trouble for keeping recovered property. Some lost their jobs.

The property, guns, and ammunition were inventoried, photographed, and held until later when the guns were returned to the gun shop owner. In a short time, the gun shop owner accused us of taking guns, as some were missing, he said. I was OK with that since I knew I had not taken anything, and I knew nothing was taken in my presence. While the gun store owner should have been grateful, he was not. His charges were out of line, in my opinion. He was apparently one of these guys who didn't like cops, so unfortunately, he could think what he wanted; I didn't care. We completed a good investigation, the bad guy was convicted, and we were accused instead of the bad guy who had the guns for some time in a barn.

That was one of two times in my career that I was accused of stealing. As I say, in situations like this, if you are right, ya don't like it, but ya don't worry about it. Bring it on, make a report, let's investigate and find out who the real thief is. Oh wait, we already have!

I was accused of taking money years later when I was a lieutenant in the watch commander's office. A citizen brought in a briefcase she had found on the sidewalk in Olathe near the door of a now closed business. It was after five o'clock, stores closed. I took custody and handed it off to my aide, who was a civilian employee. He was sitting in front of my office, I instructed him to open the case to find an owner's name if he could. He opened it and immediately said, "We have money here." I told him to count it and watched while he did so. In this briefcase was several hundred dollars and paper work identifying the briefcase owner. OK, so far we are doing good, aren't we? I called the person whose identification was in the case, and she was in my office within a half hour. She opened up the briefcase to check the contents and told me that not all of the money was there, and she indicated that we took it. She said she knew the lady who brought it to us, and she was not a thief. "She wouldn't steal anything from me." OK, so now I am the thief. Since she was convinced we took money, I suggested that she call Olathe police and make a theft report. I picked up the telephone to make the call, and as I remember, she walked out saying, "Never mind." I don't know if this was ever resolved or if she made a report, but I did. We got no apology, so she may to this day still think we took money.

Any cop who would steal a few bucks or *anything* and jeopardize his or her career, family, and reputation is rare, in my opinion—and stupid. In these cases of accusations, make a report, and let's investigate. Good or bad, the truth will be found out, whether admitted or not by the accuser. In both cases I experienced, the issue just seemed to go away.

In my career, at first I was nervous when taking the witness stand in court cases. Other than school, I had never been a public speaker, and when you are a rookie, you are under pressure, even though it may be brought on by yourself. There's a lot to digest and to learn. The stage fright doesn't last long. It didn't for me, as over time I got to where I really, really enjoyed testifying. It was fun, although it was serious business, but if you are ahead of the curve, no problem. I knew from my dad that all you had to do was build a good case and be honest and accurate, and they couldn't hurt you. I was as professional as I could be but did as I was trained to "just answer the question." I took it a step further, which really angered some defense attorneys. I gave the shortest answers I could, and they had to really fish for anything and everything! It really messed with some of their heads; body language can tell you a lot about the other side.

Chapter 31

People Who Hate Cops

Some people just don't like cops. That is, until they need one, and then it all changes. I witnessed a change in people many times. There was this guy that disliked me for some reason from my teen years all the way up past when I became a cop. That all changed one day when his daughter was in a traffic accident case that I investigated. Then we were buddies for about an hour or so and maybe awhile. Since then I see him occasionally, and he hardly speaks to me and only if I speak first. Oh well. Woe is me, right? He may just be shy? Reasons for some of this anticop behavior may be from media reports, most of which seem to be anticop these days or a bad experience with a cop, usually because of an attitude that needs adjusting; or other unfounded reasons. The current anticop assassinations in the news are sad. In my opinion, one percent of cops give all the rest a bad name. The rest are honest, caring people whose goal and profession is to "protect and serve." It's called public safety! Don't let anyone tell you different, especially the media. Mental health issues play in this as well, I once knew a guy, one of many who hated cops but only when he wasn't taking his happy pills and then cops were OK. The antigun crowd and politicians blame guns on everything under the sun. Cutting mental health budgets nationwide is what they should be looking at and fixing and the "happy pill" situation speaks for itself.

Many career attorneys handle certain types of cases whether they win or lose. Many represented undercover drug cases or other criminal violations, lost in court. Why lost? Because the crook has committed a crime in front of a witness—that's me.

At times on undercover cases, an informant is a witness, and on occasion, there's a surveillance team taking pictures or videos of a crime in progress. That's all pretty hard evidence. Not a lot of cases were covered by a surveillance team, so when undercover I was on my own most of the time. Sometimes I had a partner, especially if it was more dangerous than usual, but 90 percent of the time, it was me and the crooks.

While assigned to DEA, I went to the sheriff's office once a month to get my paycheck because they wouldn't mail it to me. The sheriff said, "I want to see you once in a while." Other than that I stayed away and here's why, one time I ran into a defendant in a courthouse hallway who saw me first as I came out of the prosecutor's office. He was sitting in the outer office waiting room. "What are you doing here?" he said. I gave him some bullshit answer, showed him my (counterfeit) parole papers, and told him I was ordered to a meeting by my parole officer who was "a real asshole." He bought it, but now ya know why I didn't go to the courthouse any more than I had to. You had to plan for these scenarios before they came up, I did most of the time.

I had close friends, relatives, and fellow officers who just knew I had to be using dope to make cases. As hard as I tried, I couldn't convince some of them that they were wrong about that. I never crossed the line. I have never used any kind of unprescribed narcotics or pot—can't stand the smell of the stuff. I was just a good actor, and I had a system. I had methods of distraction and deception, all within the law. I had to deal with accusations of lying, cover-ups, you name it, by a couple of attorneys who disliked me because when a case I developed went to court, the defense rarely won. They didn't like me, and I didn't like or respect them; however, you don't let that show in court. Show respect, be honest, be calm, be concise, give short answers, don't volunteer anything, and know your case.

Remember this, and you will hear it from me more than once: if you make good cases, and if you are honest, you are ahead of the game.

As Mark Twain said, "If you tell the truth, you don't have to remember anything."

During my career I developed lasting friendships with a few lawyers and judges, they were the good ones that I have always respected; however, a few of the defense attorneys were what we call the real "ambulance chasers." Their "fee speeches, attempts to baffle the judge and juries with bullshit" as hard as they tried were just lost in the courtroom. Some presentations were just jokes, but they still received their fees. Not being a lawyer, I don't know what is taught in law school other than rule one, but one thing that should be taught is to not show their emotions. *Rule one is that "they are the one." Rule one is all about them. That doesn't help some who just cannot control themselves. Displaying anger, engaging in physical antics, and being red faced and nearly out of control is what a few of these lawyers displayed. One lawyer wrongly accused me of breaking every law in the books in my cases. I just smiled. I was having fun with him. I knew it, but that poor bastard didn't.

I have to credit some of the assistant district attorneys (ADAs) that handled my cases in the courtroom since 99 percent of my investigations/cases were won either by jury or pleading guilty. Some of the DAs stayed in the job long enough to become very proficient in their work, they were good at what they did. The caliber of DAs was up and down due to the turnover I witnessed over the years due to elections and new district attorneys going into the job, with total staff changes in some instances.

Many times when there was a high-profile case such as homicide or others of serious nature, the DA himself would handle the case, qualified or not, and sometimes that was sad. Another thing about the prosecution of criminal cases you may not know is that a case will usually not be filed and prosecuted if it is not a slam dunk. The district attorney has to run for re-election, and cases lost in court do not help on his or her resume; only cases won help in re-elections. During my career, there were at least six different elected district attorneys in that office, and each time there was a turnover in staff. The same thing happens in almost any office, including sometimes the sheriff. What all of this means is almost constant training of new staff. In the case of the district attorney, that can mean cases lost in court due to the inexperience of some attorneys. It didn't happen very often, but it did happen; I saw it.

One of my investigations went to court with one of the aforementioned Hayes & Cop Hater defense attorneys, the main one. It was a preliminary hearing and was the result of a search warrant resulting in a heroin seizure that was dismissed because I refused to reveal the identity of my informant to the judge and defense attorney. Kansas statute did not require revealing an informant for his or her protection, and I didn't. I cannot remember the number of the statute (it was something like KSA 4something) that at the time protected informants from being revealed by an LEO in some cases, but it now is K.S.A. 45-221.10 (part c and d). In some of the investigations I worked with informants, they would have to testify in court, with the exception of search warrants. In those cases in court when I was ordered to reveal the informant, I recited the statute that protected them, and their identity was never revealed.

The judge in this case was a bully and he took advantage of his position on the bench. At one time, he had been pro-police, but something happened to change that, and he seemed to dislike most LEOs, and especially me after this trial.

One story for how he developed his hatred of cops was that he got out of his car at an accident scene to see what was going on, and a Kansas Highway Patrol trooper told him to get back in his car and leave the area.

He responded by asking the trooper, "Do you know who I am? I am Judge So-and-So." The trooper responded by saying appropriately, "I don't care who you are. You are interfering with an accident investigation, and if you don't get back in your car, you WILL go to jail." I wasn't there, but if that trooper ever ended up in that judge's court, it wasn't going to be pretty. There were other opinions on why this judge no longer liked cops or fireman but I will leave it at that, it wasn't a pretty picture.

I love telling this next story because I was having fun pissing some people off. In my case, it wasn't pretty either because Judge Jones...oops. There was a Judge Jones, so I better call this guy "Bones." Anyway, he was serious about me going to jail unless I identified my informant. He was kicking that around as he sat on his bench tapping his pencil; his other solution was to dismiss the case if I didn't reveal my informant's name to this ambulance-chasing defense attorney. I was always respectful, whether or not I respected the turd. This case and arrest was the result of a search warrant, and I wasn't about to name/burn my informant, who had been very successful on providing information that resulted in search warrants, seizures, and arrests in the past. Most ADAs and some LEOs were very intimidated by this judge and hated to present a case or testify in his courtroom. Some were actually frightened of him, and a few were absolutely scared to death, I wasn't. When I recited the statute, he became visibly angry. He sat there on the bench tapping a pencil on his note pad—tap, tap, tap, tap—and then he looked at the ADA and said, "What the hell is he talking about?" The ADA started to tell him but was interrupted. "Attorneys...to my chamber!" Oh, the chamber of horrors it must have been. They were gone for about fifteen minutes, and that always meant that they had to endure an angry rant before it was all said and done. The ADA was catching it, while the defense was loving it, a judge agreed with him—no problem here for him.

So they came back, and I was still on the witness stand. Judge Bones sat down, looked me in the eye, and said, "Now, tell the defense the name of your informant." My response was the same, and it wasn't going to change. His response was tap, tap, tap, tap, tap, and red faced and trembling, he stood up, pointed, and yelled, "Attorneys, to my chambers!" Off they went for another fifteen minutes, loud voices could be heard. There was only the defendant and me sitting in the courtroom now. This was a preliminary hearing with only the attorneys, him, me and the judge. This hearing was to see if there was enough evidence presented for his case to be bound over for a jury trial. He made a couple of smartass comments, to which I finally said, "Listen to me asshole, if you knew how close I came to blowing you away, you wouldn't be such a smartass," and I smiled. After that I just ignored him, as he just wouldn't shut up until the judge and attorneys returned from the nice little session in the chamber of horrors.

After two meetings in judge's chambers with a third coming up, the ADA asked for a short recess and motioned me to follow him to the courthouse hallway where we had a meeting of the minds. He told me, "If you don't reveal your informant's name, he's going to put you in jail! Unless I drop charges."

I said, "Don't drop charges. Let him put me in jail! If he does, I will have every confidential informant in the Kansas City area willing to work for me."

This ADA was a good man and a good guy but he feared this judge as much as any of them, he was oh so very nervous. He must have received a real ass kicking in the judge's chambers, and all the while the defense was able to sit or stand there and smirk; the judge wasn't on his butt, so he was lovin' it.

We went back into the courtroom, and I took my seat on the witness stand. Once again, the judge ordered me to reveal my informant, and the ADA said, "Judge, I am requesting that this case be dismissed." To my disappointment, it was dismissed and was never refiled. The defendant smiled, and I left the courtroom without showing my disgust with a mental-case judge who for whatever reason made a demand that could have resulted in the death of a lawful person.

That judge is now dead, and comments I have heard from several lawyers and cops go something like, "If I find out where that asshole's grave is, I am going to go piss on it. Let me know if ya find it." And I say, "You do the same. I may join you."

Chapter 32

"How Many More Times?"

Here's the rest of the story and what initiated that particular case with the out of control arrogant bully uninformed judge. I came very near to shooting this guy with a twelve-gauge shotgun at very close range. It would have cut him in half. That was the defendant in this case, and because a judge didn't know the law or had to have it his way, it was all for nothing in a heroin case with a well-known local drug dealer and user.

At the execution of that early morning search warrant, after kicking in the residence's front door, we went toward the master bedroom, knowing where it was located from information given by the informant. In the bedroom hallway, I was first in line with a shotgun. Five or Six LEOs were behind me as the perp came flying out of the bedroom naked and armed with a six-inch...OK now wait. I know what you're thinking and that's not it, but it was a six-inch .357 stainless-steel Colt Python handgun, and it was pointed at us—mainly me since I was at the front of the pack. We were all in a narrow hallway leading to the bedroom. He saw the shotgun pointed directly at him, my finger was on the trigger—no shit; it was being squeezed. I warned him, "Drop it, or you're a dead man." That shotgun barrel had to look much larger than the .357. He paused and then very slightly moved the barrel off point, and that's the only thing that saved him because I was squeezing. He took his gun off point, laid it down, and was disarmed. Not surprisingly, he was very close to shooting at us, he later said, according to sources. I am told that he has straightened out his life and gone from being a doper to a model citizen, which I am glad to hear.

On that case, I received a letter of commendation and accolades from the sheriff and my boss because I came within half a heartbeat of shooting a bad guy, and they knew it. I didn't shoot, and only I knew why: it was his body language at the time. It would have been a good shoot as shootings go. I have never shot at anyone with the intent to hit him in the arm or shoot the gun out of his hand or just wound him or her as in the movies. In the first place, not so many people are that good of a shot, and the other thing is, as I have said before, as an LEO you are trained to shoot center mass, and ya shoot until the perp goes down.

That judge didn't like me before this trial, and he really hated me now. He *really* did, because I wouldn't cave in to his unlawful order. Ya don't have to. Following that trial, I would often see him in the courthouse hallways, and I always smiled and spoke. He would grunt a reply, but for him it was painful. Again, body language tells a lot about some folks, and that is one of the tools an LEO has when he or she can spot it and understand it.

On one undercover case in Judge Sheldon's court, there was this attorney who nearly always became angry with me. I gave him no slack. I was screwing with him with the short answers and little information. All of a sudden he shouted, "Judge, will you require this witness [me] to quit answering my questions in generalities?" Judge Sheldon replied, "Mr. Buggel, if you will quit asking general questions, maybe the witness will quit giving you general answers." I just smiled. He was toast, and he knew it. Case over! That was a high point in Johnson County courts for me because when I returned to Johnson County from DEA, the judges were not the same. Federal judges required respect toward us agents from defense attorneys. It just wasn't so in Johnson County. See another Judge Sheldon story in chapter 48.

More Court Cases

I remember only a couple of my cases on trial that could have been compromised due to questions about an investigation, maybe facts, a rookie officer, an informant, an officer who wasn't prepared, or a green ADA. In any district attorney's office, there is a steady entry and exit of DAs who sign up just out of law school and then go into private practice with a company or to a law firm as soon as they can to make the big bucks. The DA's office is simply a starting point for some of them fresh out of law school, a place to gain some experience, and most can't wait to get out on their own. Many of them do end up being darn good lawyers as lawyers go. I have known many over the years, and some are friends. I just love it when this or that attorney being interviewed in the news is introduced as "a former DA" or mentions that fact on their own when they may have been an ADA for a few months or just a few weeks. To me this statement is comical and in some cases just counterfeit in nature. The truth is that in the attorney world, at times there are not very many DAs with many years of experience in that office with a few exceptions, at least not in Johnson County, Kansas. That may have since changed, but that is the way it was in having very competent and experienced ADA's. At times when your case comes up for trial, you are on your own when you have a dammed defense attorney trying to rip you to shreds and that's where I was on a few of my cases. If you are in luck, you will get a green attorney on the defense side.

In one case, I was a plainclothes detective on a burglary trial—it was a case I investigated and cleared—and there was this newbie defense attorney. He was court appointed, and it was one of his very first jury trials. He was dying. His presentation was lacking, and he was sweating, stammering, stuttering, talking with long pauses…it wasn't pretty. After all evidence had been presented and witnesses' testimony given, he was in closing arguments, and he was begging the jury not to convict his client of burglary charges. He said, "Ladies and gentlemen of the jury, please don't convict my client because of my incompetence and inexperience" (his words). I was embarrassed for him and didn't think he had the chance of a snowball in hell. He didn't; she was convicted!

His client had been in the news several times over this breaking headline about her being a "go-go dancer" at a night club. The media loved talking about it. Never mind that there was this gas station owner, the victim, who lost a boatload of cigarettes and other merchandise…the television and print media were writing and talking about her, "the go-go dancer," over and over. I had confessions from her and her two male accomplices, but they were all now pleading not guilty. This young girl sat there looking pitiful, which she was, and the jury wasn't feeling sorry for her, but I did. The other two male defendants in that case were found guilty in jury trials, on the same evidence. They all received jail time. After that trial, I never heard of them again criminally. Sometimes in your career, you will see or deal with the same people over and over and over. I didn't see any more of these characters except for one obituary I read later on; one of the men was the victim in a KCK homicide.

I had another case on trial early on, and I learned a lesson on this one. I admit that it was a borderline traffic charge on a local perp that really needed to be arrested, so I did. I went to court pretty much unprepared for what was to happen. It came back to bite me in the ass. The defense attorney on this case was an ass kicker of a defense attorney, James Bradley; he kicked my butt all over that courtroom. This was partly because of two reasons. As I say, it was not a great case, and I was not prepared for court. On top of that, I had a green ADA handling that court case. While I was being attacked, he did or said nothing, so I was fair game. I was highly embarrassed in this case, and I damn sure had learned my lesson. Make good cases and be prepared, and after that I did and I was.

One of my cases that went to trial ended up in a hung jury twice. I was as prepared as one can get, but there was just one itty-bitty item in evidence that I had a brain fart on; I could not remember it, and it was important. I couldn't remember until the whole trial was over, and then later it came to me, too late. Besides that, the juries, at least two of them, were not impressed with the informant in the case. He seemed cocky and arrogant to them. To me that was just the way he came off without any intentions. He was a cop wannabe at the time, although I think he later decided on something else. He made a few cases for me, got me laid on one occasion (I was single), and asked me to be the best man in his wedding, which I was.

On this investigation, the informant had introduced me to this car salesman who seemed to be an OK guy, but he was one of these law breakers trying to supplement his income and social drug habits with easy money, but he got caught. So here we go to his third trial in Judge Harold Riggs's court. At the beginning of trial number three, I was on the witness stand, and the judge called for a sidebar session with the attorneys. I was sitting there as Riggs made eye contact with both attorneys and me, and in a stern voice he asked (are you ready?), "How many more times am I going to have to hear this goddam case?" I was about to bust trying not to laugh. I was tired of it as well, but I wasn't going to give it up. Both attorneys looked a bit nervous. This was the most humorous sidebar I have ever witnessed in my life. Judge Riggs's body language told it all. Judge Harold Riggs was great, in my opinion—a great man, and one of the best judges we had at the time. This was humorous and very unexpected. Riggs called a recess, and he and two attorneys went into chambers. I was not called back to the stand in this case because after a short recess, the trial soon ended. They worked it out to where the defendant would plead no contest, so it wasn't lost or dismissed, just negotiated, and I was OK with that to end it.

The defendant's attorney in this case was one that just absolutely hated me. In every case he came to trial red faced, mad, eye-fucking me every time we met. It showed, and I always smiled, which made him all the madder. I loved it! I was having fun. More on him later.

One attorney who I thought was an OK guy for an attorney handled mostly drug cases. He nicknamed me "Rocket." This had to do with a couple of specific cases during my undercover days. Every time we went to court, he and others were blown out of the water because of the way the cases were handled and evidence presented. He was a good man and a fairly good attorney who had a reputation with the druggies but lost most of their cases. They apparently all didn't know this because they kept hiring him; he would take about any drug case. This guy had a booming voice like the cartoon character Foghorn Leghorn but without the accent. It was a voice that just boomed throughout the courtroom, but that seemed to work against him at times, in my opinion. He was one of these guys who really liked to hear himself talk, but all too often he tried to baffle other attorneys, witnesses, and juries alike with bullshit. It didn't work most of the time, but the druggies just loved him, and so did I. He never won! In a lot of criminal cases, crooks recommend attorneys to one another even though many cases end in guilty pleas or by jury. I have never understood that except some are the ambulance chasers and will take any case they will be paid on if the bad guys will hire them, and they did.

This attorney, I'll call him Dave, was the defense attorney on a cocaine case in which I had made several buys from a defendant. Let's call him Nick Scary. Nick was one of our rich kids who drove a high-priced car and worked in the family business, probably making a good salary. But…he was a pretty successful drug dealer, mainly dealing in cocaine. He was one of these guys who sold dope to our kids to pay for his own habit. That's no excuse; he's still selling dope. He would call me, or I would call him, and each and every conversation I ever had with him was recorded, whether on the telephone or in person. Whenever I would meet him in a prearranged location, we would sit in his car or mine to do the transaction. I had a hidden recorder that worked very well that I used on many cases, and this was one of them. After I bought a good amount of cocaine on about five different purchases, I arrested him, and his car was seized under the law. If a vehicle is used in the commission of a drug crime, it can be seized by the government, be it local or federal, and that, along with everything else, really hurts these guys. Whether you agree with this or not, it's the law, and it includes any mode of transportation, cars, boats, airplanes, and even property, including businesses or homes if they are bought and supported with drug money—and most are. So Nick was arrested, and the drug unit was making good use of his car. The case went to trial, and the ADA made his case.

So Nick's attorney made his case, and they called a witness—that's me, and only me because I never had surveillance backup on this case. After Dave set up the groundwork for his client, he started questioning me on evidence. He was really sure of himself on this one, it had to be one of the shortest drug trials on record. The defense attorney asked, "Detective Sergeant Hayes, just how is it that you know and can remember all of these facts?"

I answered, "Well, sir, I know this because each and every time I talked with Nick about ordering cocaine from him, either on the telephone or in person, the conversation was recorded. I have played those recordings before this trial to refresh my memory." (He was supposed to know this before court, but that was not my call.)

It got real quiet. Dave then asked the judge, "Your Honor, my client and I would ask for a continuance in this case." "Request granted," said the judge, and that was that as far as this case went. A plea of guilty was later made, and this is the case that earned me the nickname Rocket. Dave always grinned when we would meet and greet me, "Hi, Rocket. How ya doin'?"

Now here's an additional item on this case: Nick's car was a nice luxury sedan, which we confiscated, a very nice car. Dave was friends with the district attorney, Dennis Moore, who later became a Democratic representative in the Third District in Kansas. What Dave got accomplished was to get Moore's authorization to return Nick's car to him, and Nick was granted probation. These guys all knew each other, and they "worked things out" sometimes for favors in the future. Dave was also one of the attorneys who was making loans to another judge who had a gambling problem, one of the judges censured and removed from the bench later on. There were several judges in Johnson County that were not real good people and were censured and removed. They had a good gig, but for some it just wasn't enough. One was removed over sexual harassment, one for borrowing money from defense attorneys for gaming bets and another for cocaine possession, and there were some that should have been removed for other reasons but were not.

Enough about crooked judges. At that time, there were some really good judges in Johnson County, but if ya looked at percentages, it wasn't a pretty picture.

Funny how things go around…that green ADA and defense attorney Bradley both ended up being judges. Bradly died a few years ago, and the ADA is still on the bench.

Chapter 33

"Some LEOS Just Know Things Lilly."

Aseasoned officer who pays keen attention in his or her district becomes very aware of the surroundings and people, friendly or not. On all shifts he knows residents, local cars, businesses and buildings, and the business people. They know what's down the side streets and the alleys and what's at businesses, they know some of the crooks, and in addition, some "just know things." Clint Eastwood's character said, "I just know things, Lilly," to his girlfriend in the movie *Line of Fire*, and it's true. Some cops have "the nose," which adds to that sixth sense some have, they just know things. That comes with common sense, judgment, experience, experience, and more experience. And along with that nose, don't let anyone tell you that if ya work, you will have luck; in some cases there's a lot of luck, but it doesn't always just happen. Ya have to be doin' something. It's called work.

A cattle-rustling case reported on the northern edge of Olathe was one where my sixth sense kicked in; maybe it was just a hunch. We all knew this area crook and his brothers that we had dealt with on many occasions. I just had this gut feeling that he was good for this cattle theft, so I began driving past his house. On trash day, I saw cow bones in plain view, so I got a search warrant for his house. Detective Fred Tush and I later arrived with a search warrant, found the evidence in the house, and arrested the crook. Case closed. He pleaded guilty. He was an OK guy, but he was a thief, and while I have mixed emotions when a person steals for food, it's still against the law, and he or she has to pay the price when caught.

In my career, I worked a number of suicides, accidental deaths, vehicular deaths, answered calls on and assisted on a few homicides, but there was one suicide that bothered me. In Fairway, Kansas a man fatally shot himself in the basement of his home. What bothered me was that this man had been an LEO in another state. He'd retired because of illness, something like a type of neuromuscular disease or something of that nature. Even being from another state, he was a brother LEO. It took me a while not to dwell on that incident, but there were others.

Many cases, be they suicide, homicide, or accidental death by any means, are very troubling for some when they're new to the job. For most or some of us, we go home and leave the job at the office. My family had no idea what I dealt with unless it was in the news. I didn't talk about it at home, but until his death, my dad kept track; he knew what I was doing and what I was involved in, and I could tell he was proud of me. I wasn't going to embarrass him now, he believed.

I have friends who are lawyers and judges, and they are just the same as everyone else when it comes to judgment, careers, operations, morals, beliefs, and so on. There are some good, some great, and some not so good. There are a few, just like in every other walk of life, that were and are absolute crooks. In Johnson County, this is confirmed by court cases and news articles. As I mentioned a few judges have been censured, disbarred, or removed from the bench and should have been prosecuted. Around sixteen judges in Kansas have been removed since 1974, several from Johnson County. More on judges later.

Chapter 34

It's Better to Be Seen Than Viewed!

I have mentioned that I have heard all my life that some cops "never had to draw their gun during their career." While I know it's true for some, it is hard for me to believe because I had to "pull it" on occasions when I was a uniform officer and many times when I was working investigations, as you will see. It's nothing to brag about, but it's part of the job, and in nearly all incidents, it's all in the name of survival. It was the norm on search warrants, burglary calls, and some arrests to have your weapon or shotgun in hand as you went in. Although I'm a good shot with a handgun, my weapon of choice was and still is a shotgun. I came very close to shooting a few bad guys at close range during my career, and I probably did hit one or two, with shotgun and handgun. Most statistics will tell you that most shootings occur at very close range, not much more than six to eight feet "It's better to be judged by twelve than carried by six" is the old saying, but true it is and that's my opinion. Here's another point to ponder, the best "home defense" in my opinion is a shotgun, I tell all of my friends and neighbors this fact, ya don't have to be a great shot to save yourself, just point and shoot, very effective.

While I was assigned to the DEA, there was this threesome of bad guys who were shooting at us in Independence, Missouri. One was hit in the forehead. And then there was the Metcalf State Bank Robbery. A residential search warrant in Olathe was very close (chapter 19), and on another I was dispatched to an assist-the-officer call with one of my district officers near Desoto. A farmer had a .22-caliber rifle aimed directly at Patrolman Bob Basore with bad intentions. I don't recall the nature of the call, but upon arrival, out of the car with shotgun in hand, I warned the man that if he didn't drop his weapon, he would die, and he likely would have, we were less than eight feet apart. He paused and lowered his rifle. By now, he knew that if he didn't put down his weapon he would be history. It would have been a good shoot as shootings go, but it would have been a sad one. He was just an old guy who felt that these cops were invading his space for no reason, or so it seemed after the fact. This is one of several guys I almost had to shoot in my career; you can see how close it comes when it's to the point that it could go either way. This guy was arrested, but charges were later dismissed by the sheriff. Nothing wrong was done on our part with the incident or the arrest, and the dropped charges were never explained to me; politics? We didn't like it, but that was the way it was. I was involved in a couple of shootings and near shootings during my undercover days, more on that later.

Of the other many cases I worked as a plainclothes detective, some were exciting, some not, some were interesting, some not, but none were very boring. One case I worked involved a con artist who gained the friendship of people he came into contact with. His game at the time was selling color televisions when they were relatively new and expensive. This caper hit the newspapers. The *Kansas City Star* headline read "Police Search for Friendly TV Salesman." This guy had to be a good talker, because he was able to take orders for televisions that he didn't have, couldn't get, and had no intentions of getting. He told his victims that he was an insurance investigator and that he had access to the color TVs through sources. He showed them his gun he "carried on his hip," as his victims said. Most of these victims were businesspeople and some realtors. One of the victims bought four TVs, giving the crook $340—that's $85 a TV. Eighty-five dollars for a color TV at that point in that time seemed too good to be true— and it was, wasn't it? The unsuspecting victims told all their friends about this guy and the good deal. Word of mouth was giving him a very good business. There ended up being eight victims or more; some buying more than one TV, exactly how many victims I can't remember for sure and he was still working. I was taking more reports working the case one day, and

I got a call that the bad guy was at the business of one of the victims visiting and taking more names for orders, he thought. I went to the business, put the guy in my car, interviewed him enough to know that he would be charged, and took him to jail, under arrest. He ended up with a guilty plea and got a year in jail. I never knew if the victims got any of their money back, but they did get the satisfaction that some victims get—bad guy goes to jail. I think this guy eventually ended up in prison for something else and eventually died imprisoned.

Transportation of mental persons is a task that the sheriff's deputies are required to do. One evening my good friend and partner Robert (Bob) Mort, who was also assigned to the detective division, and I were taking a guy to the Osawatomie State Mental Hospital for evaluation under a court order. He was from very big money, the son of a wealthy Missouri politician, and probably wealthy in his own right, whether earned or not. This guy had a reputation of being crazy and doing crazy things and had attempted suicide several times. Not a pretty picture for a rich guy, but money doesn't have any boundaries, does it? Bob and I had been friends for years, so we did what friends and especially cops do. We took jabs at each other every chance we got, made fun of each other, and just generally screwed with each other. As we were driving, it went on and on without any thoughts of the guy in the back seat. We had nearly forgotten him in his restraints, and we were getting loud in our rants, laughing and having fun at each other's expense. Suddenly there was this reply from the back seat: "Well, what do you want me to say!" in a loud, confused, and angry voice. The poor guy had thought that all the bantering conversation, what we were saying about each other, was directed at him and about him. It was one of those situations where you had to be there, but we were now laughing our asses off to the point of tears, you know, the coffee out our nostrils. After that, it got real quiet until we had deposited our passenger off to where he would hopefully get some much-needed psychiatric help. We were bewildered that all the while during our conversation, which went on for about twenty minutes until he screamed out, he thought it was all about him. We felt bad for him but, in one of our black humor moments, we were still laughing for a good part of the rest of that trip. Bob and I laughed about this gig for a long time and up until the time of Bob's death. He had moved away to Arizona. We would see each other from time to time, and that incident always came up—in war stories, don't know. Every time I flew to Arizona on a conspiracy case Bob would come to Tucson and we would meet once again for a few drinks and war stories. I always missed him; great friends are hard to come by.

Here's a case you need to be aware of, and all the public needs to be aware of: carbon monoxide poisoning. Its winter, it's cold and houses are closed up. In one of the cities, I was dispatched to a house after occupants had been taken to the hospital suffering from carbon monoxide poisoning. It was a man and his two children who survived, sadly his wife did not. This could have been accidental, or it could have been a suicide, but I think the coroner classified it as either undetermined, accidental, or both. What had happened was the wife started the car in the closed, attached garage of the home, producing carbon monoxide that permeated the entire house through the furnace duct system. Luckily one of the kids awakened dad, who found that they were all groggy and sickly, and he called an ambulance, not knowing his wife was dead in the car in the garage. This mistake caused one family a lot of grief and they had a very bad Christmas that year, remembering this every Christmas thereafter...

Another death by carbon monoxide was a couple parked out in the county during winter. It was a sad case. They are all sad, but this one was a young couple who were overcome while having sex in their car. Ironically the guy died with erection; that was not put to sleep. We've all heard guys say that that's the way they want to go, having sex, but believe me, if they had seen this scene, they might change their mind.

Accidental deaths come in all shapes and sizes, as they say, and so do suicides, I'm not saying that the death of that lady and the near death of her husband and children was a suicide but I did work a few. It is said that suicide victims are/were among the most selfish people on earth. Many suicides are the result of arguments, anger, or out-of-control emotions; some are the result of sickness; and in some the victim simply gives up on life. One suicide I worked (mentioned earlier) bothered me as much as any. It was the former LEO who had shot himself in the chest due to illness. He did have the foresight before he killed himself to do it in the basement near a drain; that makes cleanup much easier than some who blows their brains all over the walls, ceiling, or other parts of the house.

Chapter 35

Eyes Wide Open

I once had a friend who had killed himself; he took an overdose of pills of some kind. So, I went to the parents' house to give my regrets. As I was talking, the mother stopped me. She thanked me but said the following: "Eddie, we appreciate your kind words, but we have accepted John's actions. It was his decision to make; he did it, so we are supporting his decision. We are OK with it." No tears or anything. I thought that was a pretty healthy attitude if you are tough enough to pull it off. I have mentioned this to others since that time; sometimes it helps.

In retrospect, whether you agree with that or not, I have always felt it was a healthy way of acceptance, especially for the actions of a loved one whose consideration didn't include his or her family. If you have never seen a person with gunshot wounds, and especially shotgun wounds, and most have not, let me tell you, it can be a very gruesome sight.

There was this farmer who walked out of the house to the highway, sat down beside the property's gate, and shot himself in the head with his twelve-gauge shotgun. This was not a direct contact wound, so it blew off half of his face and a part of his skull. It was a nice, clean wound that revealed the brain, everything, immediate death, of course. That's one example of a shotgun wound. Another is when a person puts the barrel of a gun in his or her mouth and closes the mouth around the barrel. In this situation, a whole lot happens that you might not think about. The gun goes off, and the concussion of gases helps to blow the head apart. It's an explosion and not a pretty sight...so, if you are contemplating suicide and want a good corpse to be viewed, don't do it this way, please, and don't do it in a place where your friends or relatives will see the carnage, especially your kids.

There was this woman in Wichita who continually attempted to kill herself. Call after call, she would cut her wrists but not enough to bleed out. It wasn't me, really it wasn't, but a LEO friend of mine finally held up his own arm and told her, "Lookie here. See these veins?" With his finger, he followed the veins in his arm from the wrist to the elbow. "Next time instead of cutting across your wrist, follow these veins with the razor." A week later she was found bled out in some bushes she had followed his instructions.

Here's another bit of advice: If you're having an argument with your spouse or friend, and in a rage of anger, the other threatens to blow out his or her brains, don't say, "Go ahead, do it!" People do ignorant things when they are emotional, angry, and stupid, and this was one of them. One time two spouses were arguing, and the husband, holding a pistol to his head, said, "So you want to see me blow my fucking brains out?" He then took the gun down. But the wife said, "Go ahead," at which time the man put the gun to his head, and BANG, right in front of her and in the middle of the kitchen. I knew this guy. He was always a bit hyper in conversation, but I never thought to this extreme.

Many one-car accidents are suicides, and some head-on crashes are as well. Another argument resulted in a suicide by vehicle. This person left the house, drove away going at a high rate of speed, and hit the first thing that came up, a huge oak tree. We got the call of a vehicle on fire. My district officer was on the scene before me and radioed me that there was no one in the car, but "She's [meaning the car] really burning big time." It apparently had a full tank of gas, because when I got there, it was still a roaring fire. What he should have said is that there was no one in the car that he could see, because after it burned down a bit, I went to the driver's door and saw the driver, with all her limbs burned away and the crown of her head either burned away or blown off. The brains were exposed, taking on the appearance of scrambled eggs. The remainder of that body had to be pried away from the frame of the car for the post mortem. In the case of bodies burned beyond recognition, this is usually what's left after a huge, intense fire.

Suicide is one of the most selfish things a person can do. It's bad enough if the family doesn't see you, but even worse when they see what you did to yourself and the mess, the cleanup. Again, do it out away from everyone and where kids won't discover your body.

I took a report on a missing person whose car was found above the Lenexa Kansas Shawnee Mission park lake. In the car he had left a suicide note for his loved ones. It said he was ending it all, this was in the dead of winter, and the lake was frozen over by the time of this missing person report which is now assumed suicide report. Usually when you take a report, your part of the investigation is over, but it so happened that when the lake thawed, I was on duty when the body, fairly well preserved due to the lake temperatures, floated and ended up at the dam. The dead-body smell was horrendous as usual—ya never forget the smell; it's like a snapshot. Another report was taken, and the death was ruled a suicide by the coroner.

So much for suicides. Let's move on!

I've been a deputy sheriff and a search and rescue volunteer in Chaffee County, Colorado, and I was a volunteer firefighter in Arkansas...*for two weeks*. Why just two weeks, you may ask? Read on. After passing the background checks and the grueling interviews, I was all geared up to start volunteering at the firehouse. You know, I was going to be one of those hero firemen all the media talks about. Once again I would have to attend training classes—starting all over again. I was not looking forward to more classes. That was a good part of retirement, I didn't have to do peat and repeat over and over and over as well as slobbering over the dummy in resuscitation classes, but ya do what ya have ta do, and classes were coming soon. I attended two weekly meetings and found that in this small meeting room full of firemen, about twenty-five feet square, I could almost see the wall across the room. They all smoked, and I had not been in such dense cigarette smoke since about 1975 during sheriff's office staff meetings that were just as bad until the sheriff finally stopped that. So...as a volunteer firefighter, once again, I retired.

My good buddy Byron Horn, retired KCK Police Department captain, shares these three incidents:

I was having a beer(s) at the American Legion post here in Arizona, sitting next to this guy who was telling me about his father who had been a cop somewhere. The old boy gets this call, an information call or something of that nature, and as he walks into this woman's house this friggin' monkey jumped on his back! Talk about having a monkey on your back! He couldn't get the little fucker off, couldn't get it to let go! Finally his partner got the monkey off his back!

Now, I remember a similar call. I'd just gotten inside a home (invited) and this parakeet landed on my shoulder! It startled the hell out of me! Out of reflex, I grabbed it and slung it up against the wall! Yeah! Killed it! Shit happens.

On another call, we were sent out to "talk to the lady," and she comes out to the front porch. She tells me she was concerned about this pack of dogs running loose in the neighborhood. Her kitty cat was in the front yard. I told her how dogs have been chasing cats for a long time and asked, "Have you ever seen a dog actually catch a cat?" She hadn't, but at that moment about five dogs ran into her yard, grabbed that cat, and tore it to pieces! Again, shit happens.

So as you can see, sometimes really strange things happen on the job!

Chapter 36

You're Undercover Now, You're Undercover Now

Ya get it? It's music? It's like "you're in the army now?" "You're undercover now?"

When I was assigned to the O'DALE task force undercover with the Bureau of Narcotics and Dangerous Drugs / Drug Enforcement Agency (BNDD/DEA), at the time was within the Western District of Missouri. I had always been in uniform or plain clothes (suit and tie) and had short hair. I'd never had facial hair, so it took a while to assume the look. On one of the first investigations, I was burned/recognized. Luckily he was cool about it and there were no problems, except that case went nowhere. As my hair grew and I would see acquaintances, they were confused. Here's this cop who has gone where? They really thought I had lost it, gone to the other side. In addition, some cops had to prove themselves in the assignment, just like every other assignment. "Can we depend on him?" peers would say. We all had to prove ourselves, and it was the same thing all over when I went to the DEA task force. Besides that, there were the state line jealousies that were evident, but I just ignored this. Prove yourself, and then you are one of the guys.

The BNDD preceded the DEA. Before I left, it had been changed to DEA. BNDD in Kansas City, Missouri, was under the Western District of Missouri, which included six states at the time. We worked where information and circumstances took us. That task force was staffed with officers from area metro police departments and sheriff's departments as well as a federal officer from every agency except for the FBI; it was felt that they were "above us." Funny how that worked out since the last I heard, DEA is still a part of the FBI. We were all commissioned with federal commissions/ID's as agents under the United States Department of Justice.

The O'DALE task force assignment was requested by several deputies, but I got it, much to the jealousy of at least one other deputy at the time. I will call him Dick, no pun intended—well, maybe a little bit.

My first O'DALE immediate supervisor—I'll call him Buddy—was a cocky, arrogant asshole who thought he knew it all. He was green, and we all thought this was probably his first assignment in supervision. We all had years of experience, and we were assigned with several green agents just out of the BNDD academy. The task forces were President Nixon's baby. Some thought part of the plan was to train the green agents who had no LEO experience and not a lot as far as undercover investigations and law enforcement in general, some of them admitted this. One agent told me that everything he learned was from Jerry O'Donnel who was a seasoned KCMO police officer assigned to the task force. Jerry and I worked together from time to time and like most we remain friends to this day. To some of us, including myself, as I say, the undercover part of it was all a new experience. One day, early on for that task force, supervising agent Buddy stood before us seasoned LEOs in a meeting and said, "You guys do whatever you're big enough to do. Whatever you're big enough to do, I'll cover you!" A few of us looked at each other, a bit confused, all thinking the same thing. "Did he just say what I think he said, we can break the law? And he will get us out of it if we do, if we get caught?" We didn't buy it; we just let it go. Some people think they are above the law, and it ain't just politicians.

I'm not paranoid but some people just won't like ya for whatever reason and I have my faults one of which is "I tell it like it is no matter who you are." After I was there for a few weeks, I sensed that for some reason Buddy had an obvious disliking for me and displayed it every chance he got, no matter who was present. No matter that I was an eight-year LEO veteran with street experience he didn't have (eight years is not a real long time, but street smarts help a lot) I didn't let it bother me, and it didn't take very long for me to realize why he didn't like me. The guy that didn't get my assignment, Dick, was evidently trying his level best to torpedo me and get me sent back by telling the supervisor a lot of negative and untrue crap about me. I was told in confidence that was the deal, and I don't know what

Dick was saying or what he suggested, but thanks to him I was in trouble at O'Dale from the get-go since Buddy and Dick were friends and wanted to work together. That was until I started making cases, by then I had that supervisor on "ignore" for the most part. I just smiled when he came around. He made attempts to embarrass me in front of others every chance he got, and I just smiled and ignored him. Initially when the task force began, some of the Kansas City, Missouri, guys looked down on Kansas cops, but that soon changed. If ya smile at your nemeses, it messes with their itty-bitty brains—drives 'em crazy because they never know what you're thinking, or what you know, it really bothers them.

Although I was new to undercover operations, it didn't take long for me to get my feet on the ground, and when I began making cases, I was left alone. I made a lot of cases in my first year at DEA (as well as the rest of the time I was there), receiving a letter of commendation from the task force commander, Bob Elliott. He mailed a copy to Sheriff Allenbrand listing all of my investigations and cases before I knew he had penned it. Bob nicknamed me "Steady Eddie." He always smiled when he said it, and I remained that until I left the task force. Guys that made cases made him look good and he appreciated that fact. From the task force, Bob went to another assignment in the nation's capital just before I transferred back to Johnson County. While few of them had nothing to do, they were hanging around my desk when I was in the office. One agent said, "I'm hanging around this guy—he's hot." Makes ya feel good, especially when I had a guy like Buddy standing there as I was making my reports and bagging evidence.

I got the last laugh on Buddy though, as his tenure at the task force was soon cut short by a huge national news story of the times. Did you ever hear of the Collinsville, Illinois, incident? It was all over the news, and this guy was the biggest duck in the puddle agents there said. Look it up, Buddy (I was told) was a supervisor on the search warrant where the front door of a house was kicked in, at least he was there, the occupants were restrained, and the house was searched. But as it turns out it was the wrong address; they kicked the door in on wrong house! It was the house next door that was suspect, and I have to tell you, if you have ever seen a house that's been searched for contraband in most cases you have seen a mess. There's a lot of house cleaning to be done after those capers. This kind of mistake, the wrong door, resulted in the government and police departments getting sued, which goes back to the operations commander—that's Buddy. When you're a government agent and screw up, many times that equals a transfer. Sometimes ya don't even have to screw up, but this guy was transferred out fast to Guam some said, New York or somewhere on the East coast. I never knew for sure and really didn't care, he was out of my hair. Fortunately, I wasn't involved in that case, and while things were a bit tense around the office for a while, I enjoyed it. After that incident, I would only make eye contact and smile; that was about it. Buddy knew why I was smiling, and soon after that, he was gone.

They tell me that the Guam transfer for any federal agent is similar in nature to assigning an FBI agent to Kansas City or Detroit. It's one of the last places they want to be; it's a demotion, or at least it used to be. Research the FBI agent, a really nice guy who had Lee Harvey Oswald as an informant. When assigned to Kansas City, he was FBI liaison to my sheriff's department, so we all knew him and the circumstances of the Kennedy assassination and his transfer to KC.

So here's another important FYI training tool linked to the above situation. If you ever get information on a search warrant, **"PLEASE MAKE SURE"** you are at the right address with the right crooks, because this has happened with sad endings for both sides, and it's happened several times since then. Double-check your sources and resources. The adrenaline is flowing, and ya want ta get it done, but just make sure every duck is in a straight little row. In defense of those agents in the Collinsville event, the news reported that the occupants of that house were druggies (true or not, I don't know) and busted up their own furniture and wrongly blamed the agents to make more news of that caper, and did it ever. Even though the agents were at the wrong house, the occupants were not the best of citizens, they said. There was still a monetary settlement paid, although, given all of the facts, it wasn't as much as it could have been.

Chapter 37

Things Are Not Always as They Seem

So this dirt bag looking guy, that's me, buys this house on a lake, and we were near closing time. I stopped by to visit with what would be my new neighbors. I wanted to find out if there was anything that might be a problem before I moved in. In the backyard, I met neighbors-to-be on both sides, and I asked one of them if he knew of any problems with the house inside or out. Roy Krummel, who was an over-the-road truck driver who soon became a dear friend and neighbor, looked straight ahead. He didn't miss a step, said, "Nope," and went straight to the house, left me standing there. Well, that was nice for first impressions, I thought at the time, I always had fun with this. It was the same thing for the neighbors on the other side; they were working on outside plumbing and didn't even look up at me. It was always fun because I knew in time they would all know who and what I was. At that point in time, all Roy saw was this skinny, long-haired, bearded doper-looking guy who was to become his neighbor moving next door to his family and three kids. Roy was NOT happy!

On another occasion I ran into a high school classmate, Bruce Craig at a shopping mall who knew me well and who just happened to be a Johnson County commissioner at the time. It's no exaggeration that Bruce was one of the best commissioners ever, in my opinion. He was a local businessman, and he was a cop's friend and a sheriff's department supporter. Sheriff departments need commissioners that support them. I could tell that Bruce was very confused. It was apparent that he thought I had fallen off the deep end and *had* become a dirt bag. I really didn't have time to "splain" because I was meeting a bad guy for a drug deal. We talked for seconds, short time, very short, and he walked away, shaking his head. I'm sure a call was soon made to the sheriff to see what had happened to me. Long after that meeting and after I was out of undercover operations, each time I received recognition for another five years of continuing service (we always had an audience), Craig made a point to introduce me and tell that story, telling the audience what he saw and what he thought at the time. He had been relieved, and he thought it was pretty funny; I always did too. That intro always got a laugh from those in attendance. I just smiled; I'm still having fun.

I'd been at the task force long enough that I had now assumed the necessary appearance, that of a hippie doper. On my very first undercover case following the first "burn," an informant and I went into this apartment on the Country Club Plaza in Kansas City, Missouri. There were about a half dozen people inside, so we sat around engaging in small talk, getting to know one another. Two things happened on this gig. One guy went out on the balcony and fired off a pistol they had stolen in a house burglary. Since I had surveillance on this one, I just knew that my outside surveillance team was coming in, but they didn't. I guess I was in the "prove myself" mode, because they later said they heard gun shots but were "not sure" it came from that apartment. In the end that was best, as we all would have been burned, but then the next thing that happened—and again this is on my first successful case—was that the guy sitting across the room from me was tying up his arm to take a shot and after he took it, he asked me, "Do you want some heroin?"

"Naw, I'm OK," I say. I have had a needle phobia ever since!

Nothing was gained in this deal other than experience and intelligence turned over to local police departments on the burglaries. I had really broken the ice, so to speak, and I was on a roll because by now I had developed a few informants, and I was undercover daily and lovin' it. It was really exciting, and I was having fun. I have said many times that I was having so much fun that I almost felt guilty for receiving a paycheck. Going into a new assignment like undercover activities and investigations was almost like starting over. When I was assigned to plainclothes detective, there was some hesitation because of the unknown, but it was nothing like being undercover. It didn't take long to adapt to the plain clothes detective assignment, some were able to hit the ground running. Undercover was different, besides proving yourself to your peers, you have to prove it to yourself: Can I make it, can I do it, will I have the guts or courage? Can I be cool headed in tight spots? That's where I was initially, but I was determined that I was going to give it a try, give it my best as I always tried to do, but this was all different. I could always go back to my home department but I wanted to succeed. At the time, again I had a total of eight years' LEO experience, and I thought I knew a lot about the world, but I found that there was a lot I didn't know when it came to the drug and criminal culture; I had to learn a new vocabulary and mind-set. I had to listen to music I didn't like at the time, and I couldn't believe how females of the drug and criminal culture spoke; their dialogue was the same as any drunken sailor's. We learned a lot from our informants and unwitting bad guys, I paid attention and listened a lot, and it paid off.

The offices of the DEA task force were located on an upper floor of the Ten Main Center office building in downtown Kansas City. Ya ride the elevator or walk the steps, and most of us didn't do steps, so you can imagine the looks we received from business people riding the elevators. That's until they found out who these dirt bag-looking guys were, and we did look the part, carrying goods, sledgehammers, fire axes, long guns, and so on. Who knows what we'd be carrying as we would leave and return from search warrants and raids. There still there were those that visited the building that had to wonder who we were. The body language and looks were oftentimes really comical.

Some of the antics that went on in that office were comical too, and in one case border line, against the laws of acceptance. Whatever the case, the statute of limitations has surely passed after forty-plus years, but we all should be ashamed. Our telephone numbers had previously been post office numbers, so for that reason, the phones were ringing, ringing, and ringing for the post office, and it was really really irritating. We tried our best to get it corrected by the post office and operators, but the calls kept coming. So we decided to make a game of it. When someone called, we'd try to help them by giving them the information they wanted, correct or not—information on zip codes, addresses, and other postal information. People would call, and they would be transferred around and around, put on hold, and transferred some more, and all the while we were laughing our asses off at our imagination on what to do next. One poor postal employee must have had a lot of explaining to do when he got home. His wife called in asking for him, and she was put on hold for a while and transferred a couple of times, and when we finally got back to her, she was told her husband was on leave; he'd been on leave for two weeks. This call went on far too long for her and for those that would stay with us on the phone. As I recall, the calls dropped off after the lady called for her husband. Another game we played on these phone calls was this: someone would yell "fire drill," and whoever was handling the phone call would say, "Sorry, I have to put you on hold till the fire drill is over." Then ten minutes later, the call would be resumed. Cold bastards we were.

Chapter 38

William E. Frazier "Billy"

As I said, we had fun on the elevators at the expense of unsuspecting fellow agents and especially the secretarial staff, asking each other questions when there were other people around. For example, we'd ask each other, "When did you get out of jail on that pimping charge?" Or, "When did you get out of jail on that hooker charge? How much was the bond on that?" And another was, "How much was the bond on your robbery case? Is it still pending?" "Did you beat that manslaughter charge? Howd ya do≈it?"

Now ya want to talk about looks and body language? Until other building tenants caught on, there was no eye contact; they just looked straight ahead, stone faced, looking at the doors that wouldn't open soon enough, and exiting as fast as they could when the doors did open. After they caught on, they just smiled when there were other newbies on board. They were enjoying the games we played.

We had a few agents that loved farting in the elevator, and some were really rank, and then blaming it on someone else, usually the secretarial staffers, but it didn't matter; we all had to deal with it until the doors opened and we made our escape. Some really wanted to look and smell the part. Did ya ever get on an elevator with a fat guy wearing dirty clothes who needed a shower; we had a couple that worked with us? At times I had to ride the elevators and in a car with some agents, and summer or winter, the windows in the car were down because of the smell. That was going a bit far for me. I looked the part, but I didn't smell it, or at least no one ever said I did.

Working undercover, I assumed several identities, a couple that I used for years. I had a checking account, driver's license, pilot's license, parole papers, alcohol beverage card, an attorney general agent card from the infamous Kansas attorney general Vern Miller, and several other documents under the names Ed Davis and Chris Emmons—all counterfeit but all within the law for their purpose. They all came back to my name should LEOs have had a need to know. Fortunately that never happened, except when I was arrested and un arrested at Lake Ozark, Missouri and Westport, in Kansas City and a couple of traffic accidents. It didn't go as far as to show an ID, with the exception of an Independence, Missouri, caper with me and Harlo.

Before my assignment to DEA, I worked extra for a friend who was head of security at the Jones Store at Metcalf South, located in Overland Park, Kansas. This was my first undercover work, and I was to be a "shoplifter." The Jones Store had lost televisions, so I was hired to steal a TV, so here we go. My first time out, I went to the Jones Store with my brother-in-law, Fred Plowman, who was a reserve officer. I removed a sold tag from a TV as instructed and stuck it on a more expensive TV, which we picked up, and out the door we went. It was a large, heavy, cabinet-model TV—you remember those in the seventies? As we are going toward the exit, a couple of guys in suits held the door open for us on the building's north end. We proceeded to the car where we were to load it and then drive to a dock on the back side of the building. When we got to the car, here came the same guys who held the door open for us, and one identified them as security officers. The TV was carefully put in the trunk of the car as they helped hold up the lid, no scratches, so we were ready to leave. As said, "leave" meant going to another door of the building to unload the TV and return it to the security boss. The two security guys that held the door open were now questioning us, we argued, and I was standing there as though in disbelief that we were being accused of stealing a TV? Freddy says, "We don't have to take this shit. I'm going to call my lawyer," almost convincing them that we did in fact buy the TV…we thought.

I got the main security guy off to the side and told him he needed to arrest us, as we'd been hired by the head of security. The guy with him was a skinny little guy who was a twin to "Bernard P. Milton Oliver Fife"—you know, Barney Fife of *The Andy Griffith Show* and *Mayberry RFD?* This guy was trembling from fear, like Barney Fife. I felt so sorry for him; I feared he might pee, and he may have, but he had on a long suit coat, so we couldn't tell.

Here's the irony to this TV shoplifting caper: The main security guy that arrested us resigned soon after that and went to work for the Kansas City, Missouri, PD. His name was William E. Frazier and he would soon become my partner after we were both assigned to O'DALE at around the same time. We were partners until he transferred back to his police department. During our time at DEA, we individually and as partners made more cases, at least as many as any other agents.

It's ironic how Frazier and I were similar in many ways and here's another. Retired KCMO Police Chief Larry Joiner spoke at Frazier's

funeral saying that Billy was turned down for a job several times because he had such a great job at the Jones Store and the pay cut he would suffer but he was finally hired due to his persistence. Like me, all Frazier wanted in a career was to be a cop. Here's Billy in his undercover "uniform."

Most guys assigned undercover units became investigators and surveillance team officers. Everyone wasn't successful in actual undercover work; not everyone could do it or even wanted to do it. I wanted it, I did it, and I had fun doing it, I was an actor as I have said. In my mind, there's a lot of pride when you have this crook committing a crime in your face, taking the incident to the limit. The agents that didn't work undercover were still an essential part of the task force working backup, surveillances, arrests, and search warrants, as well as being court witnesses and carrying out other duties.

I didn't wear the poncho very often, just when it was really a shaky deal or I felt the need. It hid my (legal length) sawed off shotgun very well, never needed it but one guy asked me, "what you got under that poncho!", "nothing" I replied, he let it drop but any danger with him IF there had been any was past tense, he got the picture.

"Agent Says, They're Trouble"

One cold winter evening, Billy Frazier, two other guys, and I were all undercover in pairs on two different unrelated investigations. We were working two different defendants going on at the same time in the same building somewhere near the Country Club Plaza on Main Street in KCMO. When my deal was done, I left the area. Shortly after I left, Frazier and the other agent were in a fix. They were going to be robbed and probably murdered by the crook they were dealing with; that is, the crook thought he was going to rob them. He found the wheel gun on the one agent but didn't find Billy's Walther PPK .380 automatic pistol in his coat pocket. The bad guy was forcing them at gunpoint to a back room. As they were going toward the back room, the bad guy started pistol whipping the now weaponless agent with his own gun, but Frazier and his pistol saved them. Frazier had his hand on the pistol in his coat pocket and shot the guy five or six times from the inside of the pocket, putting a bunch of holes in that nice leather jacket. The bad guy ran outside and died in the middle of Main street. Billy saved that other agent's ass that night who later said we were "trouble." I could say more, but I'll leave it at that but IF you're not out there looking for trouble you're not going to be very successful in your job.

Billy Frazier and I were both sergeants during that time and both received promotions after we returned to our departments. He retired as a major with his family (two sons who were sergeants) and his partner (me) at his side. By that time I had already retired at the rank of captain. Billy's retirement ceremony was pretty cool, with all of us standing in a line. I was surprised when he called me up to the podium and proudly introduced me as his partner in front of the attending audience, most of whom were KCMO cops, and some besides Billy are truly heroes.

We were working in Omaha, Nebraska, where the two local, longtime DEA agents were telling everyone, including us, that there was no dope in Omaha! "We have no narcotics problems," they said. "Yeah, right," we thought. We decided to prove different. Omaha was Billy's caper that he

developed with an informant. He was able to make at least forty different hard narcotics cases, all while the two local agents mainly sat on their asses as they had done for years. Following the buys, which were mainly heroin cases and some cocaine, stolen-property cases, and burglaries and armed robbery intelligence, we made the arrests. At that time, it was the biggest cooperative raid in Omaha history they reported, with federal, local, state, deputy sheriffs, you name it. We were all there, and Billy and our squad were all heroes. The locals couldn't thank us enough. It's really neat when your partner is one of your best friends, and that's what Billy was.

Chapter 39

It's Better to Be Judged by Twelve Than Carried by Six

Soon after the Omaha capers there were a few embarrassed federal agents transferred out of Omaha. Ironically one of them was brought to our task force in Kansas City and appointed our supervisor. That's the way the feds do it; when they have a misfit who can't do anything else, they make him or her a training officer or a supervisor. Keep 'em off the streets, I guess. Now I will say that is not the deal in all cases, but I saw it enough, and it happened with one guy who left our department, went to the FBI, and was put into training. He couldn't make it on the streets, I guess, as a fed or a cop, so make him a training officer? He still went around proudly telling everyone that he was an FBI agent. Some of us knew what he was. He hadn't been that great at our sheriff's office, and I couldn't believe it when he was hired by the FBI

Kidnapped!

Working undercover, dealing with crooks, with money and property, be it drugs or stolen property, there is a risk of robbery, such as mentioned in the previous chapter when Billy Frazier and another agent were going to be robbed and most likely murdered.

There are other dangers in undercover operations in dealing with the bad guys, some the same as in all areas of law enforcement. One such case was where I had bought heroin or cocaine (can't remember which) and it was what we call "turkey." Turkey is when you have been ripped off, sold some kind of powder, sugar or flour (not a controlled substance). If you don't go back to get your money and challenge the crook, he will suspect you are either stupid, a coward, or the police. Another agent and I went to the house where the buy had taken place and "discussed" the "turkey transaction" with the crook, convincing him that we better get our money back. He called his brother to get the money and a location to meet us at. So we went there and waited in our car, and pretty soon another car pulled up, and we were now looking down the barrel of a shotgun. Let me tell ya, shotgun barrels look really, really big when you're looking down the barrel of one stuck inside the driver's side window. Surveillance agents in the area saw what was going on, and as we "pulled away," cars got in front and behind this crook's car. We now had him blocked in, we thought, in front of the People's Bank in KCMO. By now he knew he was outnumbered, with multiple guns pointed at him. He panicked and put his car in gear as I dived through the driver's window in an attempt to get the keys from the ignition. Not a real smart move, but cops sometimes do this when someone is trying to escape. The guy wasn't buying any of this, and he accelerated, sideswiping a citizen's car on the driver's side with me hanging on. To this day, I don't know how I wasn't crushed between the two cars—a miracle it was. As he was accelerating and approaching Seventy-Fifth Street, I was deciding what was I going to do next (these things happen fast). Was I going for a ride that could get me seriously injured or killed, or was I going to bail out? I saw a heavy row of bushes coming up as he was going through the bank parking lot, and it just seemed to me that this might be a good place to get off. That's what I did as he made a hole through the bushes, and into the bushes I went, luckily getting only bruises and scratches.

The surveillance agents later that day told me that all they could see of me were the bottoms of my boots protruding from the bushes. This was mentioned in future training sessions **a lot** by one of my agent buddies, but he's probably now retired, so I could be off the hook. They all thought it was a real hoot. They laughed their asses off when it happened, and they couldn't tell the story without laughing. I guess I still think it was funny, and I still know I was damn lucky. One of my nine lives used on that caper.

A newspaper article with the headline "Holdup Report Proves False" reported, "Police made a fast call to the Peoples Bank, 75th & Wyandotte on a report of an attempted holdup" and found "it was a disturbance by several bearded youths with shotguns and revolvers" who got into a fight but left before police arrived.

The article didn't mention the car wreck. That would have been a hoot, a car wreck with a passenger hanging on the outside of the striking vehicle. I never worked anything vehicular like that, but I was sure involved in one. The bad guy in this event was later arrested for leaving the scene of an accident, traffic only to secure our cover.

While working undercover in Shawnee, I was involved in another vehicular accident that put my identity in jeopardy. I was buying dope on a case with a local crook when my parked car was hit by an apartment tenant. There were damages and a police report—oh crap, what to do? When the uniform officer came to work the accident, I gave him one of my undercover driver's licenses as he filled out the report. I still have copies. When I was able to talk to him without the perp, I told him the situation and who I really was. He was cool about it, and the accident report will forever read that "Ed Davis" from Missouri was the driver/occupant of the parked damaged car.

There was this employee at an auto-parts plant in Lenexa that was selling stolen parts from that plant. I bought a few parts before he was arrested, the most significant of which was a high-dollar car radio. He was a nephew of a friend of mine, and I forewarned my friend of what was going to happen, the arrest of his nephew. He was just a guy who took a chance on losing his job to have more money—easy money if ya don't get caught. While leaving to go meet this guy, I was rear-ended by another driver. By now I was getting really tired of these people crashing into my undercover car that I had become quite attached to. I went on to the meeting, or rather the stolen-property buy, and the accident was worked later. I almost got into a jam over that one. The sheriff was pissed off that I left the scene of an accident until he found that I had informed the watch commander about what was going on. The suspect was arrested after I bought several radios and other auto parts.

Buying stolen cars was another interesting case. There was this bad guy who took orders for whatever car anyone wanted to pay for his drug habit. I became acquainted with him through an informant introduction. I didn't place any particular order; I just asked him what he had that I might want. After I bought several stolen cars he had "in stock," he was arrested for auto theft, possession of stolen property, drug possession, and sales of narcotics. This guy was a sad case, hooked so bad that he had become an auto thief. He needed help, and he got it, in jail. Following picture, he and me making a deal.

Some investigations go nowhere as Billy Frazier and I experienced in a fast trip to Little Rock, Arkansas. We always kept our suitcases packed because when we had to leave, we usually had to go immediately. We drove late at night to get there, only to be called off to drive back. Whatever was going on had fallen apart; we just drove all night for nothing. The same thing happened on a Wichita trip—got there, turned around, and came home.

One afternoon Agent Harley Sparks and I were ordered, "get to Omaha ASAP." By the time we got on the road, it was dark, and we were driving into a blizzard. When we got a few miles into Nebraska, the snow was halfway up telephone poles, and the road was only one lane in places. Luckily traffic was very light. Some folks had the God-given good sense to stay home—not us! I wish I had had a camera, but we've all seen pictures of such storms. We arrived the next day driving a two-wheel-drive sedan. It had taken us over ten hours to get to Omaha instead of the usual three hours. A blizzard, ice, and snow—bad weather or no, ya still gots to go!

Some people are just sick, and in my undercover days, this was evident. Some of these were eye-openers for me. As I said, I had to learn the language, the terminology, and fast, and I had to listen to the music of the times.

The following is one example of sick people, druggies. I wasn't in the apartment on this case, but some of our agents and informants were and reported this. There was this one doper house, or "crib," as they called it, that we reported to child protection services to rescue a child. As said, I wasn't there, but as the story goes, this three-year-old female child was trained to go around the room and give the men in the room BJs. Now we all know, and those that didn't know found out what BJs were during the Clinton administration, didn't we? Blow jobs! There's no rationalization for this act with this child, and each and every one of those involved should have been prosecuted and registered as a pedophile and sex offender. Did they? I never knew, but we had done our part. If there were other cases like this, and there probably were at the time, here's why. If you went to a "head shop" in that time period, pacifiers were being sold that were in the shape of a penis. A small person's dildo? That's what it was, and in my opinion, it was sick as well. Other than second hand marijuana smoke, young juveniles being allowed to smoke pot was the only child abuse situation I was ever aware of, but some of these people were animals; they lived like animals, and there were no boundaries. And now we have the big push to legalize marijuana in all states. In the sixties and seventies, we were all talking about how these demonstrators and protestors were someday going to be running our country. Well, it's happened, and look where we are now.

Some of my fellow officers were animals and displayed this each and every chance they got. We were eating breakfast in a Lake of the Ozarks hotel restaurant when John, who had pipes (a voice) similar to the actor Charles McGraw, was asked a question. The nice-looking, sweet little waitress standing behind him asked, "Oh my, that smells so good, what do you have on?" to which John said, "I have a hard-on, but I didn't know you could smell it!" That restaurant got real quiet after the thunderous laughter at her expense from those of us within earshot. Have ya ever laughed so hard that your drink is coming out of your nostrils. That's the way it was some days when you're working with animals.

Chapter 40

Once Again

Common sense tells anyone that cops can't break the law to make a case, but some fellow officers and friends as well as some of the public think undercover cops have to cross the line. They think that we had to use dope and other criminal acts to do the job. We didn't. Some folks just couldn't believe it. Back in Johnson County as a supervisor and fellow undercover officer, it was my job to educate newbies on dos and don'ts of undercover work. I hate to say it, but in fact some officers did go over the line, broke the law, and paid the price even though they were coached and told this would happen. Break the law, get caught, and you are either fired, prosecuted, or both. I had a few friends that got in trouble even though they knew better; for whatever reason they did break the law. More on that later. But I didn't; I was just a good actor, and I had distractions to keep the attention away from me.

For example, I had an attractive, very well-endowed female informant who went on some cases with me as my "girlfriend." Her very, very large bust—big uns they were—would be partly exposed by a very low neckline, missing buttons and all…you get the picture? Bad guys did, and ya don't have to be a bad guy to enjoy the sights, do ya? They were really nice. One case was when I was buying a large amount of cocaine on the Missouri side; this guy couldn't take his eyes off her "stuff." She was pretty good at making conversation, smiling a lot, and just being a tease, and while he wasn't paying attention, I simulated snorting cocaine and just blew it off the plate. That's all you can do, simulate. I said I was satisfied with the goods, paid for the coke, and we left. The arrest followed sometime later. I used this scenario on a number of cases with this nice-looking, well-endowed informant. It made dealing for stolen property and narcotics much easier, as you can see (no pun intended), since no eyes were on me.

Soon after that caper, I left DEA and returned to the Johnson County, Kansas, Sheriff's Department to the City County Investigative Drug Squad. I was still a sergeant, second in command of the squad, I was still working undercover cases. This task force was similar in nature to the DEA task force as it was staffed by officers from most of the police departments in Johnson County, I was still having fun and loving it.

So, one day my boss, Roy Miller came out of his office and handed me the name and telephone number of a suspected drug dealer in Tucson, Arizona. "You wanna call this guy, tell him you're a friend of Keith's who told you to call, and see what you can do with this?" Miller had received the name and information from one of his informants. Sure, I said, so I made the call and got Mongo in Arizona on the phone, cold turkey.

He said, "Hello. Mongo here. How can I help you?"

"Hey man, my friend and yours, Keith, told me I could score some dope."

"Oh yeah. How's Keith doing?"

"He's great," I said and we made more small talk. Then I asked, "How about the dope?"

"What do you want?" he said.

"How about some coke or heroin? I need some of both for me and my friends."

This turned out to be one of the biggest and most interesting cases I worked. It ended with eight separate defendants—ten including the Edgerton, Kansas, delivery caper. It was over a period of months, all by telephone, with the exception of the Edgerton arrests. Out of all of the defendants, I never met any of these dope dealers until after their arrests.

I was sending buy money via snail mail, paying with money orders, personal checks, and some photocopied cash. The final transaction with these AZ conspiracy guys was three hundred pounds of marijuana which was the Edgerton, Kansas rest-area caper. In this deal, the 300 lbs. of pot was delivered to me by a couple of brothers I had been introduced to on the telephone, by Mongo. By pre arrangement, they brought the pot to an Edgerton rest area on I-35 (it's gone now) in a motor home, and that was where the arrests and seizure was made by me with surveillance nearby. After I made the arrests, I called surveillance to come on in. There was no resistance from the brothers who were arrested for possession and sales of marijuana and carrying a concealed weapon, a small, loaded .22-caliber derringer one of them had in his pocket. All defendants from the Arizona cases pleaded guilty. They were all telephone recorded and had cashed checks with their signatures, and in the case of the rest area defendants, had a great amount of dope with them. Those two guys went through the system, were bonded out, prosecuted, did prison time, and eventually were released but the story doesn't end there.

As Paul Harvey Always Said, "Now for the Rest of the Story."
A few years later, it's 1982, the two brothers and four others, two of whom were illegals from Mexico, along with an Olathe bondsman, a total of 6 defendants were arrested in Arizona in two motor homes and two other vehicles with a total of two tons of marijuana coming from Mexico to the States. The bondsman who had posted their bonds following the Edgerton rest-area bust in 1975 had gone into business with them. Some guys never learn. So back to jail they went, including the bondsman, who was now out of the bonding business and with a $25,000 bond he needed for himself. The bondsman had been a deputy sheriff years prior to this, before becoming a bondsman and now a dope dealer. I always wondered, did he post his own bond? I was saddened by this because I liked the guy, although most thought he was kind of on the fence as far as being trusted or honest. Guess they were right. Most LEOs know the bondsmen in their areas. Some are trusted and liked, while others not so much, but I still have a couple of friends that are still bondsman, and they are A-OK in my opinion.

The arrest of the Kansas bondsman with the two guys he had bonded out in the Kansas case and others had a total of six thousand to seven thousand pounds of marijuana valued at up to $1 million wholesale and $5.5 million retail at that time, according to area newspapers on January 30 and 31, 1982. It was a raid, and defendants were arrested in several different places, with two motor homes and a van full of dope, a lot of dope.

While I was working my cases, we had a "safe phone" to receive telephone calls at the office, and I had one at home. Every telephone call received or made at either place was recorded. Some calls were fun and funny—the conversations, that is. My home was on Gardner Lake, and one day as I was out on the lake on my pontoon boat idling up to the dock, the telephone I had on the dock was ringing. I let the boat idle up against the dock, still in gear, jumped off and answered the telephone; it was one of the Arizona boys calling me to sell me some dope—take an order that is. Order placed, deal consummated, but the funny thing was, when I played back the recorded conversation back, you could hear the boat motor running in the background as well as the birdies chirping and ducks quacking.

The telephone company boys were on repairs one day doing something, and the two guys were talking about the problem. Of course they didn't know they were being recorded, and one said, "Have you been in the house yet?"

The other said, "Naw. That SOB is a detective with the Sheriff's Office; he ain't never home." He was right about never being home. I was gone a lot! All hours I was..

In the Arizona conspiracy case, I worked with a task force in Tucson AZ. I later found out it's leader was the famous Sheriff Joe Arpaio. It was a dirty job, but as they say, "someone has to do it." I had to make five air trips to Tucson, four in the investigation and one for a prisoner transport unrelated. Every time I was in Tucson, I had a day to play, and there's a lot to do there; a beautiful place it is. Sheriff Joe's offices were high up with all glass exteriors, giving a 360-degree view of the city, mountains, and desert. Another "dirty job" having to work in a place like that with that view.

Back in Kansas, an acquaintance who was head of security at the Metcalf South Sears store located in Overland Park had an employee whom he suspected of stealing from the store. The suspect's MO (method of operation) was easy, as he was the guy working on the loading dock, loading merchandise for customers. But not all of these folks were customers; some were other crooks he negotiated sales of merchandise with. It was, of course, for a reduced price, and he pocketed the money, not Sears. I was introduced to this thief by an informant. We first met close to the Sears store at the old King Louie bowling alley (now gone), having lunch and playing pool a few times. I was able to convince him that I was OK because he initially challenged me, accusing me of being a cop. "You aren't the pohlece are you?" he said.

I laughed and replied, "Shit, man, I'm the fuckin' FBI, right?"

He laughed out loud, and I did too, and then he grinned, shook his head, and said, "Aw shit, man." I now had his confidence.

After that I made several buys from him. I bought tools, toolboxes, appliances, TVs, garage door openers...all expensive stuff from this guy. Every transaction was videotaped, and still shots were made by my surveillance team. I would back my truck up to the loading dock, he would load the merchandise, I'd hand him the buy money, and off I went. I made five or six buys from him, and he was arrested at the loading dock of the Sears store. All I had to do each time was to back up to the loading dock where he loaded me up with the goods, I handed him the cash and it was a done deal, drove away like any crook would do. He was later arrested, lost his job but the case was dismissed since Sears was fearful of a law suit and the security man was in the oleo for a while. We made a great case but all for not.

About undercover buy money and making cases:

"Buy money" was funds set aside and needed to make undercover buys on criminal cases, drugs stolen property etc. and was available to the plain clothes detective division as well as narcotics. There was a certain amount of money budgeted to the squad in the beginning by the public and businesses and later on by the Sheriff, the District Attorney's office and from participating police departments in the county and it was nearly all of them who funded the City County Investigative Squad or CCIS.

The following caper had to do with *Sgt. Roy Miller (later Lt. Miller) who was assigned to the drug unit from the Lenexa Police Department, he was designated squad leader, I was second in charge when I returned from DEA. Some of our squad members thought they knew it all, at least more than me and Miller, maybe they did, maybe they didn't but we were the BOSS and some didn't like us for that. There was something about guys assigned to the drug squads, a few were misfits and we knew it, they didn't play well with their own departments and that's why in some cases they were assigned to us, to get rid of them and that wasn't fair to our squad. That was our opinion that some may disagree with but who cares. One guy that thought he was a real hot shot quit a state job that almost everyone wanted to come to us, that was a clue but we had to take him. He left and bounced around at other jobs and who knows where he is now but he wasn't the only one. After their time in the CCIS some of them that went back to their departments didn't stay, either resigned or were eventually fired, some were promoted so it wasn't all negative. We had some really good guys and we made some really good cases as you can see due to their efforts. But this got ugly before it was over, I'm lying in bed one night, I'm awakened when and I hear a car screech to a stop out front, a couple of gunshots and the car burns rubber and speeds away. I figured I know who this was so I rolled over and went back to sleep. The next morning I show up for work, say nothing and they say nothing but I see the grins. I guess they thought I would panic, call the police and it would hit the papers or something but I foiled their plan, said nothing and that ended their fun. Shots fired musta been in the air, in ground or blanks because I found no damage to my house.

Miller made the mistake (they said) of "borrowing buy money" for personal reasons and the prima donnas who all used buy money themselves for personal reasons decided to rip Miller off, they went to the Sheriff while he was on leave unbeknownst to me. When Miller returned he was suspended and then dismissed because the prima donnas found that funds were missing from the bank account with Millers name on it. There's much more to this but I do not know all of the particulars (nothing criminal) other than the squad and buy money was originated by Margaret Jordan when she was District Attorney and passed on to Sheriff Allenbrand when she left as District Attorney.

I was blindsided by this whole situation and didn't do anything at the time, didn't really know what to do. What I should have done was to go to the sheriff and the DA which was Dennis Moore at the time to tell them that there were DA's, there were sheriff's department staff officers and DA investigators who all had borrowed money from the buy money funds at one time or the other as well as the prima donnas who had ripped Miller off. Miller and I talked shortly after he was suspended and he told me that the only persons in our unit that had not borrowed buy money was myself and a secretary. I told him "this is not true; I myself have used buy money when I was out working and needed cash." It was sometimes as much as a hundred bucks in my case, I wrote a check or went to the bank and it was paid back the next day. I didn't want to get into a situation as a few DEA agents who owed over a thousand dollars and had to borrow money to pay it back when they left the task force, returning to their departments. I was told in one case we had an agent who owed 5 K and he had done almost absolutely nothing but to take up space in a chair and go to college while at his DEA assignment. I knew he wasn't doing anything but it wasn't my problem. I don't even remember his name or the department he was from but that was a sad case. Most who were assigned to DEA returned to their respective departments, some got promotions and some stayed until retirement.

Miller fell on the sword and I'll tell you why, he covered for everyone, the borrowing of money may not have been wise but when you worked the hours we worked and got into a pinch for money for one reason or the other ya had to do it. It seems that the sheriff and then District Attorney, *Dennis Moore were the only persons that didn't know this. Hells bells, it's common sense, they had such funding for DEA, the metro squad, plain clothes detectives and other units so I figured everyone knew what we were doing, it **WAS NOT** stealing, it was borrowing, using as needed and again, almost everyone associated with the drug unit and the DA's Office BORROWED MONEY at one time or the other. I was so involved in my cases and trying to supervise some of these guys that using funding in a pinch to better further a case being a problem was the last thing on my mind

After Miller's departure we were all called to Sheriff Allenbrand's office where he explained Miller had been removed without specifics and told us all as he looked at me and said, "there are other problems here and they will be taken care of in due course and the chips will fall where they may." I'm thinking, "why the hell is he looking at me?" In an hour or so I found out, I was called to Major Lanes office where I was greeted by the Major and *Captain John Zemites, remember the road-block incident (I'm going to come kill you, you've been screwing my wife) where I had an unloaded shotgun for defense, that was Zemites and me. John started the conversation which was about money I had paid my informants. It appeared to those that were working and looking into this matter, including Lane and Zemites, that I had stolen money I reported had been paid to my informants. They couldn't find the receipts, that was the plan, no one outside of our squad could find those receipts, for protection of my informants. Those informant payments were in the thousands of dollars. It didn't take me but a few minutes to find out where they were going with this and I did the very same thing I did when I was testifying in court, I didn't volunteer anything and gave the shortest answers I could, I was now having fun with this. In retrospect they thought I had done wrong and they were going to arrest me. So we go along for a few minutes and Zemites gets really pissed off (I brought this up in conversation recently and he says he doesn't remember it) and says "what we are asking you Ed is this," I immediately stopped him and responded, "I know what you are asking me Captain, you are accusing me of stealing buy money." He responds by saying "Well where's the money, where's the receipts for payments to informants" and he was asking in an angry manner because he thought they had me. Again I responded, "I know what you are asking me Captain, you are saying I'm a thief", "well where are the receipts, how do you account for all of this missing money?" He asked.

I won't say where receipts were, but they were lawfully in a safe place in our office, not in any records system but it was legal and it was out of reach of the courts and defense attorneys. Only Miller and I knew the process, maybe a secretary but no one else. When I told them where the receipts were Major Lane stood straight up and said "I have to go see Dennis, Ed, get those receipts and show them to John" and the Major immediately left the room for Dennis Moore's office. I have always thought they had a warrant for my arrest and they were going to use it. YUK YUK!

Informants were interviewed in regards to payments to them for information given and their answers just poured water on the fires, what could they say, they got paid and they got paid well in some cases. As I have said before, when you're honest and ya tell the truth ya don't have ta worry about getting different scenarios, responses and covering up. That was the end of that for my part, did I get any apologies? Nope, and I asked Moore one time IF he had a warrant issued for me, he said he didn't remember the issue.

---

*After this debacle Miller returned to the Fairway Police Department later to become Fairways Chief of Police. District Attorney Dennis "the menace" Moore ran for and was elected to the 3rd congressional district in Kansas, served for years before resigning for health reasons. John Zemites is a friend but I will say this about that and he will agrees, John could be a real asshole at times.

Chapter 41

Relationships with Bad Guys And Informants?

To this day, I believe that I probably have the record for any one deputy on the number of search warrants filed and executed and confiscations made in the Johnson County Sheriff's Office on drugs and stolen property. No way to prove it, but I have witnesses/LEOs from that time that I worked with. All of these cases were legitimate, honest investigations; however, there were lawyers and a couple of judges who thought I was lying on evidence in court and on affidavits for search warrants since there were many; after me because of the number of cases I made. One judge (later removed from the bench) had "in camera hearings" with me and my informant at the insistence of the defense and then in camera hearings on about every case he handled just with the informant who they thought might trip up or make a mistake. There were none to be made. ("In camera" is a Latin term meaning "in chambers." This refers to a hearing or discussions with the judge in the privacy of his chambers with my informant and sometimes with me.) And of course nothing wrong was ever found. I just did my job honestly and made more cases much to the chagrin of the attorney and judge who hated me the most.

On one search warrant, the sheriff, Johnson County, and I were sued for 1.1 million dollars by a defendant and his ambulance-chasing attorney, the one that came to court mad all the time and absolutely hated me. When the case went to federal court, it was dismissed by an honest, long-time Johnson County lawyer who had become a judge and then a federal judge. Incidentally in that case, six pounds of marijuana was found in the residence clothes dryer, a pretty good amount for that point in time. I was a bit disappointed since I was looking forward to going back to federal court; hadn't been there for a couple of years. Again, the defense attorney was claiming that I lied on the search warrant affidavit, as he always did. It's easy testifying in court when you know the facts and you have been honest. It didn't take a lot of preparation; I just smiled and continued to mess with them. I loved it! Still do.

I think some of these cases will be interesting to most and some will be mentioned in future chapters. Because of my being a pain in their asses, they weren't happy, but in the end, some of them decided they were wrong about me; some of them, that is. I was driving some of them crazy and having fun with it because I was being honest and just building good cases; however; this one judge and one attorney never gave up. Where are they now? The judge was censured and disbarred for borrowing money from defense attorneys for his gambling problem. As far as I know, the attorney, one of them, my main critic, is still "practicing" law, but he has to be a

really old fart by now. I doubt still that he has won many cases. He and the judge had to have had ulcers as a result of dealing with my investigations and being unable to find fault or wrongdoings. They were obsessed in catching me at something; there was nothing to catch, but they were just sure that I was on the wrong side of the law.

My years of working undercover were some of the most exciting and fun years of my career. As I said, I felt guilty for getting a paycheck since I was having so much fun and excitement; I was running around in civilian dirt bag clothes, blue jean cutoffs, blue jeans and T shirts and pretty much on my own getting a clothing allowance, wow.

Many times, I've been asked about relationships or friendships with bad guys and informants. Ya spend a lot of time with them when you are under-cover. And yes, you get to know some of them fairly well, working on cases with some of them for an extended period of time. I had more than a few of these. Some were what are called "unwitting informants"—the bad guy, that is. That is when an LEO is getting information from a bad guy who doesn't know he's an LEO. Since I was older than most of them, the bad guys seemed to show respect for me and my knowledge. Some would ask for help or for my opinion on a point of interest to them. There were some of the bad guys I did like personally, but they still were drug dealers, drug users, burglars, or thieves; once they were arrested, any friendly relation-ship was over. It was sometimes sad on my part.

It was sad because some of them were likeable, however misguided they were for whatever reason and for what they were doing. Some just wanted to make an easy buck or money to keep up their drug habit. There were no long-drawn-out court appearances, no attorneys, and no judges; just pay the fine and/or do the time. Most defendants pleaded guilty since I was a witness and had evidence and documentation to the crimes.

I had an informant, Tim, who was working because he had been arrested selling me cocaine. Tim was wanting help in his case; he wanted to appear favorable to the judge. Some thought it would help. Sometimes it did, sometimes it didn't, but most judges were not sympathetic.

Now this is funny! Out one evening Tim and I stopped at a "stop and rob"—ya know, a convenience-type store. I went in to make a purchase, leaving Tim in my car. Everything seemed OK when I returned to the car, and we worked a bit longer before that evening was over.

I feel the burn!

A few days later, my banker called me and said, "Do you know some guy is passing your checks at an auto-parts store in KCK?"

"Well, sure I do, Don. HELL NO, I DON'T!"

It seems that the auto-parts store called the bank to check on Tim and found out that he was not Ed Hayes. They had a picture of Tim, who at this point had not shown a great deal of intelligence, and I guess I hadn't either, since I'd left my checkbook in the glove box of my car for Tim to steal. So, Tim stole a few of my checks, tried to pass them, and now had an additional charge of forgery and attempting to pass a forged instrument, and as "the Donald," says, "You're fired." Needless to say, he was no longer my informant. Then he claimed, "You set me up." I just laughed at him, which made him all the more angry.

Chapter 42

Smitty

*H*ere's what ya do when an informant goes bad or burns ya. The last thing an informant wants is to be found out by his buddies and fellow crooks to be a snitch. His or her life could be in danger, and some have been killed for being a snitch. We don't want that to happen, but undercover work is serious, and we do not want one of us to get hurt either. So, one of the first things you do in the education of your informant is to let him know up front "the rules":

> If you tell anyone I am a cop, if you burn me or others in any way, you will pay the price. If you don't cover me like I will cover you, we will run a news story if we have to. Your cover will be blown, they will know, and you will be toast.

I never did this, never had to, but I heard of others who said when they were burned by a snitch, they burned him, it's pretty hard core but they brought it on. Again, that's the last thing they want, and the threat of it keeps them on your side. Nothing brings more attention to a snitch than a uniform LEO who walks into a crowd of bad guys and picks one out for a private conversation. Not all CIs and even a few cops are honest, and as I previously said, I had a few friends who got into trouble when they went over the line. There was this informant, "Smitty," who had worked for an agent at DEA and was pretty well burned on the Missouri side. The agent, "Jim," called me and wanted to know if I would work with Smitty. Knowing the numbers of cases Smitty had made on the Missouri side, I said yes. I knew all about Smitty, and Jim was a friend, I thought, but what I didn't know was that Smitty was as big a crook—no, he was bigger than any of them. He came to me, and we went over the ground rules, and next thing I know he is making introductions to dealers, and I am making the buys. We had made about eight heroin and cocaine cases on eight different defendants, and then I got a visit from a defense attorney who said Smitty supplied heroin to his client to sell to me. Knowing the numbers of cases Smitty had made at DEA, I wasn't buying it. I questioned Smitty, and he denied doing this, so I let it go until another person I knew well, a sheriff's deputy on the Missouri side, came in to tell me the same thing: Smitty was giving defendants the dope they were being charged with selling to me. Smitty had given heroin to his nephew. I was still a bit in denial. I called Jim, who said he knew Smitty wouldn't do this, so I suggested that we do a polygraph test on Smitty to clear him of any wrongdoings. Jim resisted, but the Johnson County district attorney at the time was now aware of these accusations, and this was going to happen. Margaret Jordan knew (she thought) of an "expert" polygraph person in Chicago who had an impeccable reputation, so he was contracted to do the work. I especially wanted the best examiner to clear this up.

Jim in the meantime called me several times and threatened me, verbal threats unless I got the charges on Smitty dropped. Here was a cop threatening a cop, and I now became suspicious of Jim, whom I liked and had worked undercover with on occasion. I refused and got several more threatening calls from Jim, but I didn't cave. If Smitty was wrong, he would pay the price.

Unbeknownst to me, Smitty went to Chicago on his own—he didn't ask us, he just went. He took the polygraph test and failed, then Smitty went missing, and a warrant was issued. He was later arrested and jailed in Johnson County. Smitty still denied the charges, and when his court date came up, the case went to trial. During the trial, this polygraph "expert" was asked to identify the defendant, who was sitting among several people. This is a game defense attorneys play and sometimes win. If you can't identify the guy you made a case on or who you gave a polygraph test to, the case is toast, and that is exactly what happened. Said professional polygraph guy cannot identify Smitty in court, and with a big grin Smitty walks out a free person until he is again arrested on other charges. The cases made with Smitty were all dropped, and we were lucky we didn't get sued. Nowadays we would, even though there was no intent on anyone's part. Smitty eventually went to prison and may still be there.

The kicker in this case is that Jim was also found to be involved in drugs with Smitty. As a result he was fired, charged, and did his own jail and probation time. As I understand it, one of the things Jim was doing was using his status as a DEA agent to con drugs and methadone out of pharmacies and doctors. Sadly, the rest is history.

Informants are always a subject up for discussion among LEOs. Much of the time, they were working off an arrest in hopes of a reduction of their penalties or jail time, some were cop wannabes, and some were working for money; a few of my informants made some pretty good cases for money. I had a number of informants during my career, some good, some not so good, some you could trust, and others you couldn't, so you let them go. Some men, some women, some sought excitement, and some experienced it when things went wrong. Some informants just wanted to hang around with cops, hoping to get information, and some of the women wanted to get laid! They did!

I had an attractive informant (not the one with the big boobs, but she was OK too) who was able to befriend people, get into their houses, see narcotics or stolen property, and give me the information, and then I would get a search warrant. This was one way I got many search warrants, every one of which resulted in seizures and arrests. She was responsible for the seizure and arrests in the house where we found six pounds of marijuana in clothes dryer. That's the case where the ambulance-chasing attorney sued me, the sheriff, the county commissioners, Johnson County, and the State of Kansas for $1.1 million. I was disappointed when that case was dismissed by the federal judge, who just laughed at the case and dismissed it. I wanted it to go to trial. This poor lawyer couldn't win shit. I hope he reads this book. He and I are the only ones who will know who he is. He should be proud, shouldn't he?

Here's a side note on search warrants: One of our guys, I can't say which one, was probably the sire of many many children without the enjoyment, well maybe a little. During a search warrant you see many different items, personal things, sex toys, vibrators, pictures, you name it but one other thing ya see a lot are prophylactics, you know, "rubbers," sex? This guy would stick a pin in the package, thru the rubber and smash the package so it wouldn't be seen. Now when Mr. bad guy gets in the saddle, do ya think he's going to pull out to change raincoats? Naw, so there ya have it, how many 40 year olds that are walking the earth from this caper will never be known but there ya have it, he added some unplanned children to the population, be proud Bro!

Chapter 43

The Locksmith

*I*n another case, a search warrant developed with information from my informant concerned a bad guy that was possibly an informant for the FBI or someone. I didn't develop this case but as said it was developed with my informant and I was involved in the search warrant and arrests. This crook, was a burglar, a thief, a forger, and probably more. On top of all that, he was a locksmith, he had the parts, key racks, tools, blank keys, and equipment to make keys to anything. One of his specialties was cars, which was one of his MOs. He had a total key shop setup in his house— very impressive it was. One of his MOs was getting into the trunks of cars at golf courses, exercise clubs, businesses, and parking lots, some enclosed. He had mucho golf clubs, golfing accessories, and stolen property galore, too much to mention. So he was a locksmith and a golf equipment sales- man! We had to rent a U-Haul trailer or truck to confiscate all the stolen property from this house.

This bad guy and his live-in girlfriend were arrested on site, jailed, and both posted bond almost immediately. A few days after they bonded out, he got a telephone call at the house early, 3:00 a.m. His girlfriend later says, "The telephone rings, he answers, there's a short conversation, he gets up, gets dressed, and leaves. I have not seen or heard from him since." This case closed, now history. While awaiting trial, this bad guy just went missing. We never knew why for sure, but we had suspicions. We didn't know any particulars, but it was suspected that he was put into the witness protection program since we suspected he was "connected," as they say, in some way or he was murdered? Connections can be dangerous can't they.

The repercussions of this case were what I was suspended for the second time around. Besides all of the stolen property, he had a handgun and other items taken from the trunk of a DEA agent's car, the one I had worked with, Harlo—remember the Golden Point gun battle in Independence, Missouri, near Harry Truman's house? It was Harlo who was with me when we had an LEO's shotgun pointed at us.

Living across the road from a golf course on one side and a lake on the other side, I needed a golf club to hit balls into Lake Gardner with my son over a holiday weekend, so I called Harlo and asked him if it would be OK if I used one of his golf clubs that was being held for him to pick up, and knowing me, he said, "No problem." Looking back, I guess it was not a great decision on my part, since the club had been in evidence from the search warrant in the crook's house—you know, the one that was connected and vanished.

Hey, You Assholes! Get Off My Car!

I was snitched off to the sheriff by one of my insubordinate patrolmen (who was a problem child), and the sheriff ordered Major Lane to suspend me for a day, so I was to work one day off without pay. That was the order from the sheriff. This snitch was an officer that had been called down for a "visit" with the sheriff to chat about his stack of parking tickets on an undercover patrol car he had not paid attention to. While I was working this day off, on a weekend, I was sitting in line to get my car cleaned at a car wash in Overland Park. These two guys in front of me decided they didn't like each other very much for some reason. They were the two cars ahead of me, and got out of their car, said not so nice things to each other, and started throwing punches. They were both pretty good at it. This was fun to watch.

Undercover guys who want to remain anonymous usually don't get involved in situations such as this if we don't have to, so I was sitting there watching this fight, enjoying it, until they ended up wrestling and fighting on the hood of my car. It really pisses me off, so I got out with my night stick (a.k.a. Kel-Lite flashlight), identified myself, stopped the fight, and arrested them, which meant I'd hold them until the Overland Park Police arrived. Overland Park took my information, and I continued on. I didn't care what happened after that; I just continued on with my suspension day without pay. I couldn't stay out of the oleo even on a day of suspension.

Search warrants can be very dangerous, as you read about in previous chapters. Sometimes we'd end up pointing guns at the bad guys, with bad guys pointing guns at us, but there were a few times when cops pointed them at each other, and I had that happen to me several times, as both the pointer and pointee. Undercover, we all look like the guys we are investigating, and when you work with other agencies, you are sometimes not well acquainted. On a couple of occasions, as we were securing residences on the outside, search warrants and arrests, I came face to face with another officer. They and I paused (thank you, God), and we both had each other looking at the big hole at the end of a gun barrel as we came around the corner of the house. In all cases, we had just met at briefings.

It was about this point in time that President Nixon came to Kansas City, Missouri, to make a speech at the federal building near the KCMO Police Department. We were scanning the tops of buildings and building windows around the area. A couple agents and I were on top of the police department watching other buildings and the crowd from above. Although we had a bird's-eye view of the speech, there wasn't time to watch. After his speech, as the presidential limo pulled away, we could see Nixon just below us smiling, waving with his trademark fingers pointing toward the sky as they drove away heading north toward the airport to get the hell out of Kansas City.

For years, the sheriff's office had a mounted horse patrol as well as a rescue and recovery underwater dive unit and an air patrol unit, not to be confused with the prisoner transportation airplane that was in service for a few years in the eighties and early nineties. The mounted patrol and air patrol units were phased out somewhere around 1959. That was before my time at the sheriff's office, but pilot friends of mine were in that unit with their own airplanes. In the 1970s when the sheriff's office needed an airplane for some reason, *I* was the "air patrol unit."

I have a commercial pilot's license, have done some commercial work, and at that time I had aspirations of being a commercial airline pilot. I soon realized that airline pilots were not much different than bus drivers in the sky. No disrespect, because most of them do it because they just love flying that much, and most are really great pilots. As corporations get into financial trouble, the first thing to go is their pilot and airplane, so those jobs for the most part are not as solid as I was looking for.

I got over all that and stayed with the sheriff's office, volunteering my airplane as needed, which I flew on traffic patrols, for events, intelligence, surveillances, and so on. A few times the KCMO helicopter was used, and being a pilot, I usually was a spotter with the pilot. These flights were usually on drug cases and other criminal-related surveillance cases. Things don't always go great even from an aircraft. As an example, on one particular surveillance, we were in the helicopter following a white van in the Merriam/Lenexa area. This van pulled up to a four-way intersection, and guess what? Three more white vans pulled up at the very same time. When they drove away, from the air, we couldn't tell which one was which. How could this happen, you may ask? All I can tell you is that ya had to be there, but the ground surveillance was able to pick it up again by license numbers. I don't remember how that case ended, but that's how things go sometimes—some days ya just can't win; ya win some and ya lose some, and that's just the way it goes.

On another surveillance flight, Major Chuck Lane and I were flying for intelligence gathering, in a fixed-wing aircraft this time. As we were returning to home base, the engine suddenly just quit! Chuck was looking worried. I was too busy, and it was dead silent for a moment. Pilot training had told me what to do in such a situation; it's usually carburetor ice. I'd never had engine failure that sudden except if I'd turned it off with a key. Ya usually get some engine sputtering as a warning with ice, but not this time. I wasn't too concerned because we were just west of what is now New Century Airpark at over five thousand feet; a "dead stick landing" would have been easy.[4] Now I went into emergency aircraft procedures and nearly pulled the carburetor heat instrument out of the firewall. That's a plunger-type knob in the instrument panel for just that reason, and it applies engine heat to melt ice in the carburetor; it usually works. As the engine immediately started, Chuck looked at me and said, "I don't know what the hell you did, but it must have been the right thing." We were laughing, relieved—no engine failure, just carburetor ice, which on hot humid summer days is not unusual.

Chapter 44

Loose Lips Don't Only Sink Ships

During my years working undercover investigations, our unit did several wire taps. This was following the DEA assignment and my return to Johnson County. We had investigations we worked that were capers in which anyone connected should be very proud of in my opinion, all of us did one hell of a good job with the exception of one guy I will tell you about. It's the kind of things they make movies about. One wiretap was a Jo Co investigation, but we were based in an apartment complex in Kansas City, Kansas, across the parking lot from the bad guy's apartment. They were suspected of dealing heavily in cocaine and heroin. The wiretap was manned by the Johnson County City County Investigative Squad (CCIS—the drug squad) and KCK undercover officers. It was led by Lieutenant Roy Miller. I was a sergeant at the time and second in command of the CCIS task force. From the apartment we were operating out of, we could see bad guys come and go twenty-four hours a day. We were on shifts of twelve hours on and twelve hours off, twenty-four-seven. From my house, it's a forty-five-minute drive to and from the location, so you can imagine how much sleep I and the others got during this caper. By the time I got home, showered, and caught a few hours of sleep, I was back on for another shift, twelve more hours. It was grueling and lasted for around two weeks, but it was a fun, great, and interesting investigation.

On a telephone wiretap, as you listen to conversations of bad guys, ya don't have to guess about when they come and go most of the time. They will unwittingly tell you almost everything, so we followed them every time they left, everywhere. Some officers worked the wire, while others were either in the apartment or outside to follow them.

A funny thing happened during this investigation—well several funny things happened, but this was of a personal nature. I always had my kids or at least one of them for a couple days a week, usually on weekends, being happily divorced and all, as many folks experience at one time or the other. It was during this time that I missed my visitation time with my kids and was late on my child support payment, the only time ever. As exes go, we were not close, so we didn't talk a lot; for my part, I only talked to her when I had to. So, I was awakened by a telephone call during my very short sleep cycle. "Hello," I said.

"Did you forget something?" she said in a smartass tone that I was used to, I was at a loss. I didn't know what the hell she was asking me about. My world at the time was totally on the case I was working. I had not had time to think of anything else, especially her so I didn't know what the f*** she was talking about. I was really pissed because I had been awakened from the itty-bitty time I get to sleep! So I said, "What the hell are you talking about?" She said, "Well, I haven't got my check yet." I thought, "Oh shit! I have been so busy I totally forgot to mail her the check," but I didn't give her any explanation; I just said the check was in

the mail, and it was, as soon as I was on the way back to the command center on the wire. I guess ya had to be there, but I have always enjoyed that bit of experience in post marriage. My son reminds me on occasion that it's his mother I am talking about, but she hosed me each and every chance she got (not physically), and I got one in (no pun intended) on her for a change; she was stressed. She was oblivious to what was going on in my life, and I didn't really care.

So now back on point. There we were on this wiretap, following these guys, rotating on the inside and the outside surveillance to break the monotony, and we really were doing a top-notch investigation, in my opinion. We were waiting for the big score because they were making frequent air trips to California to pick up loads of dope. That's when we were going to arrest them, when they got back with a larger load, and they would tell us, wouldn't they? On the wiretap? I was having fun even though I was dog tired most of the time, but when something occurred, the adrenaline would kick in, and off I would go.

I don't recall exactly how many bad guys we watched, but there were three living in that apartment, and several others were coming and going. One day we heard this conversation; they were talking about taking this air trip to pick up a load of dope. The next day my surveillance partner and I were outside, in separate cars. We knew they were leaving, and when they did, we followed them to Kansas City International Airport. I got pictures of them checking in and going toward the gate and got some really great shots as they exited the building to their flight.

The telephones were quiet for a few days, and then we heard them talking on the telephone, saying that they were coming home. They didn't score very much, they said. We heard their schedule, so when they landed, we were there taking more pictures. I got pictures of them coming out of the gate and heading for their car—more really good shots from a restaurant balcony. These were probably the best surveillance pictures I ever took. I was proud of myself, and I was having a good time at it. We were now in the waiting stages again for another trip they were talking about, but what we didn't know was that this investigation was now OVER! The next morning I was monitoring the wiretap, and suddenly there was this "oh shit" moment and a conversation I will never forget.

"Hey man, the cops have a wiretap going on in our apartment complex. We may be getting our telephone tapped. We have to be very careful." This guy suspects his conversations were being tapped, and he was still talkin'. "My mom works at city hall [Kansas City, Kansas] and knows this cop," he said. "The cop came in this morning and saw her in the police department lobby. In conversation he told her that someone in our apartment complex is being wiretapped. He didn't know she was my mother. He knows this because he is working on the wiretap."

I nearly fell out of my chair. So now what to do? I could not believe what I was hearing, because the bad guy named the officer (my sidekick on the airport surveillance) who was supposed to be working *with us* and had now *got us burned*? We knew he was a windbag blowhard, but no one expected this to happen, even from him. We had been on this investigation for two weeks, and because some dumb-ass, loud-mouthed, braggadocios cop couldn't keep his mouth shut, couldn't keep an investigation to himself as he should, because he was trying to impress some woman, WE WERE DONE! The investigation was over. This was not the way we wanted to end it, with days and weeks of hard work by about fifteen cops blown out of the water by this loud-mouth cop. There was nothing else to do but shut it down, end it with a search warrant later that day. The other KCK cops were embarrassed because of one of their own. We recovered what drugs they had, made arrests, and that was it. Although it didn't end in the manner we had hoped, we still got convictions and got bad guys off the streets for a while, and the end result was that we had a good time doing it, most of us.

I once heard a guy say that he was having so much fun, he looked forward to going to work every day. He said, "I was loving my job so much that I felt like I should be paying them for me to work there." That was me most of the time in every division but especially in undercover investigations; I did feel guilty some of the time.

Well, get over it, right? We're not done so here's another case to remember, another to be very proud of. It's another interesting case our task force worked and is similar in nature, but it wasn't a wiretap; it was all strictly surveillance by auto. We had a couple of local bad guys who were pulling armed robberies in the KCK and Johnson County area, and they were good at it. We suspected them in up to fifteen armed robberies, and they needed to be caught. No one had been hurt yet, but they needed to be stopped. We were again working as a task force with the KCK SCORE unit and other officers from Johnson County cities. This was another one of those capers where we went to bed and got up with the bad guys twenty-four-seven; we worked their hours. However, on this case, they slept later, so that helped out a lot. It was long hours but a lot of fun as far as investigations go.

We were working out of our cars, following them everywhere they went, watching them case their prospective victims and businesses. This went on for over a week, about ten days it was, and it seemed like they would never commit. At times we had to wonder if they'd spotted us, but they hadn't, we guessed, since they were still driving around casing businesses.

One evening around nine o'clock, we followed the bad guys as they were casing a popular BBQ restaurant in Merriam, Kansas. It looked like this was going to be it. They drove by and around it several times, so I drove into the parking lot, took my shotgun out of the car, and went inside to await their arrival. As I entered, I showed my ID to the two employees. They were glad to see me, under the circumstances. There were no customers present since it was near closing time. I set up shop in a back storage room where I could see bad guys as they came in the door, and I waited. And I waited. And I waited. They drove around and by a few more times, and then for some reason, they left the area. They were followed until they gave it up for the night. I was disappointed; I just missed out on another chance to be a witness to bad guys and their deeds right in front of me. It's hard to figure out how some of these people think and why or why not they do what they do, but for some reason they didn't rob that restaurant that night. Maybe some of the bad guys develop a sixth sense, or maybe they just had a gut feeling that the time wasn't right—same thing, I guess.

A few nights later, as we were following them, we watched them drive around seemingly for no reason, but we knew what it was all about; they were casing a couple of smaller businesses in Shawnee, Kansas, located close to Merriam. They drove by this small, busy taco restaurant a couple of times and then stopped, parked in back, hopped out, ran in, and robbed it. Right in front of us they were. This was what we were waiting for, and to their surprise we were waiting for them when they came out. Astonished they were to see about twelve LEOs in their faces. They offered a little bit of resistance but to no avail; they were had, and they knew it. To me these types of cases were always fun, but I was always glad to see them end so I could rest up for the next one.

During these years we had several more wiretaps, all in Johnson County, but none were as much fun or productive as the two aforementioned investigations. We always got seizures of drugs, stolen property, and intelligence from bad guys and their associates. I recall on one search warrant that was a result of a wiretap, we were working on seizure of evidence, when the telephone rang. This was always fun for me, answering the bad guy's telephone to see where that might take us. The caller said, "Is this Jim?" to which I said, "Yes."

"Do you need any coke today, Jim?"

I said, "Yes. When can you bring it by? I need it ASAP for my friends."

"Well," the caller said, "I'll bring it right over."

He did, and fifteen minutes later we had another arrest, charging this guy with possession of cocaine and possession to distribute cocaine. I musta sounded like Jim on the telephone. That happened a couple of times during my undercover days, but it was icing on the cake so to speak; another bad guy who sold drugs to our kids and to people who were hooked was off the streets.

There was one other telephone call I took at a bad guy's house in Prairie Village. The caller said, "Is Bob there?" and I said, "No. Who's this?" to which he said, "Paul." Paul and I had a short conversation, and this guy sounded exactly like a former agent whose name was Paul and who had a distinctive voice. I never knew, but I have always wondered why Paul, if it was the Paul I knew, was calling this bad guy. Maybe it's best that I didn't know.

Chapter 45

Underwater Rescue and Recovery

In a drowning on the Fourth of July of 1967, a novice scuba diver went missing in a farm pond west of Olathe. This diver had done exactly what you are not supposed to do: he was fully equipped and scuba diving *without dive training*. On that recovery incident, Ed Hayes Jr. (my father) and I were in the middle of the pond in the sheriff's department boat while divers were searching the area. This is a good example of the need for top-water supervisors. A diver screamed out in distress, and I could tell he was in trouble; we could see he was in panic mode. "Help me, Ed. I'm drowning." I dropped my belt with my weapon to the bottom of the boat, and in the pond I went. Having had lifesaving training in my younger days, as I got to him I ordered him to roll over on his back, putting the weight of his dive tank under him so he could stay on top, and I pulled him to the boat, which was about thirty yards away. As Chuck would say, cheated death again!

The same reporter that had been at the Metcalf State Bank robbery, "John," was on site reporting live on the incident and witnessed my rescue of the diver and the recovery of the young man who had drowned. Reserve Sergeant Walter Hoeflicker found and recovered the victim who, sadly, had recently returned from a tour in Vietnam, only to drown tragically in a fifteen-foot-deep farm pond. Walt brought the young man's body to the surface, and we returned him to the bank.

Any instructor or experienced diver will tell you, ***DO NOT get in the water, do not try to scuba dive,*** unless and until you are a fully trained and certified scuba diver and ***do not dive without a "dive buddy."*** Training procedures will save your life, and training and emergency procedures could have easily saved this veteran's life. This incident sparked my interest in scuba diving, so I took the courses and qualified eventually as an open-water diver.

It's always nice to get a compliment from a fellow officer—I'll take it! Here's one in a note from then-deputy Jim Conrad regarding the rescue of the dive team deputy on July 4, 1967:

> Ed,
>
> If your next article is on underwater search and rescue you might remember this. I remember a drowning west of Olathe or Lenexa in a small pond when a diver got tangled up in some barbed wire under water and you dove in with your uniform on, less boots and equipment belt, to help him and get him in our boat. I was impressed...you were my hero that day.

As I have said, during the first three years of my undercover assignment, I went to the office/courthouse for one thing only, my paycheck, and only because the office wouldn't mail it to me. Sheriff Allenbrand said, "I want to see you once in a while."

Sometimes, actually much of the time, in those days (repeating I know) I really felt some guilt—some, that is—since I was having so much fun and getting paid for it! Some of my coworkers would agree. Anyone working in law enforcement will tell you that there are fun times and times not so fun for various reasons, but it is great to work in a job you love most of the time.

So, it was the same thing with the underwater rescue and recovery unit. Sad as it was at times, it also was interesting and at times exciting. I was in charge of the underwater and rescue unit before I went to DEA and remained so while I was there, but now the time was getting close to

the end of my undercover days. It was a bittersweet day for me when I was transferred to the watch commander's office in charge of shift operations since I had had the time of my life working undercover, wearing whatever outfit I wanted for any given day—shorts, T-shirt, no shirt, or just whatever pushed my button that day. But transfers are a part of the job. Different units give officers more experience in the profession, and ya need to do it if you want a well-rounded career experience, although most times it's not your choice.

The original dive unit was staffed mainly by reserve officers until they were phased out to my disappointment, except for one, Sgt. Walter Hoeflicker, the dive master that trained me. Sometime after the reserves were eliminated, I volunteered to manage the dive unit, so I was appointed staff officer. Walt and I trained full-time officers as search and rescue divers and managed that until it was phased out two years prior to my retirement. There were other good, experienced dive units in the area—Lee's Summit Underwater Rescue and Recovery—so Sheriff Allenbrand elected to use them as needed, due to budget constraints I guess.

While an underwater *rescue* is remote, it's not impossible, but to call the dive unit a "rescue unit" is deceiving, in my opinion. Before my time there never was a rescue; sadly, all cases were recovered drowning victims and or evidence recovery.

There were a number of dives the unit made over the years searching for weapons, firearms, and items of different crimes, burglaries, shootings, and so. What most folks do not know is that in Johnson County, there is no clear water to dive in other than swimming pools, rock quarries, and some ponds that we trained and instructed in. It's all "black water," zero-visibility diving; ya can't see your hand in front of your face. The searches are touch and feel with your hands. Put yourself in an unlighted closet, close the door and you get the picture.

On occasion Gardner Lake has a visibility of up to about five feet and we did dives all over that lake in recoveries, training and many times just for fun. If you had water that was clear at all, it was on a good day, and you only had a few feet of clear water. There was one day that we were searching for a lost wallet near the dam, and surprise, we had fifty-plus feet of visibility. This was one day only; the next day, we went back and had only a few feet of visibility. Other dives I recall were all tragic drownings. There were a couple different victims at Gardner Lake, Quivera Lake, Shawnee Mission Park Lake, many different ponds, and the Kaw River. I didn't dive in all incidents because as supervisor I was self-assigned to top of the water to monitor my divers in most cases.

One dive was at the Sunflower Village apartments west of Desoto searching for two-and-a-half-year-old Lisa Silvers, a victim of a kidnapping/homicide. She wasn't found, so the pond was drained, and she was still not found. Her little body was found in a county ditch by hunters eight months later. The suspect, her uncle, was arrested in that crime but was found not guilty by a jury of twelve men. I would like to be present for deathbed confessions with some of these people. In other incidents, victims were washed away at lake spillways, several at Gardner Lake.

One other dive case was when I received information from an informant regarding the theft of a Ditch Witch machine. This machine, according to the informant, was stolen by a politician's nephew, (he was the nephew of a governor) taken out on the ice of a pond, and sunk by using a chainsaw to cut a hole around it when he was feeling the heat. I had tried to talk to the individual but was refused contact by his attorney, so I take my information to a judge, got a search warrant and divers (I wasn't one yet), and we all showed up. I presented the warrant to the mother, who was highly pissed off at me, and she showed it. She thought it was OK, I guessed, that her child was a thief. He was either not there or was hiding; I didn't care. It wasn't enough that her "little boy" was a thief, as it seemed that it was all my fault, that I was trying to get even—for what I never knew. I thought I was doing my job. This was a fairly good-sized pond but not very deep, so it didn't take the divers long to find the machine. The pond was ice covered, and breaking the ice as they went, they hooked on the machine with a tow cable, and the truck brought it up.

This case came back to bite me in the ass because the thief's attorney called me and begged me to support charges being dropped for his client.

I didn't care if the thief was the POTUS's nephew (he wasn't). I wasn't going to support such a thing. In the first place, he was a cowardly thief, and there was also a victim in this case, the owner of the machine. Defense attorneys don't give a hoot for crime victims. Like prosecutors, they only care about their numbers; getting their clients' charges dropped or having clients found not guilty helps in getting them more clients. District attorneys are looking at reelection, and cases won are their job security. Now the reason I say this case got me bit is that this thief's attorney ended up being my ex-wife's divorce attorney, and he never forgot my decision in his case. He overcharged me and gave me no slack.

Chapter 46

The Tragic Death of Captain Bill

*I*n training exercises, we always wished for clear water, and there were several rock quarries in which we trained and practiced. One was local, and another was in or near Mound City, Kansas. Both had nearly unlimited visibility similar to a swimming pool and were fairly good sized. The Mound City quarry was an hour's drive, but for training it was great. It was approximately three acres, and as I recall, the depth was about fifteen to twenty feet. Another plus was that at the bottom was a 1970s green Pontiac four-door sedan. The other quarry was just off Kansas Highway 10 near Desoto. It is now surrounded by a golf course, if it still exists as a quarry or pool of some sort. Dive training starts with out-of-water bookwork and lectures revolving around basic procedures, equipment familiarization, emergency demonstrations, and so on. At that time students demonstrate swimming skills by getting in a swimming pool, where abilities are monitored before any other training is commenced. If you're not an excellent swimmer, ya should not be a diver. Instructors will not allow poor swimmers in their classes recommending they go back to the basics, a swim class. The able bodied student starts in the shallow end of the pool swimming laps, followed by having the mask and fins dropped into the deep end, where you have to retrieve them, put them on underwater, and back to the top ya go. IF you cannot perform these two exercises you are out of class.

By the time you graduate from each additional training exercise and are proficient in a pool, you go to a lake or pond. That's where you learn to be a diver. In the case of search and rescue you are first a diver, and then rescue diver training starts for those that can qualify. It's not a good ole boys' club; if ya can't cut it, you will not be certified.

The closest thing I remember that could have been a "rescue" was in 1978 at Pomona Lake West of Ottawa, Kansas. A steamboat replica named the *Whippoorwill* was blown upside down by what they described an F1 tornado. A call for divers went out from the governor's office to all area agencies, and I responded. Upon arrival, I found that the *Whippoorwill* had been towed to shore by well-meaning boaters in its upside-down position. I was trained to anchor any watercraft at an accident location, so it's my opinion that, if anyone under that boat had survived (other than two crewmen in an air pocket) they could have drowned during the tow.

There were sixteen passengers drowned out of fifty-eight people on board, according to some numbers. Others said forty-six aboard and seventeen drowned. Plenty of divers responded from many agencies, and by the time I got there, I was not needed in the water, so I stood by on the bank to help in any way I could. That ferry boat upside down was a grim sight with all the activity—first responders, people alive carrying the dead, all the lights.

In earlier times, the sixties into the seventies, the Olathe Fire Department and the sheriff's office deputies were close. We all had the same respect for each other, and it showed. I had firemen (more than one) tell me that they would rather work with "you guys," meaning the sheriff's department, than anyone else. "You know what to do, and you take charge," they would say, and they'd give examples of incidents that we assisted them on. We made their job easier, they said, and that made me proud.

Around 1976, staff members of the Olathe Police Department and Fire Department mentioned that they would like to have their own dive unit. They made a request, "Can you teach us?" So, Reserve Sergeant Walt Hoeflicker and I obliged. Soon we were training in a local swimming pool at the Kansas School for the Deaf in Olathe, and we were getting prepared to do a rock quarry open-water dive for training purposes. Following that dive, those that were able would go to a lake for additional training.

When we took on the training for Olathe first responders, we agreed to do it only if they would do everything we told them and in sequence; in other words, when it came to any diving, I was their boss. Once they got certified, they would be on their own, but not until. They were also told, and they agreed, that they would not do any dives anywhere unless Walt and I were on scene, no matter what. Their certification was coming soon, and I really thought we had our ducks in a row.

Late one night there was the drowning of a young man at Lake Olathe. Due to the time of day, hours had passed before it had been reported. Witnesses were gone. We elected to wait until daylight the next morning. I had not planned on using the students for this dive but had planned on having them on site during the recovery. Walt had called me the night before and said they had called him about the drowning. He had told them not to make that dive, saying we would do it the next morning and after my court appearance. "Was I right?" he asked. I replied, "Yes, of course. I thought we had that handled and understood." And we did.

The next morning I had a district court hearing on an undercover case. I was about halfway to the courthouse when I was ordered by dispatch to "proceed to Olathe Lake, without delay." I informed dispatch that I had a court case and couldn't proceed; I was going to court first. A few minutes later, dispatch called me and said, "On orders of Major Lane, proceed to Pecker Point at Olathe Lake and contact units on scene."

So I was on route to Pecker Point to see what the hell was going on since dispatch wouldn't tell me on the radio. I couldn't imagine what would take precedence over a scheduled court case, but when I arrived, I found out. There were several police cars, fire trucks, and other first responders and their vehicles, and an ambulance.

I got out of my car and was met by Fred Tush, who was now an Olathe detective (he previously worked for the sheriff's office). He said, "Too bad about Bill, isn't it, Ed?"

I said, "What are you talking about, Fred?"

"Bill drowned. You didn't know?"

"What!" My head was spinning. Ya could a dropped me with a feather. I replied, "How the hell did that happen?"

Fred said, "They were diving for a drowning victim, and something happened to Captain Bingham in the search."

I asked, "Who is 'they,' and why were they in the lake without me or Walt here?"

Fred didn't know much other than that they all (our trainees) had come to the lake to make the dive against our agreement and orders.

Here's what sometimes happens to novice, uncertified divers, even professional first responders. For whatever reason, the team wanted to recover a drowning victim to make a showing of their new dive unit and skills that were still in the development stage. On orders from someone above, they had gone to the lake on a rescue against the orders from Walt and me. I just didn't understand how someone, a supervisor, not a diver, could be that ignorant. They and had gone down on a rope search, and when they came up, there were bubbles coming from the bottom. It was obviously a dive regulator, and Bill was not with them on top water. They followed the bubbles and found Captain Bingham on the bottom. The investigation that followed showed that there was no equipment failure, and quite possibly Bill had been hit or kicked in the face, knocking his regulator off, and he may have panicked. I could never hold any responsibility in this incident against any of the dive students or Olathe fire or police. They were follow-ing orders from a supervisor in the fire department, not from me or Walt.

For obvious reasons, that was the end of the training by Walt and me for Olathe first responders, and a sad ending it was. I will add this. In the academy you will be told, "Anytime in your career, if you get an unlawful order from a superior officer, you have the right to defy that order, and you should defy that order, if you have the courage." Let the chips fall where they may after that. I wish they had done that on this occasion and called me.

Pecker Point was so named because it was a location used by lovers in parked cars—a lovers' lane. In the fifties, sixties, and early seventies, a very busy place it was. I don't know what they did there. Do you? But I do have my suspicions, don't you? I remember Captain Bill's reference to it, and we would always laugh; he thought he knew as well. Bill was a professional, a friend, and he was always a joy to work with, as we did at times when I was in uniform and on the dive unit as well. We were always in touch. He was one of the guys that was always glad to see an old friend, and he showed it every time. Captain Bill was loved and respected by all of us! And I for one will never forget him, his friendship, and his dedication to serving the public. He was one of the good guys, but they all were.

Chapter 47

Oh No! Not Another Transfer

On July 1, 1980, I was moved from investigations back into uniform, assigned to the watch commander's office. I was still a sergeant even though there was a captain and lieutenant above me. As watch commander, I mainly reported to the sheriff. There were four watch commanders—one each covering day shift, evenings, midnights, and relief. Watch commander on the day shift was mainly liaison to all department divisions as well as all courthouse offices. On the evening and midnight shift, the watch commander in the absence of the sheriff was *THE* sheriff in those days. The watch commander managed the road patrol, detectives, the jail, and any others that were working at the time. On the evening shift, we had our "aide de camp," Deputy Johnnie Boase, who was always the best supporter, backup, and help, in my opinion. Johnnie intercepted citizens who came into the office and took care of their needs or passed them on to the watch commander as needed. On the midnight shift, the WC was on his own. If he needed help, he called the jail, and a turnkey would come to help.

When transferred to the watch commander's office, I was sergeant until 1983, at which time I was promoted to lieutenant at the same position. I had achieved one of my goals, since my father had been a lieutenant when he died. My next goal was to become captain as my granddad was. Then I would be happy. I had no ambitions after that except to take whatever I was offered. As it turned out, after I was promoted to captain in staff services, I figured my next step would probably be retirement.

As I mentioned earlier in this book, when I went into the watch commander, I was supervisor over deputies that didn't even know I existed.

They didn't know where I had come from or what I had done. Many had been hired in the seven years I had been gone. Most were not even employed when I went undercover, and of those that were, they were in divisions that I only managed on the evening and midnight shifts. They knew me, and they were OK with it, but the slings and arrows continued for some time with some of the newbies who resented my presence. That was their problem, because they worked for me, not me for them. There were a few that tested me and a couple that thought they had me set up to be either moved or fired at one time, but it just didn't work out for them. When one of these guys died, I was asked, "Are you going to his funeral?" I said, "Why should I? He isn't coming to mine!"

One time, they reported me, and I was in trouble for having my dog "Bob" in my patrol car I thought. The little guy had been in my private car for a whole shift getting only a couple pee breaks so needing to work over I put him in the patrol car to take him home. He really needed to go home and take care of some business, he did. Here's the deal. I had a female deputy riding with me on that shift. When we dropped the dog off at my house, we found that the neighbors were having another one of their marathon parties, so we stopped over to visit. My surveillance team (watching me) didn't see us go next door. They thought we were in the house doin' something we shouldn't be doin', at least on duty. So I was ripped off by a couple of guys that hadn't known me for long when I was transferred to the watch commander's office. Undersheriff T. R. Lawrukiewicz called me in and quizzed me on what they thought had taken place. It was about more than the dog, they thought. I told Tom what actually had taken place, and it ended then and there; for them it didn't work out.

A word to the wise: Ya have to learn to cover your ass, especially from those that are envious, jealous, or just want your job, or those that might want you to leave the organization, and over the years I had a few of those. Ya learn to cover your ass. Something most people don't realize is that when the drug squad had the shakeup, I was for one reason on the sheriff's shit list, I asked him several times what it was about but he wouldn't tell me, denied it. He was looking for something all the time, so I had to cross each and every *t* and dot each and every i, OK, no problem. Fellow deputies would ask, "What did you do to him?" For those that paid attention, it was obvious that he was on my case. This went on for a few years and ended for the most part after I was promoted to lieutenant.

Some of us did not want to be in the watch commanders office including me but you went where you were assigned and did the job. My two-week watch commander training period was under a lieutenant also assigned to the watch commander. I now had another training officer after fifteen years on the job. By his own admission, Carl Foster was an animal of sorts. His antics in those days, while humorous for some, would now get the sheriff and others sued in a heartbeat for sexual harassment or just plain and simple harassment. It wasn't that way twenty-six years ago, and I was no angel either. Hard to believe, isn't it? Nowadays most folks, it seems, don't have a sense of humor. Carl meant well, and he loved to tease some of the deputies, and tease them he did. Some didn't mind, some did. His name calling, while not sexually orientated or vulgar, was sometimes off color and was certainly not gentlemanly even then, but some just laughed at him and themselves. Cops need a good laugh much of the time. So laugh we did, some of us.

To say that Carl was not thoughtful of others would be a stretch. He was a great guy and a friend, loyal to the sheriff and he was recommended and sponsored by my dad. Now, there's a few stories I can share but not all. One evening Carl was in one of the back offices with a female deputy, doing what I don't know, but his wife, Shirley came in and asked me, "Where's Carl?" I told her, "He's back there in the undersheriff's office, go on back." I thought no more about this until "Mrs. Foster came out, red faced and tight jawed, looking straight ahead, and exited the building. Soon after that Carl came out, the deputy he was "counseling" went back to her post, and he sat down. It was quiet for a few minutes. He was thinking, and then he said, "Hayes, from now on if my wife comes in, call me. Don't send her back to me. Call me." To this day, I don't know what was going on other than being in an office late at night, one on one with a female deputy, but the wife certainly didn't like what she saw, whatever that was. I just laughed at the comedy of the whole thing; I guess it was one of those things where ya just had to be there.

As I said, one thing Carl did with regularity was to grab coworkers in awkward places, and again some didn't care and others did; some male and female deputies enjoyed the grab-assing around. One evening the midnight nurse (who was all of five feet tall and ninety pounds) arrived for work and came in my office to chat. We were friends, and she was dating a good friend of mine. Carl grabbed her in one of his token manners (not sexual in nature), and she went ballistic! She'd warned him before. She was tight jawed, and her skin color was maroon, and she was in his face (as much as a five-foot-tall woman can get in the face of a guy who's six foot two), screaming at him, wagging her finger in his face, and just ripping him up one side and down the other. I just sat and watched. It had been a long time coming, in my opinion, and when she left, I said nothing. Another very quiet moment with Carl, and then he said, "She's crazy." It was still all quiet. I said nothing, and he looked at me and said, "She's crazy." After a pause, he added, "What do you think, Hayes?"

I said, "Carl, do you really want to know what I think?" He said yes, so I said, "Some of these people, including me, but especially some of the women, don't like you screwing with them, and I think you had better become aware of that before it's too late. Additionally, they don't appreciate you calling them heifers!"

To Carl, they were all heifers. That was the end of that conversation, but I don't think he ever messed with that little nurse again. After that we were all still friends, still are. Sometimes ya just have to tell it like it is. I've never had a problem with that.

So now my training period was over and I was on my own again.

Oh hey, that reminds me of another story about Carl, who farted...a lot...really a lot, you know, vocally passing gas, in baritone. It didn't matter who was around him, another cop, a citizen, one of the male or female civilian employees, it just didn't matter. As I say, this guy was an animal. Once you entered the courthouse through the sheriff's entrance, there was a counter that separated the staff from citizens. I saw Carl up at the counter taking a report from some folks. I was getting ready to go off duty. The report was finished, and the folks left. Carl came to me and said, "Hayes, I have to leave. I have to go home!"

"What?" I said.

"I have to go home. I'll be right back."

"Why?" I said.

Looking a bit sheepish, he said, "I thought I needed to fart, but I shit. I have to go home to shower and change clothes."

Being my normal, caring, sympathetic self, I said with a grin, "OK," and then I just busted out laughing. I know this happens to some older folks on occasion, but this guy wasn't that old. I never let him forget it, but with him, there was always something.

Carl's thing with me was grabbing me on the ribs on my right side, and I had become quite tired of it. I was standing at the counter one evening, and once again I was grabbed at the ribs, so I swung my elbow in a back motion and hit him in the ribs. I heard a loud groan, and turning around, I saw, whoops, it wasn't Carl; it was another deputy. I just couldn't help laughing, and knowing the situation, he laughed as well after he caught his breath.

Kansas Fire and Police (KP&F) was a good retirement, so when I got to the point that I was working for nothing, I chose retirement. It turned out that if I retired, money saved on clothes, travel, food, equipment, plus my monthly check, was more than I'd make if I was still working, so it just didn't compute to stay on. I had other things I wanted to do in this life, so I retired in 1993 at the age of fifty-one after twenty-nine years of service. My wife was happy for me but pissed at the same time because she had to keep working for years (as an RN) after I retired. She worked, and I played, but I didn't gloat…much.

Chapter 48

"Well, It's Johnson County, Missouri, of Course!"

*B*eing the assigned watch commander is a lot different than being out in a patrol car, answering calls or looking for bad guys, watch commander was all management duties at the time. Initially, I was a sergeant, then after a year or so, I was promoted to lieutenant.

In addition to being watch commander, I was also put in charge of the records division, which was next to my office. When I was watch commander, there were times in which there was excitement and interesting and funny things happening, and sometimes not. You could make it what you wanted it to be, to a certain extent, at times it was boring as hell. Deputy Johnny Boase, besides being our aide de camp on evening shift, was a good friend. All agreed that he was great help, and he had the respect of all of us. We had some good times and some bad times as far as incidents go. We fielded citizen complaints as we received them as well as telephone calls that came to my office. I had other duties, so as far as taking reports, I would assign duties, and when Johnny was there, he carried the ball much of the time. He did it for everyone—it was what he wanted—and it left me free to handle other tasks.

One evening shift, a guy came into the office for something, and Johnny found out that there was a warrant for this guy (we checked *everyone* for wants and warrants). Johnny was trying to get the guy to the jail elevator to take him up to be booked, but the guy wasn't buying it. He was pissed and was getting in John's face, being abusive, arguing, resisting, borderline combative, and it was at the point where we needed to end it before it got worse. I stepped out of my office as he was badmouthing John and asked (as if I didn't know), "What's going on here?"

The guy said, "He thinks he's gonna put me in jail, and it ain't gonna happen."

I looked at John, winked, and said, "Let me take care of this gentleman, John. Step into my office, sir, where we can talk about this privately."

He was willing to do that, but unknown to him, we were all in front of the door that took arrestees to the jail elevator, and in we went. As we went in, that heavy steel door slammed with a *BANG!* And when the elevator door opened, there was nowhere else to go. In we stepped, and the guy now knew there was only one place he was going, and that was up. That was where the jail was, and he knew it. Knowing he was had, he realized he'd best calm down, and he did. I could hear John laughing so hard that I thought he was going to wet himself. When I came back down from the jail, he just laughed and shook his head. This was a story he told others for years after that, but we had more to come.

Another night on midnights, I was sitting there minding my own business when I got this telephone call. That's what I did, answered the telephone when the call came into my office. It was a complaint from a woman who was absolutely going ballistic. I couldn't get a word in edgeways. She was going on and on so vehemently, cussing me out, cussing the sheriff, cussing the sheriff's department, cussing the officer who her complaint was about, saying she was going to not only get his job, but she was going to get my job and then make sure the sheriff wasn't re-elected, and then she was going to sue all of us. I finally realized that she was talking about the wrong county sheriff's office, and as a matter of fact, she was talking to the wrong state. I never knew what her complaint was about, but when I was finally able to speak, I said, "Mrs. Smith, do you know who you are talking to?"

She said, "Yes, I'm talking to the goddamn Johnson County Sheriff's Office!"

I said, "Mrs. Smith, what state is your Johnson County Sheriff's Office in?"

She said, "Well, Missouri, of course."

I said, "Mrs. Smith, you are talking to the watch commander in the Johnson County, *Kansas*, Sheriff's Office."

She said, "Ooohhhhh."

I then heard a loud click as she hung up, most likely a bit embarrassed. I was laughing my ass off. There was another strange and funny story to tell. I'm thinkin, look out Johnson County, Missouri, here she comes!

You hear these stories about cops killing or wounding a woman or a kid in self-defense, and don't kid yourself: women and kids *can* hurt or kill you. At my department, no one was ever killed by a woman, but there were a few incidents where a woman injured a deputy and put him in a hospital. Here's one I had on what had been yet another peaceful night in the watch commander's office. Johnnie had gone home for the night, and I was alone and really really scared as usual on midnights. An average-looking woman, slender and around five foot nine, came in, visibly upset, and she wanted to make a phone call, so I let her use a telephone. I allowed her to come through my office to a secretary's desk, where she made her call while I stood near her. She hung up and with the pencil she had in her hand, reeled back and tried to stab me, for what reason, I never knew. I was trying to help her out, I thought, and all of a sudden she wanted to stab me? So, I was fighting her off, holding her arm with the pencil, and at the same time calling the jail to send someone down to help me restrain this crazy woman. In retrospect, I should have just smacked her, but I didn't. I just held her back and down, hoping to keep from being stabbed. My help arrived, and the woman was put in a straitjacket and then transported to a mental health facility by one of my detectives. End of story.

There are motorcycle accidents, bicycle accidents, and accidents of any nature whereby a person experiences "road rash." It's something that we snicker about, especially if it hasn't ever happened to us. Well, I don't snicker anymore, because it has happened to me in several bicycle wrecks since then, and it's no longer funny to me; it can be very serious and painful, as I have found out. I was so "rashed up" on my left side one time that I could hardly move, and painkillers didn't help much.

That brings me up to an incident when a young man came in one evening to get some accident records information from an accident he had had earlier in the day. His mother was assisting him, as he could hardly walk. His whole body was rashed up, at least the parts I could see exposed by his shorts and a sleeveless T-shirt. He had road rash on every visible part of his body. It hurt me just to look at him, and I hadn't experienced this yet. He was on his motorcycle north of town when a deer ran out onto the highway. A deer strike on a motorcycle…ouch! So, here's a bit of advice: If a deer runs out in front of you, the action you take will be up to you at the time, but recommendations are that you do not try to take evasive action, as the accident can be worse. A rollover or something more intense may happen, as in the case of a friend of mine. He and a carload of buddies were coming back from a hunting trip, a deer ran out, and he tried to swerve to miss it, losing control and rolling in a ditch. His comment was, "If that ever happens again, I'll hit it head on." So hit the poor thing head on, but know this. If you do that, it may land inside with you. Large animals have crashed through car windshields, causing injuries, and in some instances, the driver or occupant's death. If a deer strike ever happens, it's your call, but be aware that they are out there in some areas, especially unincorporated areas, sometimes in herds, especially during the rut, the mating season. The actions of a deer are so similar in nature to a rabbit or squirrel—just as quick, but so much larger.

I didn't work this particular accident, but another deputy, a friend of mine, did. A horse was hit and came into the vehicle's windshield. I don't recall the exact outcome, but I do remember that it caused serious injuries to the occupants, and it seems to me that it may have killed one of them. I just don't remember for sure; it was years ago.

Chapter 49

First You're Married? And Then You're Not?

When I transferred to the watch commander's office, as I have said, I thought my interesting and exciting days were over. Silly me. Here's another laugher, certainly not for the poor lady involved, but it is another story to tell. I did feel sorry for her and her dilemma, and the "groom" had to be a real asshole.

On a late evening shift, it was all pretty quiet, so Johnny Boase and I were kicked back for a change, and in came this couple. They wanted to get married. I told them that there was no judge available, but they were adamant; they just had to tie the knot that night, and they would pay any price to "git 'er done."

Well, if there was a serious circumstance, the watch commander could call a judge, a DA, or anyone else in county government after hours, so I called a judge, Judge Janette Sheldon. I told her the situation, and while I was talking to her, the couple was sitting, laughing a lot, smiling a lot, holding hands, hugging, and kissing. They really needed to get a room, but for now we were on hold. A room? Probably did, probably would, but only if I could get a judge to come in to marry them. I suspected that was the deal: marry me, and then we can…I told Judge Sheldon what was going on, but she was busy. Finally she said, "I'm hanging wallpaper. Tell them if they want to give me two hundred bucks to pay for my wallpaper and get me two witnesses, I'll come in." You see, even if you get married in the courthouse, you have to pay the judge a fee. That's just the way it is unless said judge is feeling generous at the time; at times some did, and some didn't.

This couple agreed to pay her fee, so the judge was on her way. Courthouse weddings are performed at all hours when a judge is available. They're usually prearranged, but as it goes, sometimes they will come in after hours to do the deed. By the time the judge got to my office, Johnny Boase had gone home, so I had to arrange for witnesses to the marriage. Two maintenance workers were called on, that was the norm during courthouse closing hours, as they were easy to call on if no one else was available, and they enjoyed it since it gave them a break. So, the judge arrived, the couple got married, and everyone was happy, it seemed. The happy newlyweds went skipping out the door holding hands, kissing each other, hugging each other, and it was obvious where this was headed. They needed to get a room fast! We are all so happy for them, aren't we? I almost needed a room for myself.

OK, so now, fast-forward a month, five weeks or so. In came this lady again after hours—you know, the one I got the judge for and who we all got married off. She said, "I have a problem."

"What is it?" I said.

"I need to see the judge that married us."

"Why?" I said.

She said, "I haven't seen my husband since the day after we were married. He left for Wichita and hasn't come back. He won't return my calls, and I can't find him."

I was thinking, my God, that was a lot of trouble to go through for some tail, but I again called Judge Sheldon, who by now was done hanging wallpaper, and she wasn't coming in that night for anything. She said, "Tell her to come to my office tomorrow, and we will talk about it." I did, and the lady left. Judge Sheldon and I snickered on this one for some time, not at the lady but at the unfortunate situation. Who could forget it?

On my watch commander shifts, the Robert Post family came into my office, all of them two or three times. Robert Post and other family members were begging for someone to help them. They were concerned that the ex-son-in-law Daniel Crump was a violent threat to their daughter and their family. "He is crazy," Robert said. They all agreed, and I couldn't disagree. They had been to the Olathe Police Department several times and had received no help, so they started coming to the sheriff's office. Crump had already been interviewed a couple times, and at the time there was nothing he could be held on. I and others listened to their concerns, but my department was no different. Although it was an Olathe case, if there had been anything we could have done, we would have. Ya can't arrest someone for what you think they might do unless you have concrete evidence of a crime that is being committed or going to be committed. We just didn't have that proof. I had no idea what this little dirt bag Crump was capable of. I wanted so badly to tell Mr. Post to get a gun and kill the little bastard. Although I suggested that he arm himself if he had not already done so but there was no way that would help in this incident.

The rest is history. Daniel Crump put dynamite in a gift-wrapped box with a motion timer of sorts, placed it on the hood of a car in the driveway, and left. Looking like a gift for someone's birthday, the box was picked up and taken in the house. It blew apart the entire house, killing all occupants except for David Post, Daniel Crump's baby boy. Robert Post, fifty-one; his wife, Norma Jeanne Post, forty-seven; sons Richard Post, twenty-one, and James "Bobo" Post, ten; and daughters Diane Post Crump, nineteen, and Susan Post, twenty, were all killed on September 20, 1980. Other family members that were away at the time survived.

I am still to this day haunted by this case. What else could I have done? What else could we have done? As it stands, nothing at the time. I have been to Daniel Crump's parole hearings and testified against his release, and I will continue going to testify until the day he's dead or I'm gone. What was the baby is now a young man who introduced himself to me at the last parole hearing. He thanked me for coming to testify on behalf of keeping his father where he belongs, in prison.

Again, the Johnson County Courthouse is in the city of Olathe. When an incident happens in or around the courthouse, it is a city case, and that was usually welcomed by yours truly. I was sitting at my desk when this guy came to the doors, leaning against the doors and windows and bleeding profusely. He was drunk as a skunk, and all he could do was moan. Besides being in so much pain, he was simply bleeding all over the place. Except for Johnny Boase being our crash dummy years ago, I didn't have a lot of sympathy for drunks of any origin. Still don't; it's a self-induced event. I had dispatchers call city police and med act, and I gave the guy what aid I could. Blood was all over the front-door glass, inside and out, and the floors, and when city officers arrived, I cheerfully turned the entire situation over to them and called maintenance to clean up the mess; that's what they do.

The paperwork on anyone brought to be jailed had to be screened by the watch commander before the prisoner was taken to the jail making sure he or she could be booked without any problems or incidents. Mainly it was to see if it was a good arrest, or if there were any injuries to the prospective inmate or other extenuating circumstance, whether it be by a county, state, or city officer, bondsman, or otherwise. If a prisoner was booked and later was injured and taken to the hospital, the hospital billed the county, and the cost was on the taxpayer—you and me. But if prisoners went to the hospital before booking, the price would be between them and the hospital.

On an early midnight shift, a couple of bondsmen brought in this guy for a charge of failure to appear on their bond. He appeared to have been beaten up. This happens sometimes when you resist arrest but that wasn't the case as I learned later, he had banged his head against a concrete wall causing injury to himself in the Shawnee Police Department. One of the bondsman was Jack Hartman who I have known for years. I told Jack that this booking wasn't gonna happen until this guy was examined at a hospital and returned with a hospital release. Then I would allow his booking into our jail, Jack was always cooperative so off they went. In my opinion, we had some pretty good guys that were bondsmen, and I got along with all of them. Even the one that was arrested with the Arizona boys until he went to the other side.

So, the bondsman took this guy to the hospital, and he was examined, released, and returned to the jail. Having a hospital release, I now allowed them to take him up to be booked. At this time he was a petty criminal, although he had been convicted for murder as a juvenile. He was serial killer Richard Grissom.

Chapter 50

"Ed, I've Been Raped!"

For the rest of my career, I still commanded the underwater rescue and recovery unit, until it was disbanded around 1990. The last dive we made was during the winter in a frozen retaining pond toward the south end of the New Century Airpark. In the late evening or early morning hours, a lady had lost control on the icy road and went off the road, through a field, and onto the icy pond. The ice was not thick enough to hold up the car's weight, and it broke, collapsed, and her car sank with her in it. Early the next morning, a passing motorist saw tire tracks going to the pond, and a small portion of the top of the car was visible above the ice. At the time the dive unit had nine equipped divers. Not all would or could respond to one incident, nor was it necessary. I had two divers on scene that went into the water under the ice and had immediate equipment failure because of air pockets. Once you get in, you stay in; if air hits your regulator, (for you non divers it's the breathing device) it can freeze, meaning no air, and theirs did. Now that left only me, so I suited up and went in. I made my way to the car and hooked up the tow-truck cable. With the cover of ice on this small retention pond, the water was very clear, but there were air pockets around the car from the passenger's compartment and trunk that remained under the ice. When I came up from the bumper to look inside the car, I was out of the water, in the air pocket, and *MY* regulator froze. It snuck up on me, and I was in trouble before I realized it. There's another one of my nine lives used up. For a moment I actually thought I might drown, but then I went back to survival mode: "Never, never, never give up!" (A Winston Churchill quote that has saved my butt on several occasions.)

I calmed down and got as deep a breath as I could manage and expelled enough water so I was able to have strength enough to get past the ice to open water. So out from under the ice I came and stood up. The top-water crew saw me sputtering as I came out of the water and nearly yanked me in half with the attached safety rope around my body. The car was towed out, and the victim was recovered. She had been unable to escape the submerged vehicle. She died from drowning because of a head injury, according to the coroner.

In a previous chapter, I mentioned convicted serial killer Richard Grissom, now residing in Lansing Prison for the rest of his life. IF there's ever a son of a bitch that deserved the death penalty for what he did to his victims it's Richard Grissom. He was the killer of three beautiful young Johnson County women. Going back to the seventies, I had met Grissom when I was living in apartments at Eighty-Seventh and Pflumm Road in Lenexa. He was working as maintenance, a painter, or both, living in a nearby apartment. I was acquainted with some of the ladies in the complex who were friends with him. That's how we first met. As far as I can remember, I never saw him socially, just in passing.

At the time, there were problems with prowlers and thefts around the apartment complex. Just after midnight one night, as I arrived home and was parking my car, I saw this movement in bushes across the parking lot. I had my flashlight, and as I walked toward the bushes, this shadow jumped and ran. I went after him but lost him in the darkness behind the apartments. So, I had seen the prowler, and I suspected he knew who I was by the way he lit out.

A couple of weeks later, around 2:00 a.m., I got this telephone call from a friend. She was crying and saying, "Ed, I've been raped!" I went to her apartment, and she told me where the rapist went, out her sliding glass door. I went out briefly and returned to take her to the hospital for emergency care. Before we left, I called Lenexa Police and told them what had happened and that we were on the way to KU Med Center. At the hospital, Lenexa detective sergeant Ellen Hanson (later Lenexa chief of police) arrived and got the entire story, and the rape kit was gathered for evidence.

It was summer and hot, so the lady had her ground-floor door open with the screen door closed, when she was awakened by this young black guy who entered via the sliding screen door, threatened her, raped her, and left. I have always suspected that Grissom was the prowler and also the rapist of this lady but probably will never know.

The next time I saw Grissom was the previously mentioned incident when I was watch commander and he was brought in, injured, by two bondsmen.

When the news of the missing young ladies came about around 1989, somewhere in the news Grissom was mentioned as a suspect, and the search was on. Grissom was then found driving one of his victim's cars in an apartment complex in Lawrence, Kansas, but he was not held at the time, the homicides were not known by the officer. Upon learning his status of suspect, LEOs then tried to make an arrest, but he eluded them when he jumped from the second-story balcony in that complex, ran, and escaped. He was later arrested at Dallas/Fort Worth International Airport.

During Grissom's trial, I was present nearly all the time for security reasons. He was taken several times to judge's chambers, along with the judge, defense attorneys, and prosecutors—no LEOs in chambers. Knowing that Grissom was very capable of jumping from second-floor balconies (as he had in Lawrence), I had to wonder if he could get through the windows in the judge's chambers even though he was shackled with leg irons. I knew that if he tried, it was doubtful that he would be stopped, so every time he was in chambers, I was outside the chamber windows two floors down. If he jumped, we would meet again. He didn't.

Grissom was convicted of three counts of first-degree murder, one count of aggravated kidnapping, four counts of robbery, two counts of aggravated burglary, and one count of misdemeanor theft. He appealed and lost and now resides in Lansing Prison, where he'll be for the rest of his life, we hope. In all, he received four life sentences. Grissom is suspected to have murdered an additional victim in Wichita, Kansas, and had been charged with murder and incarcerated when he was a juvenile. The bodies of the three Johnson County girls were never found, and Grissom won't talk. There are some pretty gruesome scenarios suspected in what this animal did to those girls he tortured and murdered.

When I was transferred out of the watch commander's office to staff services, I was also put in charge of courthouse security, such as it was at the time. Another deputy and I were sent to San Antonio, Texas, for a one-week seminar on courts and courthouse security. Present were LEOs, judges, and court personnel. This was in the early 1980s. When we returned, we made our reports. At the time only one judge, as I recall, cared about courthouse security with metal detectors, checking everyone who came in the doors for court or for whatever reason. So, the courthouse stayed wide open until 1988, at which time what they didn't think would ever happen,........ happened.

Chapter 51

"What Are You Gonna Do? Arrest Me?"

*B*y this time, I was liaison to all courthouse offices and personnel for the sheriff's office, so when something happened in or around the courthouse, employees usually called me. I knew nearly all courthouse employees either by name or sight, and most knew me. I was also liaison to the district attorney's Office of Protection from Abuse Division as paper work for protection orders started with the sheriff's office and I usually handled them personally. At the time the folks we worked with in the DA's office were very efficient and very dedicated to the people they served, and it wasn't always women being protected. Some of these cases were sad, some tragic, and some humorous. The one thing that I always stressed in these cases was that the term "protection" order is false. It is ONLY a piece of paper, and that document WILL NOT protect you if the person you are being "protected" from has ill intentions. If you need real protection, I suggest you get a gun and learn to use it!

Several things happened during this time period, and sadly what happened next involved a couple in court going through divorce hearings. The man became enraged enough that the judge in the case fearing, for her life, retreated to her chambers, closed the door, and hit the alarm. By the time deputies got there, the guy had left. It was not known if he had a gun in the courtroom, but either he did or he got one from his car, because he had a handgun. Here's another thing about protection orders. **If you have been served a protection order, you WILL lose possession of your weapons if you have any**. When this guy's ex-wife exited the courthouse with their twelve-year-old son, the guy walked up to her, shot her several times, and then he shot himself.

I'm in my office when I got a telephone call that there had been a shooting on the courthouse south lawn, the deputy caller said that he believed that Bondsman Jack Hartman was involved since he was very close to a victim. Several of my deputies and I that were present in the office went to the scene a half block away from the sheriff's office. It's funny, the deputy that called me didn't go to the scene which he could see from his office, he stayed put. By this time the judge, her bailiff, and other courthouse employees were all gathering around, too close, as this poor woman was taking her last breaths. Her sucking abdominal wounds told it all; she would not survive, and the husband was deceased, having put the gun to his chin and shooting himself. There was confusion around the crime scene as freaked-out witnesses and some LEOs thought that a bondsman at the scene, Richard Grissom's bondsman, was involved. He wasn't.

When my deputies arrived at the scene minutes later, I ordered the crowd that had assembled, with more coming, to stand back. Their distance to the female victim was just a few feet when I got there. The Olathe city police had not arrived. Some of these folks witnessed the shooting and were gasping, crying, and wringing their hands. They had never seen anything like this before. I ordered uniform officers to get ropes and rope off to protect the crime scene as they arrived.

Luckily the young son was spared. I met him about fifteen years later and didn't realize for several more years that he was the young son of the couple in this incident. One day my wife was telling me the story, and I finished it for her; she hadn't known that I was there. I have talked to the son at length since that time, and surprisingly, he's "well adjusted" when ya figure what he had gone through and witnessed. In spite of all of that, we had become friends.

We were working on my house one day, and I hadn't mentioned to him that I was at that crime scene. As I said, he was twelve years old at the time and didn't remember me or anyone being there other than the officer who had put him in his patrol car. I had been walking on eggs on this for some time but felt the time was right, so I asked the question, "Shaun, are you aware that I was the first officer on the scene when your father shot your mother?"

Shaun should have been a cop, because he said, "Oh? So, you have met my parents?" Now…that's a cop's style of black humor, and even I was a bit surprised at his response. He went on to tell me that his dad had attempted suicide several times, so this was not such a big surprise to him, other than the fact that his mother was murdered at the same time. Shaun is now married, has been for years, and he and his wife both have good jobs, a good life, and are really doing well.

New to Staff Services was another period of learning, along with jealousies, injured egos, and anger. The slings and arrows began once again. I had a couple of subordinates that felt they should have been promoted to my position, and I had a supervisor, Dick that didn't like me for personal reasons. At the time I was still lieutenant. One of my jealous, pissed-off subordinates turned some of the deputies against me. He was always a step behind me and he thought I'd gotten his job, and he was going to get even. You're one up on these kinds of people when you know what they are doing, and they fool only themselves. I also still had the other supervisor on my case.

The situation with Dick never changed until I was promoted to captain. Once I was his peer, he no longer had control over me. I only mention this because I don't care which cop shop you work at, you will probably have some of the same issues to experience at one time or another. This is especially true if you go by the book. Some don't like that, and they don't like honesty; it is a threat to some of them under you and over you.

Now in staff services I was out of uniform, back in a suit. A KCK attorney came into our offices, giving my ladies a hard time, and he proceeded to get on my case as well. I was brand new to the division at the time and was unable to help much other than to calm him down as much as I could. He left and later found out he was mistaken and out of line, and the next day he delivered a bouquet of flowers to the secretary he had given the most trouble, and he apologized to all of us. I invited him into my office to talk, and he saw the name plate on my desk, at which time he asked me, "Are you any relation to Captain Ed Hayes who worked at the Kansas City, Kansas, Police Department?" To which I proudly told him, "Yes, he was my grandfather." It turns out that he knew the entire family, had been classmate and real good friends with one of my aunts. How good? We never got into that. I don't know, but he was astonished at who I was and was very moved. After that we were good friends with no problems. He turned out to be a standup guy, in my opinion, because of how he handled his mistake with my staff, and he thought we were all OK too. He made it a point to tell our sheriff how great we were every time he saw him; some other attorneys were just the opposite.

Being a courthouse liaison, I made daily visits to different courthouse offices. One day I was in the county clerk's office when a smartass character stepped up to the counter and started giving one of the ladies hell over an issue. It had something to do about a payment of some sort, and the clerk was trying to "'splain" to him the process. She was just doing her job, and he wasn't buying it. I was standing near her and him. He was rude but not combative, so I just allowed him to let the rope on out until he got to a point to where this needed to end as he said, "So what are you going to do, arrest me?"

I stood there making eye contact and said, "Nope, she's not going to arrest you, but I will if you don't stand down and listen to reason. These ladies are just doing their job. They don't make the rules, they just do their job as required and described, and they don't deserve the BS you are giving them." He backed off real quick, apologized, and became very cooperative. We are now pals.

Chapter 52

Once a Misfit Leaves an Organization, Another Will Be Hired

to take his place! This works out nearly each and every time, and not just at the cop shop.

When I was promoted to lieutenant and later captain in staff services, I had male and female deputies and civilian subordinates in my divisions. Most were loyal and very capable employees, while some, but very few, were an absolute pain in the ass. We hear leaders say, "I never asked anyone to do anything I won't, don't, or didn't do." I went a bit further. My goal was for all employees to have the same work ethic as others in the divisions. If they didn't, it would be so noted in regularly scheduled efficiency ratings that had an effect on their pay scale, giving them a personal reason to excel. Some worked out, and some didn't. Some leave the division or the sheriff's office altogether to become someone else's problem.

When I assumed command of staff services, I had this one civilian employee that had the perfect job: she didn't do a lot, and she got away with it. For years she had only been required to work a couple of hours a day, unbeknownst to most. She was very competent in her work, but she had her former supervisors and the sheriff conned into thinking she was the only person that could do her job, not realizing the very few hours of the day it took. I had complaints from other employees, and what I saw was a person that was milking the system, so this person who had been a friend up to now soon became an enemy—it was her call.

The More People Who Despise You at the Time of Your Death, the More You Have Accomplished!

I required her to go to work, and she hated me for it. It wasn't easy, as there were still a few supervisors that didn't believe me and still backed her, including my captain. Instead of just having her do the job that took a couple hours of the day, I changed her job description to require her to do more work and gave her more assignments, which she resented. On the sheriff's time, she was no longer able to file her nails, talk on the telephone all day, or research her catalogs since she now had to perform like everyone else. This was sad and funny at the same time because within a short time she had been found out by most other commanders and the sheriff.

After that Undersheriff John Foster would walk by her desk grinning making comments about her position and she hated it. He loved to jab her, he was a big tease, her coworkers loved it because what they had been seeing for years and couldn't do anything about had been corrected.

I was working away at my desk doing stuff captains do one day, when my door slammed shut, and there she stood with her hands on her hips, jaw tightened, and red faced, screaming at me. She'd gone berserk! It seemed that she didn't agree with a decision that I had made, and she was going to take me to task. I looked at her and calmly told her to sit down. She did. I then told her to cool off and leave my office, and later she, I, and her immediate supervisor would talk. She later was invited in with her lieutenant, my subordinate, at which time she apologized, and even though she didn't like it, she did do her job after that. She hated me, for it but oh well. It's still there even after retirement. I saw her at a shopping center one day and spoke to her, and she pointed her nose at the sky and walked by, saying nothing. I smiled. There's a thing called administrative courage, and like it or not, sometimes ya have ta do what ya have to do. That's if you want to be successful in your job, your life, your own skin. Some do, and some don't.

When you are supervisor on any level, new problems and situations will exist, and a biggie is your subordinates' performances, attitude, and morale. Egos and hurt feelings fit in there somewhere as well. You have a choice. Do you want to be a good supervisor, a good coach with good results, or do you want to be friends? Friends you had may now become not so friendly under your command. If you do your job, some may become your enemy. As you have read, I had some as I did my job, and sometimes it was difficult.

Your department should have efficiency rating reports for all supervisors to complete on all subordinates. A meeting will follow for direction, praise or not and feedback. I had subordinates that were sergeants when I was a lieutenant and sergeants and lieutenants when I was captain. I did efficiency reports on them and they did efficiency reports on their subordinates. Their report then came to me for my approval or not. In doing an efficiency rating on a friend, how do you think it will go? The answer is that in some cases the supervisor will go lightly on his or her friend, and in doing this, they are not doing justice to the friend. It's the "country club" syndrome. Once you get into management, you will be better off not to party with your subordinates, for several reasons. If you want your subordinates to grow, to develop in their position, but you are not honest, how will that person know where and how to improve and grow?

I had a subordinate that just couldn't understand why he could not get a promotion; his main problem was that he tried to baffle everyone with bullshit. Ask him the time of day, and he would tell you how to build a watch! I coached him and I coached him, but he just wouldn't listen. He was never promoted above sergeant even though he was very competent in his job. I told him what he needed to do, how he needed to change, and I begged him to do so, but you can only do so much. He didn't like me for that, and the funny thing is that when I retired, his job became a lot less attractive because of circumstances in his position; he was transferred to permanent evenings. My supervisor wanted him to go to the evening shift, but I resisted, saying, "I need him on day shift. Give me another sergeant if you want one on evenings." We were left alone. I was allowed the freedom to run my divisions as I wanted, but after I retired, this guy's new boss evidently didn't, and it wasn't very long before he retired.

Now here's another one that came back to bite me in the ass. There was this detective that wasn't lazy; he just wouldn't do his job. He was very unhappy where he was at, and I wasn't happy with his performance. I counseled him, I coached him, and I told him, "You won't get a transfer as long as you do not do your job." Well, unbeknownst to me, his wife worked for my favorite commissioner, Bruce Craig, and Bruce, or someone in that commissioner's office, went to the sheriff, and the man was transferred to the division he wanted to be sent to. Politics works in strange ways, doesn't it? After that deal, I did a bit of research before I made another idle threat, but I did learn a lesson and found it a bit humorous at my expense.

Something else relating to administrative courage is accepting the responsibility of changes your bosses want. If they order you or suggest something and you agree or not, as far as anyone else is concerned, that order is from you. Two situations come to mind. One was that one of my subordinates was your stereotypical "heavy cop." He was neat and clean but seriously overweight. The statement made to me was that if he ever wanted another promotion, he had better lose some pounds. OK, so I told him this, and he went on a diet and successfully dropped to his weight and was promoted to lieutenant when I became captain. He kept if off until I retired, and he never knew that the order came from anyone else but me.

Another was when an hourly staff member, a lady who had been a very good friend of mine, was reduced in her classification. She got a position and salary reduction because of some mistakes that were made; I don't think they were her mistakes, but she got the blame. I did what I was told and this was painful for me, but it was done, and to this day I am no longer a family friend. They speak when I see them, but that's about it.

No! In Trouble over an Assist-an-Officer Call, really?

I've mentioned the guy, Dick, who didn't get to go to DEA when I did. It's a long story, but it begins when I was uniform patrol sergeant and he was a detective. We had this assist-the-officer call, a triple beeper, and when you get triple beeped, everyone goes. It's a two-issue situation: one is the protection of your fellow officer, and the other is that ya don't wanna miss anything happening that may be exciting. This was around 1968, and the call was at a small beer joint in what was at the time the "colored" side of town. Yep, we had that then, and this was their beer joint and it was rockin.

Other sheriff's deputies and I arrived, and the folks were raising hell inside this bar while the city officers at the scene were just standing around outside, apparently knowing not what to do. I was told what was going on. There was no cooperation from the bar owner, and unruly patrons were taunting the cops. "What can we do?"

I walked into the bar, unplugged the jukebox, and announced, "This bar is closed! Everyone out!"

You would have thought the building was on fire as they headed for the door. When I walked out to the street, Dick had a black kid pinned up against a car working him over—self-defense, I was hoping. Soon the kid was unarrested and released. I had no reason to think otherwise, so no problem here in my mind, but it was different when the sheriff got a phone call, a complaint, and he called me in for explanation. He did that a lot!

When the boss "invites" you to his office, you go, like it or not, and it's usually pretty serious when it's him and not your immediate supervisor. I went of course, not knowing why or what was coming, as usual, and he asked me, "What were we doing answering bar calls in the cities?"

I was thinking, "What the..." and my answer was, "From day one, Sheriff, we are trained to respond, and it's always been my understanding that when a triple beeper is transmitted, we all go. Was I wrong about that in our department, Sheriff?"

He looked down at his desk, was quiet for the moment, and replied, "It was an assist-the-officer call? I didn't know that." He didn't know the nature of the call, so I was OK on that, but then he wanted to know why Dick was beating up a kid on the black side of town.

I told him the kid was going after the detective, so he was restrained, the problem was defused, he was unrestrained, and there was no arrest. "I guess if the guy wants to make a big deal out of this, we can go arrest him and give him something to really complain about." So now we were OK on that, and I was excused, but I never knew what Dick dealt with in his meeting with the sheriff, or did he even have one? Did he think I ripped him off? Again I never knew.

I once told the sheriff in one of our heart-to-heart conversations, "I will not be a snitch on some of the petty things that go on in this department;

however, I will report things of importance or that are unlawful." This wasn't well accepted, but he knew where I was coming from; he knew it was my father's ethics. They had been good friends, so he knew my father well. On occasion, whether I liked it or not, I did what I had to do and made no secrets about it. Read on about the Teamsters.

As an administrator, you will have subordinates make attempts to tell you something petty in nature. That's gossip, and if you want snitches on the little stuff, it's your call. I would tell them before they got very far, "Do you *really* want me to know about this?" Usually they thought better of it.

Chapter 53

I Win the War

There was this other guy who was married and was messing around with a married civilian clerk. They were whispering sweet nothings over the telephone from her work station while he was out in the patrol car or off duty. At the time our sheriff frowned on these situations, even divorce but over the years there were others, some in command positions so ya never heard anything unless you were involved. Other than that, what's the problem with this, except being unfaithful to your spouse? IF someone is not faithful to his or her family, how can you trust them? So back to "sweet nothings" it seems that our dispatchers were listening to their calls and conversations. They thought it was funny, and they were laughing and talking about it.........a lot.......... big time. I told this guy about the situation just as a word to the wise before many others heard about it. He grinned and said it wasn't true; he denied and denied. I told him, "Personally I really don't give a shit." But I said, "it looks to me like the evidence is in, and if I were you, I would be more careful about talking on an eight-line telephone with lights." He still was in denial, at which time I told him "Look, I don't care. You have been warned. You can do what you want with this. I've told you, and I'm done with it. It doesn't go any further by me." And it didn't till now.

I didn't talk about this to anyone else, and it seemed to go away for whatever reason, except for the fact that both divorced their spouses and married each other. I really hated this deal because her husband was a friend of mine and a policeman. I never even talked to him about this deal. I just stayed out of it, and again.........no one gets shot, sometimes ya have to wonder why.

Now there's the DEA assignment that I got and Dick didn't, time for payback? I was still a lieutenant and I now had Dick as my immediate supervisor and he didn't want me in his divisions in the first place. Seems like everything goes around and comes back. In my mind, this gets humorous as well. I swear this guy helped my promotion to captain by the unintended actions and consequences toward me as a result of his actions, it backfired on him.

Here's the deal. He presented me with my biannual efficiency rating, (even lieutenants get the presentation) smiling, and it ain't good. What he presented to me was the only rating in my entire career that was not excellent. I had never received negative reports in my ratings from anyone, and I had never felt the need to make any comments on my ratings from any supervisor. This one was different, and I didn't hold back since many of the grades and ratings were just average, in my opinion I wasn't average so I wrote comments.

After reading the ratings and my comments, the sheriff "invited" both of us to his office for discussion. I sure spent a lot of time in that sheriff's office during my career, but it always seemed to end up well for me, it really did. Several times he thought he had me, but it just didn't work out. For much of my tenure in the watch commander's office, I was in the shithouse. Some including me thought the sheriff wanted me gone over the shakeup in the narcotics division; somehow he blamed me for what went wrong. I wasn't about to give in to him and quit as others did when in my position, and I didn't. What went wrong was that we had a bunch of prima donnas that we were trying to control, and they didn't like it.

So here we go. I welcomed this next meeting about my efficiency rating. I was really looking forward to it. I was calm and cool because I was right and I knew it; Dick was not, and he knew it. He sat there wringing his hands and fingers, sweat on his lip, and we three chatted. I presented my case, I was nice, to the point, and although I could have said a lot more, I didn't. He was soon done making his case, and so was I. The sheriff then says, "OK, Dick, you're excused, you can go." Dick left, somewhat relieved that his part of this was finished.

The sheriff then told me, "Ed, I cannot reverse a report from one of my captains, but I want you to know that I think, I know you are doing one hell of a good job, and I appreciate it." He continued, "And I want you to know that this rating will never hurt you."

So now I have not only won the battle, I have won the war, and that made me feel better, but I still had this damn thing in my personnel file that was mainly forgotten until promotions for captain came around again, and it wasn't very long. In the meantime, I was left alone by Dick.

I was invited before the civil service board for my promotion interview for the captain's position. Having been a deputy for twenty-four years, I knew some of the board members; I had been there before. One of them, Andy, asked me about the efficiency report signed by Dick, whom he knew as well. "Explain to us this average efficiency rating, Ed."

I didn't flinch. I was ready for this, and I kept my reply simple: "Well Andy, here's the deal, with this supervisor there is a personality conflict. I cannot tell you folks what it is all about because some of it is personal in nature for him and could be embarrassing but I can tell you about the interview he and I had with the sheriff." I repeated what the sheriff told me after Dick had left the office, "I think you are doing a hell of a good job, Ed, and this rating will not hurt you." I went on to say further, "That's it, and that is all I will say on the matter." I was thanked and dismissed, and that was apparently enough. I was soon promoted to captain with their recommendations. As I say, I won the war, Dick was now once again one of my peers. He could no longer screw with me, and I was left alone by everyone else up to the day I retired. Some say when Dick retired he was in conflict with the sheriff so what goes around comes around doesn't it? I think in the end that the sheriff finally figured out that some of these guys he trusted were playing him, that's speculation on my part and from what I have heard. Here's something you need to know and understand, that sheriff's department and that police department doesn't belong to anyone but you and me. This concerns all of us, we need to pay attention and learn what they do, what are their jobs by states statute and are they doing it right? IF not do your job!

Some sheriffs are scared to death of being sued, and as lieutenant and captain the divisions under my command were subject to just that if someone screwed up. I ran it right, and the sheriff knew it, I had his back, and he now had mine.

On another occasion, I had a deputy that was lazier than hell and I couldn't do anything about it until I had a whole stack of incidents, almost any one of which could have gotten him fired. I coached him, his lieutenant coached him, his sergeant coached him, and he was just this poor guy we were picking on. Since he was black, the sheriff was fearful of a lawsuit. So I had this stack of complaints (nine inches high) and took them to the sheriff. "It's time, Sheriff," I said. Well, apparently the sheriff didn't think I could handle it by myself, so he had one of his aforementioned "pets" sit in on the dismissal interview. I didn't trust or respect this "pet" because of what he was—not one to be trusted but I had no choice. We were going over the complaints on this guy, and we were about done when the guy says, "I have a question for you, Barney. I heard they made you a sergeant, and you couldn't even pass the written sergeants test. Is that true?"

Well, it was, and it was common knowledge and ya coulda heard a pin drop. It was like the air got sucked out of the room, and I coulda fainted from the lack of oxygen. It was absolutely true, even though I had to keep the guy that was a million dollar moment. Many upper-and lower-ranking deputies knew it was a fact. We didn't like it, we knew about it, it's what is called politics. We all had to pass the test, but he didn't, the only one and that's how tight some of the snitches in that office were with that sheriff. Other sheriffs? I don't know about the rest. The end result was that this guy, the one we were about to fire, didn't get fired for obvious reasons, and that came back to haunt us later.

Chapter 54

Tony Lane

About Orders of Protection and Restraining Orders

I have mentioned orders of protection in the past, but in my opinion, there isn't enough said about this court order to potentially keep danger away from persons who feel threatened. It is just a piece of paper, and it won't protect you if someone wants to harm you. I have said in the past, if you feel truly threatened, get a gun and learn to use it. Get a shotgun if you don't feel competent with a handgun. I tell anyone who asks, a shotgun is the best protection you can get for home defense, in my opinion, since hand grenades and mantraps are illegal. When bad guys hear you shuck a shell into the shotgun magazine, they seem to respond positively in one way or the other unless they are absolutely crazy or on drugs, some run. It's psychological; most understand.

If you are fearful of someone or for someone in your family or otherwise, do your homework. If you don't know what to do, call the police, the district attorney's office, or your lawyer for help. Don't delay. If you are in immediate danger, get out and away from the threat; go to a safe place. There are safe houses that are available places to stay, and the DA's office, law enforcement, and others can help you with that accommodation. There are many cases of victims who had an order of protection filed and were killed anyway. A mentally distraught or suicidal person doesn't care anything about a piece of paper or court order meant to protect anyone. ***The emotions of people under stress cause some humans to kill or injure others.***

Several incidents I experienced in Johnson County have been mentioned, and a couple of others come to mind. One was a lady who moved from Saint Louis to get away from her former boyfriend, but he found her, followed her to Johnson County, so she came into my office to get an order. After all of the paper work was finished and the order was filed, she asked me to accompany her to her car, which I did. She was shaking in fear. I never heard anything back from her, so it was presumed that the person finally left her alone. Others were the Post family and the incident on the courthouse south lawn. I don't recall if there was an order issued on either one.

A local media personality came in one day very visibly upset and fearing for his life because of his wife's brothers who had threatened him and beat him up. It was obvious that he was beaten and bruised, and he was sure they were going to do it again. So as you can see, it's not only women who ask for an order of protection or a restraining order.

Tony Lane

Joseph F. (Tony) Lane's career began at the Johnson County, Kansas, Sheriff's Department. He was one of those guys who wanted more, but what he really wanted was always in law enforcement. He was hired by the Lakewood, Colorado, Police Department when he resigned from our sheriff's office. Tony was the only one from the JCSO that I remember who went to Lakewood, but there were several other Johnson County City LEOs that saw an advantage in Lakewood, which at the time had a new "concept." Lakewood's officers wore blazers instead of uniforms. Many thought that was pretty cool, so Lakewood had many applicants.

Following his tenure at Lakewood, Tony went to Great Bend, Kansas, as police chief for a few years and then on to Rangely, Colorado, for yet another chief's job. Ya see where this is going with some guys? Well, many were not as successful as Lane since he was always "stepping up" instead of screwing up. In 1987 Tony left Rangely after being hired once again as the police chief of the small town of Castle Rock, Colorado, population eight thousand, with a department of twenty officers. By the time Tony retired after twenty-four years, that department had seventy-five officers, a new police department quarters, with a population of seventy-five thousand citizens.

Besides being police chief, Lane had become an established wildlife photographer and writer, and I am told he had bit parts in several movies filmed locally in Colorado.

As chief of police, Tony Lane was interviewed by Mike Wallace of the *60 minutes* TV program over a Castle Rock case in which a man had kidnapped and killed his three children in 1999. The man's wife at the time had alerted and asked the Castle Rock police to find and arrest her estranged husband, Simon Gonzales, who was under a court order to stay one hundred yards away from the house; he didn't. He had taken his children, ages seven, nine, and ten, as they played outside and later called his wife to tell her that he had the girls in Denver. Later that day he drove to the police department parking lot, firing his weapon, and was killed by the police in self-defense. It was a suicide-by-cop incident. He had murdered his children. They were found dead in the back of his truck.

I watched that interview in which Wallace tried to put Castle Rock and its officers in a bad light "for failing to act," as Wallace suggested. He was making every attempt at the "gotcha questions." And Wallace was really making an attempt to put Chief Lane on the spot, but he was outmatched. He didn't know Lane like I do. Tony let him go on for a few minutes and then responded, "Well Mike, if we had a crystal ball in which to see what people will do, if we did, this would have turned out differently, wouldn't it?" That was pretty much the end of that interview because Wallace knew he was toast. The bad light he was trying to shine on the police had failed. That interview was in 2005, the year before the Gonzales lawsuit was settled. You can see that interview by going to *60 Minutes* All Access, I am told.

The fact is that the public and especially some media like to bash the police when something as tragic as this happens, but it's not the fault of anyone in the cop shop; they do what they can by law. Sadly, in cases such as this, people do what they do, and we respond in whatever way we can at the time.

In Denver the lawsuit was filed by Ms. Gonzales, suing the city and the Castle Rock Police Department. The case eventually went to the Supreme Court, ruled as follows in June of 2006: ***"the Police do not have a constitutional duty to protect someone."***

That doesn't mean that we won't. Those in law enforcement all feel badly, very bad, when tragedies happen, but until there are "crystal balls," as Chief Lane fired back at Wallace, nothing will change. People do what they do, and law enforcement officers respond as needed and do what they have to do. As we know, "when a crime is committed, initially the police get only the ending of the story. From there begins the rest of the story, the beginning, and the middle." I was reminded of this when I heard a similar quote on television a while back. It's what we all know on the job, and it's a fact.

Everyone liked Tony, he was a real trip, and we all hated to see him leave when he did. While at JCSO, he worked in the uniform division.

Some of his shenanigans were comical. We all laughed then and still do. It wasn't uncommon for him to pick up his relief holding a huge snake in one hand and arm and the steering wheel with the other. He loved snakes, especially big snakes. On one occasion a snake got away from him, and under the seat it went. They almost never got it out because it was all coiled up in the seat frame. How about the hay bales for his animals in the trunk and rear seats of the patrol car? Now that was all funny! It was a good thing that we always had four-door cruisers. Picture of Tony and me in the early years, 1966.

Chapter 55

Chatty Cathy

This is a guy I am proud of, his accomplishments as an LEO are outstanding, his history goes waaaay back to 1970. When the Johnson County Community college opened in the fall of 1969, it began in an older beautiful stone grade school building in Merriam, Kansas. Ju Co as it's called had a very good enrollment the very first year of over 1200 students.

Sheriff Allenbrand had this wild idea that college would make better cops and those already in our department wanting promotions had to be working on a college degree or already have one. College educated cops are better? This may be true in some cases but experience tells me the best cops are those with street smarts and common sense. I'll go further and say I don't even think college makes a better administrator, chief or sheriff.

I've seen some real disappointments.

The sheriff's office hired several people during that time with a huge education that couldn't tie their shoes and didn't work out. Over the years many college students and graduates have been hired who made very good officers, some excellent. Now college is preferred in most departments, with a college degree your foot is in the door...

So here we are, me included, going to college. Like high school I didn't like it, I've already told you I was the kid that watched the clock on the wall. Getting out of high school was like a prison release for me, like my divorce. My college curriculum was Pud I and Pud II and I finally lasted long enough to get a masters degree....Naw, I'm just shitting you, my degree was as low as they go but it did allow me to get promotions.

In my classes there were mostly LEO's since it was Administration of Justice so I knew many of my classmates. There was this one little skinny kid with a mouth like a jaybird who obviously seemed to hate cops and he wasn't bashful about it. He questioned what cops do, why they do it and was critical every step of the way and he was good at bashing current LEO events. At first he was pissing some of us off but after a while we were laughing at and with him. So this went on for the entire semester, school was out, no one killed him and some of us actually liked him, giving him the moniker

"Chatty Cathy" after the children's doll. So now I have my first year of college under my belt and a short time after that it becomes "holy shit," Chatty Cathy **IS HIRED** by the sheriff's office! I couldn't believe it!

Well, Chatty Cathy AKA Craig Hill is assigned to the dispatch office and he's a good one, most everyone now is liking him. When ya like someone ya play jokes on them don't cha. Well, we did, joke after joke after joke so here's some examples. When you looked out the dispatchers window the parking lot was below and Craig loved his

Mustangs, a new one every year it seemed. So he's working in dispatch and we jack his car up, just the rear wheels barely off the pavement. He gets off work gets in his car and we are all watching as he starts the car, wheels are spinning, he gets out with this puzzled look, sees what is going on and looks up to the windows and doors knowing that "we gotcha." And what assholes we were, no one went out to help him get the car off the blocks. Some did go out and watch and tease as he was getting the car off the blocks.

Next...Like I have told you, if you are a dispatcher and a good one, everyone in the county knows you. On an evening shift as officers from throughout the county arrive to drop off their prisoners at the jail none are surprised to see Craig sitting in an office chair handcuffed to the jail elevator bars in the corner. We are able to watch the show via the jail elevator camera. This went on for a couple of hours until someone, maybe even me went out and uncuffed him. It had to be very lonely sitting in that elevator until the next officer arrived, he was begging them to let him go and no one would. EVERYONE alive still laughs about that one.

Now here is my favorite, I am picking Craig up; he's going to work a shift with me on his day off. I'm sitting in the patrol car when his wife walks out with him to get in her car, I turn on the siren when she's in front of my patrol car and of course she jumps, we all laugh and go on our way. A few days later Craig calls me, says "I'm sure glad you hit that siren because Susan *WAS LATE*."

No wait! I forgot this. IF you haven't seen some of the movies that I have seen in regards to the orneriness of cops this will make a believer out of you. When they got married we did the shivereeeeee thing, you know, the redneck event where you vandalize or destroy someone's house and contents? With the help of Craig's sister in law and coconspirator who was *supposed* to be watching the house while they were off on their honeymoon, had a key. So we enter the house, put their water soaked underwear in the freezer, moved furniture around, some in the basement, put closet doors on bath room doors, bathroom doors on the bedrooms. We put Jell-O in the toilet, short sheeted the bed which was put in the basement, put the mattress in the shower, removed all the light bulbs, put stickers simulating bullet holes on the sliding glass doors. We put bird seed in all the sheets, removed the telephone earpiece, put honey on the outside of the ear piece which ruined Susan's hair when she tried to call her father for help. The key to the house was left on the kitchen table with the lyrics by our buddy and fellow officer, Don Hostmyer, "I got a brand new roller skate you got a brand new key" plus the big welcome home sign. Susan was very pissed off until she found out that the "bullet holes" were not real but that was a month or so later. This was brutal and we deserved a huge payback but who could beat that, put a family and a family of cops together and they go to work. At Hills retirement celebration I shared these stories, of course it made the folks laugh.

And let's not forget the mannequin in his bed covered up, he gets home after a midnight shift dog tired, goes into the bedroom and sees this human sized lump under the covers that I had placed there overnight , Craig says he almost shot the mannequin.

Besides being a good dispatcher Craig was eager to learn, he was hooked since that college class with all the cops. He later told me that he enrolled in that class since he was interested in law enforcement and "holly crap," found out that he was in a room full of cops. We had become friends so he comes out a lot and rides with me on his off hours. He also rides with other sergeants since they go on almost every call so he's learning like I did, from seasoned street cops and his goal is to be a street cop or a detective, the sky's the limit. It doesn't take very long to see that it's going to be dispatch for a while as he is in a long line of street cop wannabe's. He stuck it out as long as he could, two years resigning to go to another department. The Leawood, Kansas

Police Department was relatively small at that time with 15 sworn officers, when he retired Leawood had 100 officers.

Craig worked for Leawood for 33 years starting out as a uniform patrolman, then detective, captain of detectives, retiring at the rank of deputy chief but that's not the entire story. While at the department Craig developed into a great investigator on children's crimes.

In 1983, after investigating the abduction of a 10-year-old girl, Hill and six other Kansas City area police officers co-founded The Lost Child Network, one of the first nationally recognized child resource centers in the country.

The network is dedicated to the education, awareness and recovery of missing and exploited children. Hill' s experience with missing children cases included the recovery of several missing children over the next 15 years:

- two girls missing for 2.5 years from Topeka, KS, who were recovered through a national photo distribution program
- 6-year-old girl missing nearly 6 years, who was recovered with the help of an age- progressed photograph distributed by ADVO
- tracking of a paroled sex offender to Daytona Beach, FL after the abduction and murder of a Pittsburg, KS student
- overseeing the 2.5 year investigation and later arrest of a 29-year-old Connecticut man for the abduction and homicide of a teenage girl working at a community swimming pool in Kansas

In 1998, The Lost Child Network merged with the National Center for Missing and Exploited Children, becoming its fifth branch office. Hill was then appointed to NCMEC's Board of Directors.

In September of 2005, Hill accepted a position to serve as the National Director of Crime

Prevention Training, a program designed to provide law-enforcement officers with information about the dynamics of crimes against children and effective prevention strategies.

Where is Hill on the scale of good, great, exceptional LEO's? Nothing in this career report is exaggerated, I think his accomplishments speak for themselves. Things add up if ya stay on the job for 35 years if you work at it and this is an excellent example of a long and successful career.

Chapter 56

Peyton Place at the COP Shop? Welllll....

The Johnson County Sheriff's Department that I worked, for over twenty-nine years is the biggest sheriff's department in Kansas, and in my opinion was and is the best with the best equipment, staffs, divisions and departments that taxpayers' money can buy. Its crime laboratory achieved the ranks of about half of the accredited laboratories in the US for its state-of-the-art operations. With the exception of one modern-day sheriff, they, the sheriffs in that department, all have been the best qualified as well. That's my opinion, and that includes current sheriff Calvin Hayden, elected in November of 2016. When Kansas was a territory and after it became a state, the sheriffs did what they could with very limited staff and equipment. The modern-day development began some say with sheriff Bud Billings in the 1950's and continued with Sheriffs Burger, Thomas, Allenbrand and continued with Sheriffs John Foster and Frank Denning. They should all to be commended for how they continued in a winning way.

Having said that, I will mention a few negative situations that developed not unlike any other cop shop or business, human nature becomes ugly in some instances. I do know that no one while on the job during my time has been a real crook. No working deputy has been arrested for anything on or off the job as far as I can remember, although a few should have been. A few have been dismissed because of an error in judgment, and in my opinion. a few were dismissed that didn't deserve it. We had a few drunks; some of them left, and some of them dried out. That's no different than any other police department or business of any kind, alcohol and drugs are a problem. A couple deputies that left where in serious trouble after they left the department.

You will learn to protect your assets around cops just like everyone else, and I did when I was married or when I had a significant other. My wife and I became a couple a year before I retired, so she wasn't familiar with department goings-on but she knew how it was in the hospital.

There's a greater KC police department where for years it seemed that everyone was screwing some fellow LEO's girlfriend or wife, so the rumors went. Wife swapping and all the like went along with such activities it was rumored and where there's smoke? There were divorces, a couple of wives killed in so-called accidental shootings, and one LEO went to prison for killing his wife. It just wasn't a department I could have stayed with although I did have LEO friends employed there and they were good people, good cops who just shook their heads like the rest of us. Pay attention, and you will get lessons in fraternization, which may or may not be for you.

When I first went on the job, I fraternized with coworkers, and it was fun (I mentioned activities of some in those days), but later on, other than at work, I had only a few LEO friends that I wanted to spend time with. Work was enough. I got tired of talking cop shop off duty, and that's what a lot of cops do when they're together, on or off duty. When I left work, I left work, unless I was on call. I was tired of some of the BS, and I was tired of the police radio. I hadn't had a police scanner in my home or personal car after my first couple of years on the job. So most of my friends were civilians, and I didn't talk cop shop with them unless I was asked about something specific. Marrieds messing with marrieds happens in any organization and my sheriff's office was no different than any others.

I'll add this about me, I wasn't married during most of my LEO years so while I ain't the perfect little angel I wasn't trying to screw some of the married ladies working in the courthouse or elsewhere as others, a couple I know of were. I shared with them that my opinion of them was "Lowlife" but it didn't matter to them, they just carried on.

So I guess in writing about these few incidents, I realize that my department was not much different than the aforementioned police department, was it? Except no one was shot or killed and that was close to miraculous. There were other officers within our department over the years that ended up with affairs and divorces, and a couple of those officers were pretty high up in rank. I can count more than I have fingers that I know of just off the top of my head, including a married female deputy screwing a trustee in the jail kitchen bathroom. The "trustee" position wasn't supposed to include that type of perk, but he was doin OK, being in jail and all wasn't he? She was either fired or allowed to resign.

Chapter 57

Retired!

You will recall from the first part of this book that I went into police work as a lifeboat to escape what I felt was a boring job at General Motors. That's a great job for some, and they make a good living, but it wasn't for me, and I knew it.

I was just this immature, skinny kid twenty-three years old. I didn't have a clue of what I didn't know, and I was dangerously naive and uninformed. Many younger applicants are of the same cloth. As young as I was, I did have an ace in the hole as I have said: my dad, who taught me a lot before I was even hired as a reserve officer, and then others who'd been trained by him, I matured quite a bit by working as a reserve and paying attention to them and my dad although my mother always asked me "when are you going to grow up?" She finally gave up!

You can get some of the same help, a heads-up, by signing up with a department that employs reserve officers, paid or not. Your pay will be an education. You can also become a civilian volunteer, as my good friend Roger Thomas is. They do different tasks such as mail delivery, DUI lane assistance, and other services for the public and for the department, which frees up an LEO who's needed on the streets or other places saving funds for the budget. A lot of departments have this program, and the help is greatly appreciated, and again, you get a real education about how things work in the justice system.

It's always been my opinion that everyone should have to spend either a couple of years in the military or at the cop shop, or better yet, at both places so you will better understand the game before you go on a criticism streak on something you know nothing about and look stupid.

Here's another theory I have. These idiots that are burning buildings, throwing rocks at the cops and other first responders should be immediately drafted into the military, sent to the front. That would stop that crap in a hurry, but off the soap box I am.

In my years of interviewing prospective LEO wannabes, I always asked, "Why do you want to be an LEO?" One answer that always amused me was, "I want to help people." That may be true for some, but it's not a good reason to get into law enforcement, in my opinion, because whether you want to help people or not, you will on occasion "help people." You will also hurt some people in many ways: arrests, appearance notices, traffic infractions, death notifications, protection orders, and divorces. Some will despise you for this, some will not, but as an example, I had a very good friend (I thought) whose wife's father had been investigated and arrested; it was something very serious, so she hated cops. We were no longer friends when I became an LEO—that was her choice. At the time I didn't understand this, and you will also know those who themselves have had an unhappy (arrest or otherwise) experience with the law. Most mature folks will understand that, whatever it is or was, it wasn't the cop's fault; he or she was just doing their job for we the people.

Yes, for the most part people bring whatever it is onto themselves, but it's still a part of the job and you will be able to help or hurt people, but you really need a better reason to get on the job. You might remember my friend John at GM who just couldn't hack it because of the sadness for him in *hurting people*, the job wasn't for him, but he was still proud of having been an LEO, and he didn't discourage me in what I was about to do.

Regardless of what anyone thinks, law enforcement is a noble job. It's a job that will make you proud, for those that stick with it. Even for those that don't, for most there's still the satisfaction in having been an LEO, like John. Your friends will either like you or not. I lost a few friends when I went on the job, and it hurt, but that was their call for whatever reason but likewise I gained more friends than I lost. Some, like my coworkers at General Motors (except for John), will think you're crazy, but you have to do what you want to do despite opinions from folks that don't know. Buck up, develop a thick skin, and go for it.

In the beginning I went into law enforcement for a trial period of two years max. I found out what I wanted to do after a few years, do a good job and *retire*. I think I did OK. Will you? That's your life and your call. Good luck for those that go on the job, and I hope I have educated some on what the job of an LEO is about and what you may expect. If I have, I have once again done my job. Best of luck and best regards to all in law enforcement and their supporters. They need it, they deserve it, as well as our support and thanks to all for doing a job that most can't or will not do. Last but certainly not least, God Bless those who have given the ultimate sacrifice for you and me including our military hero's and God Bless America!

END OF A TRUE STORY

Ed Hayes AKA "two dawgs" is a fourth-generation law enforcement officer with a degree in the administration of justice. He is part Cherokee Indian on his grandmother's side (though he doesn't know how much yet) He retired from the Johnson County, Kansas, Sheriff's Department at the rank of captain after twenty-nine years on the job. During his career in law enforcement, he worked in every division of the sheriff's office, including nearly three years on special assignment with the Justice Department as a federal agent with the Drug Enforcement Agency in the Western District of Missouri. He worked undercover investigations for a total of seven years in narcotics, stolen property/burglaries, and other criminal investigations.

Since retirement he has done volunteer work in several areas, including being a member of the Chaffee County, Colorado, Search and Rescue north team as a rescuer and rescue pilot. He was appointed to the Chaffee County, Colorado, Jail Committee during the planning process of a new jail in Salida, Colorado and was a member of the Chaffee County Airport Board of Directors all before he moved from Colorado. Hayes is a life member of the NRA and a member of Oath Keepers. He is a member of the National Association for Search and Rescue, an SAL Member of the American Legion, and a past member of the Kansas Peace Officers Association and the Kansas Sheriff's Association.

An avid outdoorsman, Hayes is a commercial pilot a glider pilot, a glider tow pilot, *was* a sport parachutist, a downhill skier, amateur racer and a certified open-water scuba diver. He bicycles for pleasure and exercise, loves motorcycles and ATVs, and was a home builder. In his lifetime, he has lived on a lake and at an airport on the White River in Arkansas, and built a house near Salida, Colorado, among the "fourteeners."

Currently Hayes works on his own projects including administrator for FNCIC web site which is Victims of Illegal Alien Crimes (voiacus.org). Hayes joined this cause over ten years ago after he became a member of the Minuteman Civil Defense Corps. He was appointed states director of

MCDC for Kansas and Missouri, rising to executive director before he resigned, citing incompetence in leadership.

For the past few years, Hayes has written published articles and a column for the *Johnson's County Gazette* newspaper, where he is a senior contributor. The column is about law enforcement and Johnson County, Kansas, law enforcement history, as well as other related subjects (and some not related). In addition, Hayes has had numerous articles published in other media outlets over the last decade.

Hayes resides in the Metro Kansas City area with his wife, Pat and has three children (one son and two daughters), two grandsons and three little kids in puppy dog suits. Hayes gives talks regarding law enforcement and the careers mentioned in this book, contact him at americanpatriots@sbcglobal.net

CPSIA information can be obtained
at www.ICGtesting.com
Printed in the USA
LVOW08s0004041017

551101LV00001B/119/P